FIRE IN THE HEAD

FIRE IN THE HEAD

SHAMANISM AND THE CELTIC SPIRIT

Tom Cowan

HarperSanFrancisco

A Division of HarperCollins*Publishers*

FIRST EDITION

Library of Congress Cataloging-in-Publication Data

Cowan, Thomas Dale.
    Fire in the head : shamanism and the Celtic
spirit / Tom Cowan. — 1st ed.
      p.   cm.
    Includes bibliographical references.
    ISBN 0-06-250174-7 (acid-free paper)
    1. Celts—Religion. 2. Shamanism.   I. Title.
BL900.C69 1993
299'.16—dc20   92-53909
                                     CIP

93 94 95 96 97 HAD 10 9 8 7 6 5 4 3 2 1

This book is lovingly dedicated to my sister Gail.

ACKNOWLEDGMENTS

I wish to give special thanks to Susan Lee Cohen, my agent, whose encouragement and professional advice is always most helpful; to my editor, Barbara Moulton, for her early interest and enthusiasm for this book; to Lisa Bach for her wise and inspired editorial suggestions; to Jack Maguire, Edith Borden, Tom Sheeley, and Debbi Sheeley for reading the manuscript and saying what they thought. I am also indebted to my many teachers and mentors, both here and beyond.

CONTENTS

INTRODUCTION

THE PROBLEM
OF CELTIC SHAMANISM

Our search for the Celtic shaman
is a sweeping and fascinating task for we are dealing with two sets of
phenomena—shamanism and the Celtic spirit—both of which have survived in various parts of the world for thousands of years. Shamanism in
Western Europe goes back at least 20,000 years and possibly even further.
Some of the first evidence of shamanism can be found in the scenarios
painted on the cave walls at Lascaux in southwestern France and at Altamira
in northern Spain. These mesmerizing drawings suggest an extremely
archaic, but highly accurate, rendition of the shamanic experience such as
shapeshifted individuals that are part human, part animal, and part bird; a
human figure lying in a trancelike state; animals swarming in a stampede of
spirit and power; and strikingly clear symbols of birth, life, death, and
rebirth. The sources of such images are not lost in the past. They are part
of the human psyche, and similar images can be found in the descriptions
of shamanic journeys undertaken by modern men and women who practice
shamanism in the major metropolitan areas of the twentieth century.

Core elements of the Celtic spirit have also endured with a remarkable continuity from the sixth and seventh centuries B.C. down to the present day. In the contemporary Irish blessing, "May the roads rise to meet you, the sun warm your face, the rain fall gently on your fields, and the wind be ever at your back," we hear echoes of an ancient Celtic vow calling on the elements to witness the pledge of loyalty: "May the skies fall upon me, the sea drown me, and the earth swallow me up, if I break faith with you!"[1] An Irish monk in the early Christian era expressed the same references to the powers of nature in explaining Christ's death on the cross: "At [Christ's] death no fire came upon his captors to burn them, no great flood rose to sweep them away, the earth did not open to swallow them up, the sky did not fall to crush them."[2] Whether blessing a friend, or pledging one's loyalty, or commenting on a possible retribution for Christ's suffering, the Celtic spirit expresses an intimate relationship with the natural world. A shamanic rapport with these elements is reflected in this strong continuity of imagery and sentiment. The Celt, both ancient and modern, expects wind, sky, sea, and sunlight to respond to the heartfelt call, just as the shaman expected the herds to come at his or her call so the tribe could begin the hunt.

Shamanism

The word *shaman* comes from the Tungus tribes of Siberia and refers specifically to a man or woman with a special type of spiritual power. Shamans were visionary, ecstatic healers, or what today we may call "spiritual consultants," who worked in a trance state. In recent years, however, the word has been applied loosely, and often inaccurately, to many types of spiritual and healing practices associated with tribal cultures, everything from using drums and rattles in ceremonies to honoring an animal totem. In 1951 Mircea Eliade, one of the foremost authorities on shamanism and archaic religions, addressed this problem in his ground-breaking work, *Shamanism: Archaic Techniques of Ecstasy*, which is still one of the major sources for understanding traditional shamanic practices found the world over. Eliade discouraged an indiscriminate use of the term *shaman* to designate "any magician, sorcerer, medicine man, or ecstatic found throughout the history of religions." He pointed out that such usage would render the notion of shamanism "at once extremely complex and extremely vague" and ultimately it would "serve no purpose."[3] Nevertheless, over the last forty years, a growing enthusiasm for shamanism has brought the term into modern parlance where it enlivens discussions of religion, spirituality, healing, environmentalism, and lifestyles for the future. Clearly, the term (as well as the practice) has an importance to play in the evolution of human consciousness far beyond the specific cultures of Central Asia where it originated.

We should not let the extended use of the term *shaman* blur the sharp edges of authentic shamanism, and neither should the purist's usage of the term prevent us from recognizing truly shamanic phenomena appearing in cultural contexts far removed from the Tungus tribes of Siberia. We need to be flexible in using the term since shamanic experiences and practices are found in almost all native cultures and are currently being revived among modern people who have never crawled into a Scythian sweat lodge or spent a night alone on the Siberian tundra.

Shamanism is fundamentally a way of viewing reality, and a method or technique for functioning within that view of reality. The shaman perceives the universe in ways different from other men and women, and has personal experiences in the universe that seem to transcend those of other people. The core elements of shamanism found in most cultures with a solid shamanic tradition are: (1) Shamans can voluntarily enter a unique visionary state of consciousness during which (2) they experience a journey into nonordinary realms of existence where (3) they acquire knowledge and power for their own use or for others in their communities. These three features comprise what many shamanic practitioners today call *core shamanism*. Because the nonordinary realms are for the most part immaterial and to a large extent imaginal, shamans speak of them as spirit realms and the entities encountered there are considered spirits.

I have qualified the terms immaterial and imaginal intentionally because the realm of spirit, or nonordinary reality, is greater than our human perception of it and often defies most descriptions of how we expect it to operate. For example, the spirit world seems to be immaterial, or nonphysical, but activities performed in that world often have astounding repercussions in ordinary reality. In healing, for instance, a shaman may journey into nonordinary reality to retrieve the soul of a dying person or to remove the causes of illness that may appear as insects or demons. In such cases, the shaman treats the invisible, spiritual nature of the sickness, yet the physical body recovers. The same is true of the term *imaginal*. For example, a shaman may journey to a place in nonordinary reality and speak of it as a realm of the spirit world, then later learn that such a place exists in ordinary, physical reality. It may turn out that other shamans have also traveled there (either in the body or out of the body) and are also familiar with it, thus indicating that the Otherworld has an existence independent of the individual shaman's imagination. In addition, the widespread testimony to the manifestation of spirit entities in the physical realm suggests that they too can appear and operate in the ordinary, physical world, at least partially independent of the imagination of the person seeing them.

THE CELTS

The Celtic tribes occupied and dominated central Europe in the sixth and seventh centuries B.C. In the fourth century they reached the height of their prominence and expanded westward, to the south, and to the east. They were a formidable people. In 390 B.C. Celtic tribes sacked Rome and instilled a terror into the minds and hearts of Roman citizens that persisted for centuries. In 279 B.C. a warring band of Celts attacked the sacred shrine at Delphi in Greece. Eventually the migrating Celtic tribes founded outposts and settlements across the entire European continent, from northern Spain to Turkey, from the British Isles to the shores of the Black Sea.

The word *Celt* comes from Greek and Roman writers who used it rather indiscriminately to refer to the various tribes that occupied Europe to the north and west of them. But these tribes were never united into a "Celtic nation." In fact, the idea of national unity was as foreign to them as was the notion of a common racial or cultural identity. They had different languages, different tribal names, and diverse lifestyles. Some Celtic peoples lived in peasant farming communities, others in powerful strongholds dominated by charismatic chieftains. In some places they dwelt in peaceful hamlets, while others lived in militarized hill forts. Many Celtic centers became the nuclei of present-day cities such as Paris, London, Orleans, Bourges, and Budapest. Others were temporary encampments that have disappeared in the mists of history.

Nevertheless, most modern Celticists view the tribes as constituting a distinctive ethnic group. In spite of real differences among individual tribes, important racial and cultural continuities bound them together. Classical writers, such as Livy, Strabo, Caesar, Tacitus, Pliny the Elder, Posidonius, Herodotus, and Diodorus Siculus, from whom we derive much of our knowledge of the ancient Celts, recognized them as a distinct race with similar customs, values, institutions, and beliefs. Celts were fierce, boastful, and enthusiastic warriors; compared to Mediterranean peoples, they wore unusually colorful clothing, jewelry, and body ornamentation and flaunted their tastes; they were metalworkers who turned out a recognizably Celtic product; they were fond of storytelling, poetry, song, feasting, and drinking. As a people they were hospitable, family-oriented, and loyal to their clan and tribe. Physically the Celts were taller and fairer than people in southern Europe, with lighter skin and hair (although there were also dark-haired Celts), and often blue eyes. They also shared similar religious beliefs, such as the immanence of the spirit world and the immortality of the human soul.

Classical writers, who often denigrated Celtic spirituality as superstition, frequently commented on the Celts' intense obsession with spiritual matters. Celtic scholar Anne Ross notes that "the Celts were so completely engrossed with, and preoccupied by, their religion and its expression that it was constantly and positively to the forefront of their lives."[4] She points out that the diverse Celtic tribes did not share a religious *system* in the sense that a consistent spiritual orthodoxy colored religious practices from the Atlantic to the Black Sea and from the Baltic to the Mediterranean. Nevertheless, in spite of many variations in style and form, it is valid to speak of

Celtic religion as having a similarity of ritual and spiritual practices, the same blending of the natural and supernatural that accounts for the strong strain of mysticism running through Celtic thought and culture. "All these," Ross claims, "indicate a basic religious homogeneity which is indeed remarkable."

There are striking parallels between the patterns of Celtic tribal life and that of Native Americans. Like American Indians, the Celts lived in diverse, scattered tribal units, sometimes banding together for specific trade or military purposes. As peoples who practiced an indigenous, earth-centered spirituality, the Celts and Native Americans share many animistic beliefs and practices, along with a common attitude and respect for the land and the spirits of the land. Their fate was equally similar and tragic. Like Native Americans, the Celts suffered from the advance of other settlers. In the second century B.C. Germanic tribes from the north advanced southward, and in the first century the Dacian peoples (in what is today central Romania) moved against the Celts from the east. In 58 B.C. Julius Caesar marched into Gaul, a Celtic territory, and conquered it. By 84 A.D. Roman armies had marched all the way to northern Scotland. Eventually the majority of the Celts were defeated, absorbed, or pushed westward by an advancing, militaristic Roman civilization. Today, like Native Americans, many modern Celts are struggling to save their languages, literature, and folk customs, including older religious practices, especially in the few pockets where Celtic civilization survived most intact.

The Roman historian Tacitus perceptively explained the Celts' fate in terms that would be repeated many times over the course of history when European settlers and developers clashed with native populations in other areas of the globe. Tacitus noted how some Celts eventually "spoke of such novelties as 'civilization,' when in fact they were only a feature of their enslavement."[5] The conquering Roman armies and settlements brought a measure of peace often for the first time to fierce tribal rivalries. But the conquered tribes paid a high price for the Pax Romana: cultural independence and identity. The material amenities brought from the Mediterranean were accompanied by ideological requirements that destroyed the cultural values and beliefs that had shaped the Celtic way of life for centuries. In time, older Celtic customs gave way to Roman practices, in spite of Rome's official policy to retain and adapt native customs wherever possible. Inevitably, succeeding generations of young Celts were Romanized (and later Christianized) through education and training.

Our search for the Celtic shaman begins with these ancient tribal peoples who once dwelt in thriving, prosperous communities across the European land mass and who sowed the seeds for the rich Celtic heritage we know today. Squeezed out on three sides, some Celtic people migrated westward, settling in territories that today constitute the Six Celtic Nations: Ireland, Scotland, Wales, Brittany, the Isle of Man, and Cornwall. The regions that retained Celtic customs most successfully were those where the Roman armies never invaded: Ireland, the Highlands in Western Scotland, and the mountainous regions of Wales. We will not confine the phrase "Celtic spirit" solely to the values, beliefs, and lifestyles of these early tribes. Shamanic features can be found embedded in the Celtic spirit throughout history. To understand Celtic shamanism we will range far and wide, as the wandering Celts themselves would certainly have appreciated.

It is a testimony to the survival and durability of the Celtic spirit and its shamanic qualities that in every age, specific social types emerge that retain the vestiges of an older, deeper stratum of belief and practice that we recognize as shamanism. Druids and priestesses, bards and poets, legendary heroes, mythological gods and goddesses, Christian monks and saints, mystics, witches, and healers—what separates these individuals over time and space, and by the advancing scientific, technological culture of the modern world is not as strong as what connects them: solid spiritual values that have remained constant over centuries. That rich strain of mysticism, which the Romans labeled *superstition*, was in fact the backbone of Celtic spirituality. It is also the philosophical basis for shamanism, a feature that makes the Celt, ancient or modern, a prime candidate for shamanic experiences. In terms of core shamanism, there was probably never a time, nor will there ever be, when the true Celt does not believe in the unseen Otherworld and the possibility of journeying there to discover the mysteries of the divine universe.

◆

FIRE IN THE HEAD

In the 1890s Irish poet and nationalist W. B. Yeats entitled a poem "The Song of Wandering Aengus."[6] It begins:

> I went out to the hazel wood,
> Because a fire was in my head,
> And cut and peeled a hazel wand,
> And hooked a berry to a thread . . .

With this fishing rod, made from a tree long believed by the Celts to have magical properties, and in the enchanted twilight of early dawn, when "moth-like stars were flickering out," Aengus catches a silver trout that he takes home to cook. But while he is building the fire, he hears someone speak his name and looks over to where he had lain the fish on the floor. It had transformed into "a glimmering girl/With apple blossom in her hair." After calling out his name, the faery girl runs out the door and disappears in "the brightening air" of day. Aengus vows to find the faery maiden and grows old searching for her "through hollow lands and hilly lands."

Yeats's Aengus may have been a shaman. He had the fire in his head that shamans everywhere believe is their source of enlightenment, illuminating visions of other realities. The shamanic journey begins and ends in the mind, in an altered state of consciousness, regardless of any other worlds, independent of the mind, the shaman visits along the way. Following the light of his vision, Aengus journeyed through the "hollow lands" that lie just below or behind the denser terrain of ordinary reality. In some respects, Aengus's journey is a classic shamanic soul journey, illuminated by the imagination. But calling attention to that does not lessen its authenticity, for the imagination is the shaman's visionary tool that describes the contents of the imaginal realm of consciousness, and the survival of shamanism over the last 20,000 years strongly suggests that the tool works.

Each culture's shamanic lore reflects the distinctiveness of that culture, just as each shaman's adventures reflect what is most unique to that shaman as an individual. One would expect this of an experience that is at once personal and transpersonal. The content of the shaman's visions is shaped by the beliefs and expectations of both the shaman and the culture. The fire in the head is personally enkindled by the shaman, but the kindling is collected, in part, from the beliefs and values of the culture. The silver trout, the hazel wand, the spirit girl with apple blossoms in her hair, the Hollow Hills—these themes are recognizable to many Celts, whether they are shamans or not. They are part of the Celtic folklore within which the Celtic shaman operates.

In Celtic lands a strong belief in the immanence of the Otherworld persists even today. Modern Irish storytelling abounds with ordinary people who hear the songs and merriment of the faery folk, encounter troups of faeries, and slip into the twilight of the Otherworld, where they undergo adventures that rival the accounts of the greatest shamans. These ordinary folk are by no means trained in shamanic techniques of ecstasy, but a culture that takes such experiences for granted tends to reinforce their spontaneous occurence. From a Celtic perspective, the shaman's world of spirit and power seems always poised to break through ordinary consciousness— while fishing for trout, while lighting a fire for breakfast.

We do not know if Yeats's Aengus ever found the spirit woman who apparently changed his life forever. One can hope that he was successful, that he found her, and that he could

> . . . kiss her lips and take her hands;
> And walk among long dappled grass,
> And pluck till time and times are done
> The silver apples of the moon,
> The golden apples of the sun.

VARIETIES OF
SHAMANIC EXPERIENCE

There was drumming in the hills around Edinburgh. A 1684 account published in London to prove the existence of witches and spirits describes a lad named "the Fairy-Boy of Leith in Scotland" who took his drum every Thursday night to a hill between Edinburgh and Leith. Here the "boy of the fairies" beat his drum while men and women passed through invisible doorways into another realm containing magnificent chambers filled with festive revelers eating, drinking, dancing, and making merry. After enjoying this otherworldly gala, the men and women flew in spirit to faraway places, such as France and Holland, before returning to ordinary reality.[1]

Who was the faery boy of Leith? Who were the men and women able to pass through invisible doorways? And where did they really go?

Contemporary shamanic practitioners, who use shamanic drumming methods to create the visionary state of consciousness for journeying into nonordinary realms of experience, would readily recognize this scenario. They would have no trouble explaining the boy, his drum, the entrances into the Otherworld, the spirit revelry, and the soul flight to France and Holland. All over the world, people are once again practicing the ancient methods of shamanism in drumming sessions similar to these reported in seventeenth-century Scotland.

Shamanism is a worldwide phenomenon that has survived in various forms beyond the hunting-fishing-gathering societies of 20,000 years ago. As mythographer and scholar of world religions Joseph Campbell points out, shamanism is "the essential component of an immemorial tradition, to which a number of characteristics and related features are attached, of which some may be accented in one region, others in another, but always in relation to the unmistakable crisis of vocation" that calls a man or woman to become a "walker between the worlds" of ordinary and nonordinary reality.[2]

To adapt a phrase from William James's classic work, *Varieties of Religious Experience*, there have been, and continue to be, varieties of shamanic experience. Contemporary shamanic practitioners may not be living and functioning as the classical shamans in traditional tribal societies because modern society does not currently acknowledge and support "fulltime shamans." As would be expected in an industrialized, urbanized society based on increasing specialization in almost every field, the many roles the shaman once played in archaic societies are now distributed among various professionals such as doctors, therapists, artists, entertainers, and clergy, to name a few.

Is shamanism among contemporary shamans in native societies and among shamanic practitioners in urban settings a diluted form of the shamanism of old? It may be if there is credibility to the old Siberian legend about the super-shaman Morgan-Kara. Legend has it that after Morgan-Kara retrieved a soul which the High God was holding captive in a bottle, the High God split his two-headed drum with a thunderbolt. Ever since, the shaman's drum has only one head, and shamans have never been quite as powerful as Morgan-Kara. (At least not in Siberia.) So the current generation of shamans, whether they were trained by native elders or contemporary teachers of shamanism, may not be as powerful as the original shamans of the past.

With or without the theory of "shamanic decadence"—that contemporary shamans are pale reflections of the shamans of old—we have clearly lost the rich, supportive shamanic culture in which shamans once operated. Since the Scientific Revolution around 1600, the dominant culture in the West has repudiated the visionary and mystical traditions of perceiving reality, on which shamanism is based. Understandably, most people today know little about shamanism. But strong or weak, recognizable or obscure, shamanism has not died out, nor is it merely the vestige of some long-forgotten spirituality. It has much in common with mystical and esoteric traditions in all cultures, ancient and modern. People around the world continue to have spontaneous shamanic experiences. Under different names, and with different explanations, the core shamanic experience is still a vital part of human life.

The visionary experiences reported by shamans of ancient times continue to occur today among men and women in modern Western cultures, as well as among people still living in tribal societies. Anthropologist Michael Harner, who pioneered methods for teaching core shamanism (the basic elements of shamanic practice stripped of specific cultural trappings) and making it relevant to contemporary society, notes in his classic work, *The Way of the Shaman*, that "shamanic methods are strikingly similar the world over, even for peoples whose cultures are quite different in other respects, and who have been separated by oceans and continents for tens of thousands of years."[3] Some anthropologists explain this by the theory of dispersal, that shamanism originated among one group of people who then migrated, carrying the tradition with them to other parts of the globe. But what Harner and others call core shamanism may be a normal human archetype. Campbell points out that "the central nervous system of our species has hardly changed in the mere 12,000 to 15,000 years following the period of the shamans of the caves" and that a "similar human strain" runs through all the manifestations of shamanism wherever it is found.[4] Perhaps in each of us there is an innate image, a not-fully-conscious hope, of a man or woman who knows methods of journeying into unseen realms with the help of spirit companions and returns with wisdom and knowledge that can heal the human spirit.

◆

THE SHAMANIC ARCHETYPE

What is the essential archetype of shamanism that is activated in every century among certain men and women, and thus gives rise to the varieties of shamanic experience? In part, the archetype consists of the core elements of shamanism: the journey into nonordinary reality; the help of spirit guides, usually in the form of animals; and the return with some knowledge or power to serve others in the community. In addition to these core elements, the essential archetype includes:

> some type of traumatic initiatory crisis, often involving a debilitating, life-threatening illness for the candidate (although some shamans realize the call more slowly as their innate mysticism gradually evolves into stronger and more intense relationships with the spirit world);

> the ability to make succeeding journeys into the Otherworld at will;

> a transformed vision of reality that includes a sense of oneness and interrelatedness of all created things with the power or life-force that pervades the universe;

> and the ability to "work magic," that is, to heal, see, and control ordinary reality in ways considered extraordinary by community standards.

The full shamanic experience occurs in a trancelike, nonordinary state of consciousness, which Harner has labeled the "shamanic state of consciousness." The physical and psychological ramifications of this state of consciousness are currently being studied, and it appears to be a unique mode of awareness similar to, but significantly different from, other visionary states such as dreaming, hypnotism, uncontrollable hallucinations, revery, out-of-body experiences, and near-death experiences. In spite of its differences, the shamanic state of consciousness has something in common with each of these, and people trained in shamanism can enter this state at will because they have mastered "archaic techniques of ecstasy."[5] The most common method of creating the shamanic state of consciousness is by listening to a mesmerizing sound such as the monotonous beating of a drum, the clicking of sticks, the shaking of rattles, and/or engaging in a repetitive activity, such as clapping, chanting, and dancing.

What distinguishes the shaman from other mystics and magicworkers is the journey into the Otherworld and the faith and trust in the shaman's helping spirits and otherworldy teachers for acquiring the power and wisdom the shaman will share with the community in the form of "shamanic services" when he or she returns. Shamanic services are many and varied, such as divination, healing, dream interpretation, rites of passage, soul retrieval, and other public, private, communal, or personal rituals a client may request. While a shaman's particular magical talents and skills (such as divination or weather magic) and visionary truths (harmony of the universe or explanation for evil) may be found among nonshamans—magicians, wizards, psychics, sorcerers, or spiritual healers—what distinguishes the shaman is that his or her power comes directly from otherworldy journeys in the company of personal helping spirits.

The shamanic archetype, therefore, manifests in most cultures as a combination of activity, vision, and service. The activity is the trance-journey into the Otherworld with spirit companions. The vision is of nonordinary realities that reveal the spiritual nature of the universe. The services are wide-ranging skills and talents of a psychic-spiritual nature to heal or benefit others. The specific energy of the shaman archetype activates hope and fear about the soul's eventual and inevitable journey into the "greater universe," which is also referred to as the Spirit World, the Void, Eternity, the Collective Unconscious, the Kingdom of Heaven, or the Mind of God. Individual responses to the shamanic archetype vary from person to person, possibly from moment to moment, for the image behind the figure is, of course, each person's own Self, an initiated and transformed Self called upon to explore the "greater universe" before the actual death of the body and to return to share the experience with others.

TAKEN BY THE FAERIES

A common Celtic view of the initiatory journey into the spirit world is an abduction by faeries, who may also be called the "gentry," "the good people," or the "people of the sidhe" (the older gods and goddesses who dwell in the Hollow Hills). "Taken by the faeries" is the phrase often used to explain the bizarre behavior or the debilitating illness that in traditional shamanic societies would have been explained in terms of the candidate's vocational crisis—the call to become a shaman. We must fully understand this concept to appreciate its shamanic elements.

To be "taken" into Faeryland, or into the sidhe (pronounced *shee*), can occur in several ways. Sometimes a person stumbles into Faerie by making a wrong turn on a well-known path or, as the Irish say, stepping upon a "stray sod." In older myths and more recent folktales, a person is lured into the realms of the Otherworld by a faery man or woman, or by a faery animal, often snow white or colorless. A variation on this more active entry is to fall into a deep sleep or be lulled asleep by faery music or the singing of magical birds. Accounts of faery abductions indicate that the person "awoke" to discover himself or herself in the faery kingdom.

In ordinary reality, the individual's family and friends notice that the person has been "taken" because of a strange illness or depression. A woman may act oddly or listless, or go to bed for long periods of time. A man may be depressed or "not himself." Friends will say that the faeries have him. It is not unusual for the length of the illness to last seven years, which is often the number of years attributed to the initiatory illness in classic shamanic societies. It can, of course, last much longer. What is happening during this time? How can we explain a person staying critically ill, behaving in a socially unacceptable manner, or remaining psychically confused for a period of many years?

It is not unreasonable to consider that those taken into Faerie are truly physically debilitated; it is not just in their minds. This is in keeping with accounts of the shamanic initiation illness; the shaman's call is at once a spiritual, psychological, and physical crisis. An inability to concentrate, loss of memory, depression, and sleep disturbances coincide with the classic behavior of the shamanic candidate who seems to be not "totally present" or "all there" during the period she or he is undergoing the most intense phase of the initiation and the transformation of vision. As the Irish say, when a man "gets a touch" from the faeries he starts to act "silly." Physical pain in the joints and muscles might also reflect, in ordinary reality, the beating shamans undergo in their visionary experiences in the nonordinary realm. The wife of a Siberian shaman relates her husband's experience: "He had been ill for seven years. While he was ailing, he had dreams: He was beaten up several times, sometimes he was taken to strange places."[6]

Who are the faeries? Unfortunately, the image of faeries in the popular mind is a drastic distortion of Celtic faery folk. Today faeries tend to be dismissed as imaginary creatures resembling butterflies or winged elves, gossamer beings flitting around in the moonlight, usually at the far end of a typically English garden. Our contemporary view of faeries is English, not Celtic. Anthropologist Margaret Murray[7] and writer Diarmaid Mac Manus,[8] lay the blame on Shakespeare's doorstep, claiming that the Bard was the first to portray faeries as diminutive sprites with gauzy wings, popping in and out of our lives somewhere near midnight. Shakespeare's *The Tempest* and *Midsummer Night's Dream* have fixed this image in the Western imagination, only to be further developed by nineteenth-century fairy tales (and the artists who illustrated them) and in the twentieth century by Walt Disney studios. To understand the real power and presence of the faery folk and their relationship to Celtic shamanism, we must look back to the earliest accounts in Celtic mythology where the ancestors of the present-day faeries first appeared.

In Scotland, Ireland, Wales, Brittany, Cornwall, and the Isle of Man, faeries are not consistently viewed as diminutive sprites, even though the term is used loosely to include many types of small spirits, and a common reference to them is "the wee folk." Faeries can be any size. In some accounts they appear slightly larger than human dimensions, even up to fourteen feet tall; in others, they seem smaller than mortals. The fact that Celtic traditions are filled with accounts of mortals and faeries intermarrying and producing faery children indicates that, when they want to, they can be the same size as human beings. Murray points out that even Shakespeare knew that faeries could be human size, for in *The Merry Wives of Windsor*, Anne Page, a mature woman, dresses like a faery and expects to be taken for one. Clearly, not all faeries look like Tinkerbell.

In his collection *Irish Fairy and Folk Tales*, W. B. Yeats warns that faeries "have no inherent form but change according to their whim, or the mind that sees them . . . Do not think the faeries are always little. Everything is capricious about them, even their size."⁹ In other words, Celtic faeries seem to behave and act like spirits everywhere. From the shaman's point of view, spirits are highly personal, and no two shamans may have exactly the same experiences with the same spirits. Even today among shamanic practitioners, people with the same power animal, such as Raven, Bear, or Eagle, will have highly personal relationships with that animal and describe its powers and behavior in very different ways. It is not strange, then, that we find among those willing to speak about their faery faith, an amazing variety of beliefs, from the belief that faeries are fallen angels (but not evil ones) to the belief that they are either disembodied spirits or nature spirits (elementals), to a belief that the dead live among the faeries and for all practical purposes become faeries themselves.

One of the more intriguing insights into the spirit world, an insight that reappears throughout Celtic faery lore, is the apparent need for human contact on the part of spiritual entities. For reasons not always clear, the faery folk, the old Celtic deities, the people who dwell in the Hollow Hills, actively want to share their secrets, wisdom, and power with us. Seeking human companionship, they either enter our world of ordinary reality or take us into theirs. It is almost as if they recognize in us companion spirits, temporarily assigned a mortal reincarnation, and that their involvement in our lives, even when mischievous, is to assist us in some important way. They may be necessary both for our survival as a species, and for our individual, incarnated spirits (our souls) to prevail and eventually transcend the earthly, human condition. Shamans and Celtic visionaries recognize the interdependence between spirits and mortals as being a major component in the structure of the universe.

◆

The vestiges of Celtic shamanism, fragmented though they are, shine bright and clear, for the Celtic spirit and personality is a fertile breeding ground for shamanic experiences. We could find no better prism than the Celtic soul through which to view the brilliant rays of shamanism, so that we can study them in greater depth and detail, and trace them back, individually or collectively, to the clear crystal center. To give the reader a cursory over-view of shamanism in a Celtic context, let us consider five candidates for Celtic shamans, about whom we have varying degrees of information, but enough to stir our imaginations about what might have been a rich sha-manic stream in European spirituality.

BIDDY EARLY

Biddy Early lived in County Clare in western Ireland in the mid-nineteenth century and was known as a "wise woman," a euphemism for "white witch." The local Church authorities remained suspicious of her power until she died. As a child, Biddy Early was able to see and talk to elemental spirits and faeries. They became her playmates. It was generally agreed that, as an adult, she received her knowledge of medicinal herbs from "the earth folk (faeries), who taught her how to use them for magical and semi-magical purposes."[10] She cured illness, recommended medicinal remedies, and foretold the future. She also offered on at least one occasion to perform a type of spirit retrieval for a woman who wanted to see her dead child.

In the early twentieth century, Lady Gregory, a folklorist, Irish nation-alist, and friend of W. B. Yeats, interviewed people in County Clare who remembered Biddy Early and recorded several accounts of her shamanic powers and experiences. Some people thought that Biddy Early received her power to cure from her dead brother who had lain under a white thorn tree for shade while he was ill. She went to the tree to cry every day for a year after his death, "and then he brought her under," meaning he took her into the Otherworld where he gave her the knowledge of curing.[11] Neighbors claimed Biddy Early was taken to the spirit realms for seven years, a common length of time for faery abductions. It is not unusual for a shamanic candidate to be trained by the spirits of deceased relatives or ancestors.

At some point in her life, Biddy Early began "seeing" cures and future events by means of a blue bottle, which she would shake until a mist formed inside. As the bottle cleared, she could see the illness and its cure. Sometimes she looked into the bottle to foresee a future event. Biddy Early received the blue bottle from the faeries by way of her eldest son who also had a personal relationship with the "earth folk." One day he stopped to play a game of hurly with them (faeries seem to need mortal players for hurly every now and then), and as a token of their appreciation, they presented him with the blue bottle with instructions to take it home to his mother. The bottle became her power object, although she could "see" and cure without it. She left instructions that after her death it was to be thrown into Loch Kilgarron where it remains to this day, even though there have been numerous attempts by scavengers to retrieve it. Returning a power object to Faerie after one's death is a common Celtic theme.

Biddy Early "may have been in a trance" when she did her work, as one acquaintance put it. She was known to go into a small shed behind her home at night where she consulted with her "invisible friends," the faery folk who were her helping spirits.[12] This small, undoubtedly dark enclosure, isolated from the distractions of her home, would have facilitated the visionary state of consciousness that she needed to journey into the nonordinary realm where she met her "friends." Biddy Early appears to have practiced her form of shamanism with considerable regularity. One observer thought she was "walking with the faeries every night."[13]

Throughout her life Biddy Early engaged in an ongoing feud with the local priest and bishop who feared that her powers were from the devil. On more than one occasion the clergy visited her to discourage her shamanic practices. Obviously part of their worry was that her widespread following among the peasantry threatened their authority. But Biddy Early never "mended her ways." She remained lax in her own church observances, had several husbands, and drank probably more than was good for her. But at the end of her life, she sent for the parish priest during her last illness. She died in 1873.

FURSEY

The eighth-century monk and historian, the Venerable Bede, relates the shamanic vision of an Irish nobleman named Fursey who set up a monastery in England. Although never ordained a priest, Fursey, as a child, displayed the type of meditative, mystical behavior typical of Irish lads destined for the priesthood and similar to the dreamy, distracted children who become shamans in other societies. In her studies of the shamanic personality, Joan Halifax calls this youthful interest in spiritual discipline a "proclivity for the sacred"[14] that alerts adults in the community, particularly older shamans, that a particular child is a prime candidate for shamanic training. Bede tells us that at a young age Fursey practiced "monastic disciplines" and read "sacred books."[15]

At one point in his life, Fursey fell sick and, "quitting his body from the evening till the cock crew," was "lifted up on high . . . by the angels that conducted him." From the celestial heights he had a vision of the wickedness of the world. His three angelic "conductors" showed him enormous bonfires, hideous devils, terrifying bouts of spiritual warfare between good and evil spirits, and other typical medieval Christian scenarios.

On this journey an "unclean spirit" threw at Fursey the body of a man "whom they tormented in the fire." The flaming human projectile scorched Fursey's shoulder and jaw, leaving a visible burn mark on his physical body. Throughout the rest of his life he bore "the mark of the fire which he had felt in his soul." He seems to have relished his reputation as a wounded healer, much like shamans in other cultures. Undoubtedly the scar increased his credibility as a wise man familiar with heavenly realms. Before his helping angels returned him to his body, they gave him "wholesome advice for what ought to be done towards the salvation of such as repented on their death-bed." Thus Fursey received classic shamanic training in death counseling and later served in the role of psychopomp, a person who leads the souls of the dying into the next world.

Another classic shamanic power was Fursey's ability to generate his own internal body heat to withstand intense cold. As Bede describes it, "in most sharp winter weather, and a hard frost," Fursey could sit "in a thin garment when he related (his vision), yet he sweated as if it had been in the greatest heat of summer." Eliade offers dramatic examples of the shaman's ability to resist cold. Eskimo shamans, for example, must be able to withstand freezing temperatures as proof of their shamanic initiation.[16]

◆

Explorer/ethnographer Knud Rasmussen relates the case of a shaman who spent five days in icy water without falling ill, and without the aspirant's clothes getting wet.[17] Not only did this shaman have control over his body temperature, he was also protected from the natural effects of water.

FERGUS

Many Irish tales describe encounters with the "little people," commonly understood in the popular imagination to be dwarfs or elves who play pranks on unsuspecting mortals. The tradition of these mischievous pranksters runs strong through Irish folklore as it does in shamanic literature around the world. The fear of faeries has persisted among Celtic peoples well into modern times. Possibly as the original Celtic shaman was absorbed into Christian traditions and later devalued in a scientific age inhospitable to the shamanic vocation, fewer and fewer Celts knew about or remembered the traditional techniques of psychic protection or safe methods of encountering spirits.

Fergus, the hero of a traditional Irish tale, seems to have stumbled upon a method unwittingly. One day he fell asleep on the seashore, possibly in a trance or a deep dream state, and a troup of leprechauns tried to carry him off. But he awoke and grabbed three of them. "Life for life," they demanded, meaning they would give him a gift if he did them no harm.[18] Having considerable patience of mind and realizing his advantage, Fergus asked them for the ability to travel under lakes, waterfalls, and seas (all common entrances to the Celtic Otherworld).

The dwarfs granted him this request, except they put a taboo on journeying under a particular lake in his own neighborhood. The dwarfs then put special herbs into Fergus's ears, and after that "he used to go with them under seas." Another version of the tale attributes Fergus's power to a magical cloak the leprechauns gave him. When wearing it, he could pass under seas and lakes and enter the realm of Faerie at will.

Fergus's "deal" with the dwarfish spirits seems quick, straightforward, and to the point. Many people learning to journey shamanically for the first time are surprised by the fact that they just do it, and it works. Although performed with great ceremonial care from then on, journeying into non-ordinary reality is a matter-of-fact activity. As modern people we may start out distrustful of the spirit realms and find it difficult to accept and understand how the spirits need and desire to associate with human beings, and how they make it easy (within limits) for this to occur. One of the distinguishing marks of the shaman is conscious mastery over the journey into nonordinary reality after overcoming initial fear. He or she does not remain a confused visitor in the Otherworld, but becomes a master explorer of nonordinary terrain. And yet, almost as if the spirits want to save us from hubris, they often throw in some hitch or taboo. It might mean, as in Fergus's case, that we cannot enter the Otherworld through a lake in our own backyard.

CUCHULAIN

In Irish mythology, Cuchulain, the great warrior hero, suffered a faery sickness as part of his introduction into the Otherworld.[19] One day while hunting birds near a lake, Cuchulain fell asleep near a menhir, a standing stone marking a spot of great power and often a connecting point with the spirit world. Unbeknownst to the hero, the two birds he was pursuing were really Fand and Liban, two faery sisters who were actually pursuing him. Then, either while asleep or upon awaking, Cuchulain encountered the two women, one dressed in red, the other in green. Laughing at him and striking him with a whip, they continued to beat the hero until he was almost dead. The warrior went to bed with a strange malady that no druid or doctor could cure. He remained bedridden for a year and did not speak to anyone, until on Samhain Eve (the night before Halloween), a spirit visitor appeared to him, singing a curing song, inviting Cuchulain to follow him into the Otherworld.

Cuchulain then returned to the menhir where he was first faerystruck. Here Liban appeared to him and persuaded him to enter Faerie to help her people fight an enemy. In exchange, her sister Fand would become his wife. Cuchulain accepted, won the faery battle, wedded Fand, and stayed with her for a month. Then they returned to the world of ordinary reality, where

Cuchulain was confronted by his mortal wife Emer. Druids gave the unhappy couple magical drinks of forgetfulness, one for Cuchulain to forget Fand and another for Emer to forget the incident. Mananan, the Sea God, provided an enchanted cloak that would forever keep Cuchulain and Fand apart. This seemed to work; domestic happiness returned to Cuchulain and Emer's household, and Cuchulain never returned to the Otherworld until his death.

The man or woman being initiated into shamanic mysteries commonly suffers a debilitating illness during which he or she has the first meaningful encounter with spirits who use the delerium or coma to introduce the aspirant to the shamanic state of consciousness. For example, Kyzlasov, a Siberian shaman, was ill for seven years. According to his wife, "Sickness seized him when he was twenty-three years old, and he became a shaman at the age of thirty."[20]

When the potential Celtic shaman recovers from the illness, he or she may have no conscious memory of the journey, and may suffer considerable memory loss about what occured in ordinary reality as well. Many individuals reject the shamanic call during this crisis journey and afterwards continue to live their lives as ordinary men and women. They do not choose to become shamans. Some "refusers" become what I call "dysfunctional shamans," people who know and understand the power of the shaman, and to a greater or lesser extent are haunted by it, but are reluctant to exercise that power in their own lives.

Dysfunctional shamans seldom regain their former enthusiasm for life. They seem to be adversely marked, condemned to a life of listlessness. Many die shortly after returning to ordinary reality (which the Celts naturally blame on the faeries). This is not greatly different from accounts in other societies in which refusal of the shamanic vocation results in continued illness, lethargy, and death. The German ethnopsychologist Holgar Kalweit describes this rejection of power as an attempt to close the doors of perception after they have been opened and we experience "a more diverse and varied world." He says "they cannot be closed again; otherwise the impressions streaming though these doors will congest, swamp everything, and drown us in an *uncontrolled* mystical vision."[21] In terms of the shamanic archetype, these individuals suffer great psychic damage in their attempts to repress the shamanic energy they once experienced so dramatically, an energy that the true shaman would learn how to master.

TUAN MAC CARELL

An Irish monk of about the sixth century named Finnian of Moville discovered an old pagan warrior living nearby, Tuan Mac Carell. He invited Tuan to the monastery to tell stories about the Old Ones of Ireland. Tuan accepted and related heroic tales about the settlers who first came to Ireland in mythological times. It was not an unusual repertoire of stories, except for one incredible fact. Tuan claimed to have been present from the very beginning and to have participated in the Irish history he was retelling. In fact, Tuan's narrative is a perplexing blend of ancient mythology, history, and autobiography. As Tuan tells it, each time he was on the verge of death, he shapeshifted and was reborn as a strong, vigorous bird, animal, or fish from whose perspective he continued to witness the history of Ireland. By his own reckoning he lived 320 years before being reborn as a man.

Tuan's transformations and rebirthings represent a strong shamanic tradition. As a man he lived "from hill to hill, and from cliff to cliff," in the wilderness. In his own words he was "hairy, clawed, withered, grey, naked, wretched, miserable." Then "as I was asleep one night, I saw myself passing into the shape of a stag" and then he was "young and glad of heart."[22] As a stag Tuan became King of the Deer, the Animal Master associated with shamanism since the paleolithic era. Whenever Tuan grew old and prepared to die, he was transformed into a boar, a hawk, or a salmon. The cycle of animal transformations was finally interrupted when, as a salmon, Tuan was caught by a fisherman and broiled for the wife of Carell, a local chieftain. She ate the fish and, nine months later, gave birth to Tuan Mac Carell.

Tuan relates that he always visited a particular place, a power spot, for these transformations to occur. He also fasted for three days and nights in preparation. The isolated haunts in woods and caves and the physical suffering of fasting are customary traditions of shamans. These rituals prepare the shaman to see the animal spirits and to shapeshift into their forms on soul flights into nonordinary reality. Tuan undoubtedly experienced his various transformations while in trance states, and as creatures of air, water, and land, he acquired intimate knowledge of the natural world to complement his knowledge of Irish history. He became a seer, poet, storyteller, and a carrier of the folk memory. He could teach the inner mysteries of both ordinary and nonordinary reality.

DEITIES, HEROES, AND SUPER-SHAMANS

Historically, epic poetry and cultural mythology may have originated in the visionary work of a people's shamans. In his vast study of comparative religion, Mircea Eliade speculates that the material that becomes a culture's mythology is derived in part from the journeys of historical shamans into the Otherworld. In his words, the core stories were "of ecstatic origin in the sense that they were borrowed from the narratives of shamans describing their journeys and adventures in the superhuman worlds."[23] Certainly the oldest tales and legends about the origins of a people and their culture heroes had to have been first articulated by someone who today would be said to have a "creative imagination." I use this term to refer to a person's ability to describe and impart shape and structure to visionary experiences, not to imply that the products of the imagination are fantasy, mere speculation, or raving hallucinations that have no basis in ordinary or nonordinary reality. Even if the products of the imagination are in some mundane sense "not real," certainly the human being in whose imagination they occur is real, is historical. It is similar to arguing that both a dream and the content of a dream are real, but each in a different way. Of course, the dreamer, too, is real, also in a way that differs from the dream and the dream's content.

If Celtic gods, goddesses, and heroes are viewed in this light, then we have several possibilities for interpreting them and several windows through which to look for the original Celtic shamans. The deities and superheroes might have been spirits encountered by shamans on their Otherworldly journeys, which became the material for stories to educate, enlighten, and entertain their people and to bolster their reputations as shamans. In time, as shamanism declined in favor of a more structured priesthood (as Joseph

Campbell has argued),[24] the stories were told without their original shamanic context as simple, straightforward tales about gods and goddesses.

Another way to interpret stories about deities and superheroes is that they were originally stories about historical shamans themselves possibly based on their journeys into nonordinary reality. Shamans, like most people who claim magical powers, are routinely perceived as larger than life by their communities, so it would not be surprising to find that stories about their activities (especially after their deaths) had a supernatural quality. As stories about shamans were told and retold from generation to generation (and as belief in shamanism declined), the heroes of the stories were turned into gods or other supernatural heroes, since feats of magic and power would no longer be attributed to mere human beings.

Strong evidence that the tales were originally about humans, not deities, is the education and training (the fosterage) of the hero. Although the hero in many tales is presented as a god, his birth, upbringing, and initiation into the mysteries of magic indicate that he or she was not born with such knowledge and skill. The hero had to learn it, like a mortal. It is indicative of the close link between shamans and mythological heroes that the hero's training and initiation resembles the same procedure as those for a candidate for shamanhood: abduction by spirits, magicians, witches; training in magic and ecstatic techniques; an isolated childhood in the woods or a distant land; a series of magical tasks and insurmountable obstacles to overcome; and finally, initiation into adulthood/shamanhood.

Mircea Eliade makes an important point in this regard, concerning the true nature of the shaman, one that is not discussed very widely or openly among contemporary practitioners of shamanism. Namely, the shaman is, in some sense, a spirit. He or she can, while in a nonordinary state of consciousness, transcend the human condition and function as a spirit. Says Eliade, "By crossing, in ecstasy, the 'dangerous' bridge that connects the two worlds and that only the dead can attempt, the shaman proves that he is spirit, is no longer a human being."[25] If this is true, we can better understand how stories about the accomplishments of gods and superheroes could be attributed to shamans and vice versa. The shaman, more than other people, shares in the spiritual nature of the gods and goddesses.

◆

This spiritual aspect of the shaman's nature seems to be a bit embarrassing for modern shamanic practitioners, judging by the great reticence surrounding it. We live and practice in a society that does not recognize the daily presence and influence of spirits, and our culture generally does not accept the notion that a human being can "become" a spirit. Perhaps in spite of our commitment to the principles and practices of shamanism, we are still children of our age, and we feel more comfortable "explaining" the shamanic journey in psychological terms (archetypes, the collective unconscious, the active imagination) rather than in the older framework of spirits and spirit world. But in doing so, are we underestimating the shamanic experience, our practice, or even ourselves? As shamanic practitioners, do we become spirits in making the "dangerous crossing" into the spirit world? And are we, as Eliade notes, in some sense "dead" while we journey, and therefore, in some sense, no longer human beings? If the shamanic journey is a form of rehearsal for death, then perhaps modern shamans should emphasize this aspect of shamanic practice if they hope to function as counselors for the dying.

For a variety of reasons, we find that Celtic deities, human heroes, and shamans share the same types of magical powers such as control over weather, the ability to shapeshift or transform someone else into another shape, and the power to heal illness or restore the dead to life. We also have reason to view the nature of individual characters from more than one perspective: deity, superhero, and shaman.

However we choose to view them, the legends of Celtic heroes can serve as the accounts of even more ancient gods and goddesses, or even of ancestral shamans. If we remain flexible in our interpretive approaches, mythological tales will serve us as important cultural artifacts that shed light on the Celts' understanding of shamans and shamanic experiences.

SHAPESHIFTING, SEVERED HEADS, AND THE WEB OF LIFE

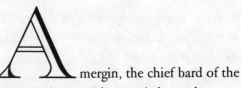mergin, the chief bard of the invading Milesians, stepped on Ireland's shores with a poetic boast that continues to haunt the Celtic imagination.

> I am the wind that blows across the sea;
> I am a wave of the deep;
> I am the roar of the ocean;
> I am the stag of seven battles;
> I am a hawk on the cliff;
> I am a ray of sunlight;
> I am the greenest of plants;
> I am the wild boar;
> I am a salmon in the river;
> I am a lake on the plain;

◆

I am the word of knowledge;
I am the point of a spear;
I am the lure beyond the ends of the earth;
I can shift my shape like a god.[1]

The "Song of Amergin," considered to be one of the oldest Irish liter-ary works, reflects the victorious spirit of the Milesians, who were among the original settlers in Ireland. It also captures an ancient human aspiration that colors future Celtic folklore and literature, namely, the identification of the bard or storyteller with the inner life of his subject matter, or in sha-manic terms, the ability to shapeshift into the spirit of other created things.

In a similar vein, the Welsh bard Taliesin sang:

I have been in many shapes:
I have been a narrow blade of a sword;
I have been a drop in the air;
I have been a shining star;
I have been a word in a book;
I have been an eagle;
I have been a boat on the sea;
I have been a string on a harp;
I have been enchanted for a year in the foam of water.
There is nothing in which I have not been.

The remarkable proclamation in this last line, the ability to "be in" everything in creation, is a key component of shamanism. The shaman's "techniques of ecstasy" are not just techniques for standing outside one's own consciousness, although getting outside one's self is the first movement of the soul on the shamanic journey. The next step is what truly distin-guishes the shaman from other out-of-body sojourners: the ability to enter other realms of existence, participate in the secret lives of other creatures, and communicate with their inner spirits. The ability to send one's own consciousness into the consciousness of another entity—whether it be the wind, a hawk, a string on a harp, or an entire landscape, either in this world or the Otherworld—and return to one's own self is at the heart of the sha-man's journey.

This chapter will explore the ancient practice of shapeshifting as a key element of the Celtic spirit. The art of shape changing is dependent upon an equally ancient understanding of the universe that Celtic peoples retained well into the present era—the interconnectedness of all created things, commonly referred to as the Circle or Web of Life. Like a Celtic braid, looped back upon itself and entwined through its own twistings and turnings, the continuity of existence is an unbroken chain linking all elements of the universe. Shamans' abilities to shapeshift are directly related to their understanding that on the Web of Life all created things share in the same power, and can *exchange* power, life, and consciousness. Recognizing that creation is more loosely knotted than it may seem, shamans enter the experiential state of other entities and allow other entities to share in the shamans' own conscious experiences. It is like trading heads for a time, or emptying your own head so that it can be filled with new perceptions and new life. The pagan Celts had a strong fascination with this concept. Taken to its most extreme realization, it meant severing a head from its body, preserving it, and honoring it.

The Shifting of Consciousness

In order to journey into other realms, we must do more than get out of the body; we must get out of the head. The shaman is a master of escaping the mind-body matrix that characterizes ordinary consciousness and entering the shamanic or nonordinary state of consciousness. In this dreamlike state the imaginal realm reshapes itself, creating a placeless, timeless field in which the shaman can participate in the consciousness of other creatures. It is at this point that shamanic journeying and shapeshifting share a common enterprise. Shapeshifting requires reshaping the imaginal realm, and consciousness becomes *objectified* in some other thing. Journeying reshapes the imaginal realm, and consciousness becomes *geographied*; it becomes the spirit world in which the shaman will travel. Shapeshifting is consciousness-as-object; journeying is consciousness-as-landscape.

Journeying and shapeshifting are both forms of entering or merging. In journeying the shaman enters the spirit world. In shapeshifting the shaman enters the spirit of an animal, plant, or object. In both cases, the shaman's imaginal realm reshapes itself (spontaneously and by the will of the shaman) so the shaman's consciousness can flow into and merge with the consciousness of something else. To a greater or lesser extent, depending on the power or desire of the shaman, some percentage of his or her consciousness becomes the consciousness of the other thing, and some percentage, usually smaller, remains the shaman's so he or she retains control over the experience and can return to the ordinary state.

Shapeshifting, like the shamanic journey, begins in the mind, in the imagination, which is the shaman's tool for describing the content of the imaginal realm, or nonordinary reality. Once the shaman's consciousness has shifted, its inner structure has reshaped itself, and the shaman participates in the consciousness of another animal, plant, or object. The shaman's aura may actually take on the plant's shape or radiate the energy associated with the animal. Finally, when these changes have occurred, and if the shaman is powerful enough, the physical body is transformed so others can see the change. The shaman will then look and act like the animal, plant, or object.

Although the physical transformation may be the most dramatic aspect of shapeshifting for onlookers, it is not the most important. Were a shaman to shift his or her physical body without the important shift in consciousness, the feat would bestow little power or knowledge upon the shapeshifter. It would be form without substance. It would be mere showmanship, lacking the deep identification of subject with object, an identification attested to by many shamans who become their spirits or, in some rare cases, are temporarily possessed by them.

There are interesting ramifications to shapeshifting both for the shaman and other members of the community. In Senegal, for example, the Badyaranke people claim that a person's soul can dissociate from the body by its own volition and appear in the form of any natural object. Encountering natural phenomena that appear to behave suspiciously or unnaturally is a perilous event. An animal, a tree, the wind, or a storm may be the soul of a hostile shaman or magician. Of course, there is danger for the shaman, too, for he or she could be captured, injured, or killed in this other form.

Shamans interviewed by anthropologists and explorers over the last century claim they acquire their power from the animals and spirits of nature, sometimes from a direct identification with nature. This means that they merge their consciousness with the elements of the universe through the shamanic journey to the realms of spirit. They shapeshift into the animal from whom they seek knowledge and power. Ward Rutherford, who has studied and written about many forms of archaic religions, suggests that such shapeshifting experiences may have been a prerequisite to becoming a bard,[2] and since bards and druids became almost synonymous, we can suppose that it was a requirement for druidry as well, and that both bards and druids acquired their powers from shapeshifting into nature, the elements, and animals.

Druids were the archshapeshifters in ancient Celtic culture. Through spells and incantations, druids cast enchantments over men and women, turning them into animals, birds, plants, and natural objects. The druids' "magic sleep" may have been a hypnotic trance similar to the shamanic trance in which they changed their shapes or delved into the deeper, unseen realms of the Otherworld. The druidic teaching of metempsychosis—that the soul survives death and passes into other forms of existence—strongly reflects the view that the spirit is maleable and capable of partaking in the physical and spiritual life of other things.

Nowhere is shapeshifting more dramatically expressed than in the complex lives and escapades of Celtic heroes and deities. We have seen how Tuan Mac Carell spent periods of time as a stag, an eagle, and a salmon during which he learned the history of the Irish race and became wise in the ways of transformation. Fintan, another mythological shapeshifter, spent many centuries in various shapes, observing the history of Ireland and becoming a link in what he called "the continuity of existence."[3] The witch-goddess Morgan, one of the nine sisters who guarded the Cauldron of Rebirth, is described by the poet Taliesin as one who "has learned the uses of all plants in curing the ills of the body; she knows, too, the art of

changing her shape, of flying through the air."[4] Her comprehensive healing knowledge, plus her ability to fly and shapechange, strongly suggest that
she derived her magic from the same source as shamans.

In some instances, universal knowledge comes instantaneously to the
neophyte, almost like a flash of mystical insight. Such was the case of Taliesin, who, in a reversal of the usual shamanic training, received the shaman's
vision first and then was initiated (and tested) in a death-threatening and
ego-shattering round of events. It happened this way. The goddess Cerridwen asked the young boy Gwion (later called Taliesin) to watch and stir
her cauldron in which she brewed the drink of inspiration and wisdom. She
had planned to give this potion to her son to make him a sage and seer to
compensate for his lack of physical beauty. Three drops of the potion spilled
on Gwion's finger, and he immediately stuck the finger into his mouth to
cool it, whereupon he received the cauldron's gift of wisdom. The rest of the
brew turned to poison, cracked the cauldron, ran out on the ground, and
eventually polluted a stream and poisoned the horses who drank there.

Cerridwen was furious that the boy had snatched the cauldron's power
right out from under her nose. Gwion fled her wrath, but she pursued him
in a shapeshifting race. He turned himself into a hare; she changed into a
greyhound; he, a fish; she, an otter; he, a bird; she, a falcon. Finally he
changed himself into a kernel of corn, but she gulped him down as a hen.
Later she rebirthed him as the child who would grow up to become the
great poet Taliesin. Ironically, Taliesin was beautiful (his name means the
"Radiant Brow"). But Cerridwen's fury was unabated. She wrapped Taliesin
in a leather bag and threw him into the sea. He was rescued and lived to
become the poet who would later boast that there was nothing in which
he had not been.

THE RESHAPING OF TIME

So central to Celtic mysticism is the experience of participating in the
myriad forms of creation that it even extends into the ability to shift consciousness into human history. Even historic events can be bent and turned
around on the braid of time. In a long poem Taliesin recounts all the

moments in human history that he personally witnessed. The list is impressive, going back to the very creation of the world as it is described by Christian apologists. He claims to have been present "when Lucifer fell into the deepest hell"; he "carried the banner before Alexander"; he was "in Africa before the building of Rome"; he accompanied "Heon to the vale of Hebron"; he was there when "Absalom was slain"; he boasts that he was "patriarch to Elijah and Enoch"; he "was in the Ark with Noah" and "witnessed the destruction of Sodom and Gommorah"; he sailed with the surviving "remnant of Troy"; he "upheld Moses through the water of the Jordan"; he was "with the Lord in the manger of the ass"; and he announces, "I was at the Cross with Mary Magdalen."[5]

In many cultures, shamans are keepers of the folk memory, and memorize the people's history, reviewing and reliving it in their journeys into nonordinary reality. In fact, most archaic societies have periodic rituals in which they re-enact the cosmogonic myth of the people. They recreate the primordial time, the Dreamtime as the Australians call it, when supernatural beings created landscapes and the first people. Shamans relive these sacred events in their journeys. In time their understanding of what they have learned from older shamans and what they have experienced firsthand in trance may become blurred. There are several complicating factors. Some shamans get old and senile, and their recollective faculties are less sharp. Also some of their experiences in trance contain information they may have originally received from their own mentors years before, who in turn may have had an equally muddy view of actual history, personal visionary experience, and the shared visions of their own associates.

The point here is not the historical accuracy of the events they know about and/or have personally witnessed. The point is that shamans embody the inner and outer history of their people, and their tales blend both personal journeys to the Otherworld and the collective history, both sacred and profane, of the entire tribe. If the exact particulars are muddled in fact and fancy—and they are—the result is not necessarily due to the shaman's penchant for deception. A shaman may not be lying in his or her boasts of being omniscient and omnipresent. In nonordinary reality shamans are everywhere and capable of knowing all human knowledge.

The Severed Head

The last line of Amergin's song, "I can shift my shape like a god," provides an insight into how the Celtic shaman acquired far-ranging knowledge and transformational powers. This rendering of the line calls attention to the practice of shapeshifting as a function of divine power, strongly suggesting that the essence of the Divine is change, transformation, and creative renewal. Other translations make no mention of shapeshifting or transformation. They are concerned with fire and the head. Among the alternate translations of "I can shift my shape like a god" are:

I am the god who fashions fire in the head.[6]

I am the god who fashions fire for the head.[7]

I am a wizard: who but I sets the cool head aflame with smoke?[8]

I am the god who creates in the head of man the fire of thought.[9]

I am wisdom: who but I cools the head aflame with smoke?[10]

Collectively these different versions agree on two points more concerned with shapeshifting than might first appear. Shapeshifting occurs in the head and is analogous to fire, the most radically transformative of the elements. Put simply, the last line may be paraphrased: "I am the fire of imagination" or "I burn with visions of another world." We can enrich our understanding of the shapeshifter's primary tool, the visionary imagination, by looking at both of these aspects: fire and the head.

The ancient Celts were famous (and infamous) for their cult of the severed head. Celtic warriors flaunted their enemies' heads, either tied to their horses or worn around their own necks, practices that disgusted the Romans and terrified enemy tribes, as was intended. Severed heads were impaled on gateposts and placed outside doorways; some were raised on stakes for protection, and others were embalmed and preserved in special chests, kept by relatives as family heirlooms. Fragments of skulls were worn as amulets. Gilded skulls were used for sacred drinking vessels, and less embellished skulls were used as cups at wells.

Caches of skulls have been found in storage pits in Danebury in southern Britain. Heads sculpted in stone and stylized skulls carved in temples and monuments by Celtic artisans can still be seen in France at the oppidum of Entremont and at Roquepertuse. In temple architecture skulls were given a place of honor and carefully inserted in specially carved niches. Some sculpted heads depict two or three faces. Was the sculptor hoping to indicate the head's magical powers to see in more than one direction, perhaps forward and backward in time, or into other imaginal realms of being, the realms behind the eyes? Was the sculptor trying to express a concept of the visions that appear in the "head-behind-the-head"? As Celtic scholar and archeologist Barry Cunliffe maintains, it is very difficult to interpret all the findings and locations of sculpted skulls and severed heads.[11] But one thing is clear from the care and reverence with which they were treated. The cult of the human head was more than pagan bloodthirstiness.

Quite the contrary. The severed head was, in Celticist Anne Ross's estimation, a religious symbol as representative of the Celts' spirituality as the sign of the Cross is for Christianity. The symbol of the severed head "sums up the whole of pagan Celtic religion," says Ross, and in its various iconographic and literary expressions we find "the hard core of Celtic religion."[12]

The Celts believed that the soul was immortal and that its earthly housing was the head. Possessing someone's head was the same as possessing that person's soul, spirit, and personal power, analogous to the practice found among some cultures of eating the heart or brain of a noble warrior or admired enemy in order to ingest his strength and prowess. The ancient Celts believed that the head could remain alive after death and decapitation, moving, talking, singing, prophesizing, and entertaining with stories. In some legends a severed head presides over the great feasts of the Otherworld.

From a shamanic point of view, it is very likely that the skull or severed head was one of the shapeshifter's primary power objects, a physical tool that represents and contains the sacred. Amergin's provocative statement about building fire for the head strongly suggests this. As a shamanic symbol the skull is not merely empty—it is *emptied*, hollowed out, prepared for another kind of consciousness. Lame Deer, a Sioux medicine man, explained that the traditional sweat lodge ceremony before a vision quest had the same effect. "It seemed to have made my brains empty," he said. "Maybe that was good, plenty of room for new insights."[13]

As a power object or magical tool, the skull represents what the shapeshifter must do with his or her own head in order to assume the consciousness of another creature. The mind, emptied like the head, must be recast as the shamanically trained smith recasts metals; it must be infused with the fire of imagination that begins the transformation into another form of consciousness. Like the Hollow Hills or the faery mounds, the smooth, rounded skull, cleared of ordinary consciousness, becomes the gateway through which the shaman journeys into the Otherworld. To borrow a term from the Huichol Indians in northern Mexico, the skull contains the *neireka*, the portal in the mind through which everyone passes at death into the Next World, but through which the shaman knows how to pass and return in this life.

There are other clues that the severed head is a shamanic symbol of transformation. A Celtic shrine at Roquepertuse consists of three upright columns with a horizontal lintel, typical of the rougher dolmens found throughout Celtic lands. In the columns are carved niches that contained human skulls. On the lintel is a bird, poised to take off in flight. In shamanic traditions the bird is a prominent power animal or spirit guide, representing the soul's flight into other worlds. Also at Roquepertuse is another stone bird holding in its beak two heads facing opposite directions, a motif strongly suggestive of the shaman's dual consciousness.

THE MYSTERIOUS BATTLE AURA

In Celtic legends fire in the head is also indicative of a warrior's battle-consciousness, another kind of altered state. The great warrior Cuchulain, for example, exhibited the "hero's light," or flaming aura, around his head when he was excited and frenzied for battle. When the light appeared, he could perform his famous "salmon's leap" and cover great distances or heights. As he raged in battle, he magically revolved within his skin so that he could fight in all directions. His hair stood on end with drops of blood or sparks of fire at the tip of each strand. In the pitch of battle fever the "hero's moon" rose from his forehead "as thick as a whetstone," and a stream of black blood geysered from his skull as tall as a ship's mainmast. The heat from his body warmed three vats of water. One would think that the pyrotechnics erupting around Cuchulain would have eliminated the need for actual armed conflict. But undaunted enemies rose to the challenge and failed. On one occasion Cuchulain juggled nine captured heads in one hand and ten in the other. When he finally met his own death and was beheaded, his head was placed on a rock that split in two.

Celtic scholar Marie-Louise Sjoestedt has shown that many root words for *hero* in Indo-European languages contain the idea of fury, ardour, tumescence, and speed.[14] The hero was the ardent one, filled with blazing energy, overflowing and erupting with power and life. The frenzied pre-battle rituals that Celtic warriors conducted in view of their enemies could have been exercises to build up "battle heat," as much as they were a form of guerrilla theater to terrorize the enemy before the battle began. It is not inconceivable that the custom of fighting naked was also a strategy to put the warrior in an altered frame of mind, although it too was a tactic to unnerve and distract the enemy. In any event, to their enemies, Celtic warriors seemed to be reckless, bizarre, and out of their minds.

Another variation of the mysterious aura around the head is seen on stone carvings of Celtic male deities. Those found at Heidelberg, Pfalzfeld, and Holtzgerlingen in Germany show two thick, turbanlike lobes surrounding the top of the head. Do they reflect the two hemispheres of the brain? Do they portray the hero's light or the intensity of mental energy needed to shapechange? Celtic scholar Proinsias Mac Cana suggests that the lobes on these pre-Christian carvings indicate the sacred or supernatural.[15] Later in the Christian era, the solar disc, or halo, behind the head of a saint was the artistic conceit for suggesting the same sacred quality. In fact, Celtic monks were frequently seen with a brilliant, otherworldly light shining around them. Such a light burned around St. Columba when he was alone at his prayers. When his fellow monks spied on him, they found the entire church filled with light. A column of light, similar to Cuchulain's battle-frenzied shaft, rose flaming from the saint's head. It is also interesting that at these times of intense prayer, angels were seen to hover around him, whispering in his ear. Most likely, Columba was in a trance and communicating with his helping spirits.

The flame of thought in the mind, whether kindled by druid, monk, wizard, god, or the heroes themselves, is analogous to the intense body heat typical of shamans in northern Asia. Similarly, Tibetan monks, trained in yogic traditions that originated in shamanic practices, can raise their body temperatures to melt snow. In some cultures a feverish physical state accompanies the nonordinary state of consciousness, a condition the !Kung in Africa call "boiling energy." We have seen that the ability to produce intense body heat and resist cold is a sign of shamanic election among the Eskimo. The explorer Rasmussen found an Eskimo shaman who explained: "Every real shaman has to feel an illumination in his body, in the inside of his head or in his brain, something that gleams like fire, that gives him the power to see with closed eyes into the darkness, into the hidden things or into the future or into the secrets of another man."[16] Michael Harner describes the Jivaro shaman of the Amazon as one who gives off light, "particularly in a 'crown,' an aura from the head" when the shaman is in an altered state of consciousness. It can only be seen, however, by another shaman who is also in an altered state of consciousness.[17] Whether visible to others or not, the internal light or fire is a key element of shamanic experience.

Skulls, Cups, and Cauldrons

The use of emptied skulls as drinking cups at wells is another strong indication that the severed head was a shamanic power object. The sacred well is, in Celtic tradition, an important entrance to the Otherworld. Some skulls found at the bottom of wells might have been former drinking goblets that fell accidentally into the water; or they might have been placed there purposefully as reminders to those who gaze into the depths that here is an entry to another, deeper world, a world that in shamanic terms resides in the head. Anne Ross maintains that the large number of skulls found in pools and wells, along with pottery and sculpted heads, definitely links the head with the realm of the divine. She notes that in some places the skull was considered to be the guardian of the well and hence a guardian to the Otherworld.[18]

A head's guardianship of the gateways to the Otherworld could be dramatically symbolized in rituals that use a skull as a goblet, especially rituals to initiate aspiring druids into the priesthood. Druids used skull goblets in sacred ceremonies. The Roman historian Livy writes that a skull was used as "a holy vessel to pour libations and as a drinking cup for the priest and the temple attendants."[19] Since details of druidic rituals have been lost over time, we can only speculate about the nature of the ceremonial drink. But based on what we know from mystery cults and initiation rituals in other cultures, the candidate was often given a mind-altering drug to induce visions and open the doorways of perception to nonordinary realities.

It is not a far stretch of the imagination to suppose that the druids, whose traditions can be traced back to ancient Greece where such mystery rites were common, also developed rites of initiation that used a mind-expanding drink. We can track the ecstatic practices of the druids even farther, into the very seat of classical shamanism itself, Siberia. Historian of European magic and witchcraft Carlo Ginzburg has pointed out the confluence of the Celts, Thracians, and Scythian tribes in the area of the lower Danube.[20] The Scythians north and west of the Black Sea had a strong shamanic culture, derived, according to Ginzburg's theory, from their contacts with Central Asian shamans. The Scythians built sweat lodges, similar in construction to those in Native America, in which they burned hemp seeds on the heated stones. The fumes produced ecstatic states of pleasure, much the same as those recorded by travelers who witnessed similar ceremonies among the Siberian shamans. Curiously, the Scythians were also fierce headhunters, thus providing another link between Celtic customs and shamanic practices in Siberia which also incorporated the use of skulls.

The very early Celts in the lower Danube could have used hallucinogenic techniques borrowed from the Siberians by way of the Scythians. They might have used the sweat lodge with mind-altering herbs, and they might have given novice druids (and others) hallucinogenic drinks in skull goblets. And assuming such was the case, since the effects of drugs are felt in the head, and since the head housed the immortal soul, the symbolism of the skull-as-goblet would not have been lost on the perceptive druids who were trained in myth and symbol. Since the head represented an aspect of the Divinity to the Celtic imagination, using the skull as a goblet for a drink that leads the initiate into the divine mysteries makes perfect sense from a magical point of view.

The Roman writer Lucan describes a Gaulish practice of ceremonially drowning a victim in a cauldron. "A man is put head-first into a full tub, so that he is suffocated."[21] The scene on the Celtic-made Gundestrup cauldron (c. 200 B.C.) seems to be depicting this brutal sacrifice. However, another, more humane, interpretation is possible based on our understanding of the sacredness of the head and the well as an entrance into the Otherworld. But to reach this interpretation we must consider another cauldron, the Cauldron of Rebirth.

Originating in Ireland, the Cauldron of Rebirth found its way to Britain where it was kept by the High King, Bran the Blessed. Later it was returned to Ireland. As time went on, Bran led his armies across the sea and invaded Ireland to rescue his sister Branwen and retrieve the Cauldron of Rebirth. During the campaign the Irish used the cauldron to restore their slain soldiers; a dead soldier who was put into the cauldron returned to life the next day, although he was stricken dumb and unable to speak about his experiences in the Otherworld. The scene depicted on the Gundestrup cauldron seems to reflect this process. Lined up are warriors waiting to be put headfirst into the cauldron. Above them is another line of warriors on horseback, riding off presumably to fight another day.

Thus the cauldron functions as a miniature well, or an entry into the Otherworld. Rather than being used to drown a victim (which, of course, is also an effective method of entering the Otherworld), it is a container to receive the bodies of the slain, headfirst, who are revivified by the potion inside. If the cauldron is over a fire (there does not seem to be a fire on the Gundestrup scene, however), we are once again back to the notion of the shaman's fire in the head. In this case, the head is put in first, then the entire body, and the spirit is quickened and brought back to life. In the literary accounts of Bran's raid in Ireland, the cauldron is indeed heated before receiving the bodies of the dead soldiers.

This tale connects our themes of shapeshifting and severed heads in yet other ways. While fighting the Irish, Bran is wounded in the foot by a poisoned arrow. He commands his men to cut off his head and take it back to bury in London. But in the meantime he promises that his head will continue to talk to the men, entertain them, and serve as guide through the Otherworld. His explicit instructions are for the men to spend seven years feasting and listening to songs from the birds of the goddess Rhiannon, whose music created a trance state in listeners, thus lulling them into nonordinary reality. After this the head continued to converse for another eighty years while the seven warriors pursued their feasting and otherworldly enjoyments, forgetting all the sorrows of ordinary life. Their sojourn in the Otherworld was filled with joy, mirth, and what must have been an interminable, but hopefully interesting, discourse from Bran's talking head. One of these seven warriors was Taliesin.

Like a Celtic knot, the themes of shapeshifting, wisdom, rebirth, severed heads, and magical cauldrons are braided together through the episodes of Taliesin's life. He received wisdom from Cerridwen's cauldron when he tasted the magical brew that had spilled on his fingers. To elude her anger, he shapeshifted into animal forms and, as a kernel of corn, he was devoured by a hen. Later, as a baby, he was cast into the sea wrapped in a leather bag that was meant to suffocate and drown him. As an adult, Taliesin accompanied Bran's army to Ireland to retrieve the Cauldron of Rebirth, decapitated the British king, and journeyed to the Otherworld where he continued to be initiated into the secrets and mysteries of the cosmos.

Clearly we are working with a complex set of interlocking symbols and images, but the classic elements of the shaman's initiation is a key to understanding them. Although they seem to defy time and space, as visionary experiences they form a coherent whole: death or near-death experiences and the resulting transformations of consciousness; the help of animal spirits and the ability to transform into them to receive their specific energy and knowledge; the journey into nonordinary reality; the realization that all creation is interchangeable, and in some sense, one. It is hard not to imagine that Taliesin was a Welsh shaman, a master of ecstatic states.

The Skull of Wisdom

The severed head as a source of truth, wisdom, and healing is a common theme in Celtic culture. In addition to the Welsh tale of Bran, ancient Irish accounts tell of severed heads which, when placed on stone pillars, would talk, sing, and even move around. In some tales, including stories about Christian saints, the severed head causes a spring to flow forth at the spot where it is laid or staked. Inevitably, the waters that flow from it contain magical healing properties. For example, according to a Christian legend, St. Melor's head was fixed on a staff which, when stuck into the earth, turned into a beautiful tree, and from its roots a continuous fountain of water began to spring forth. The waters were, as might be expected, medicinal.

The severed head as the source of truth and wisdom is found in other cultures. In Greece, for example, Orpheus possessed many shamanic skills: the ability to heal, cast spells and enchantments, divine the future, establish a rapport with animals, and, most importantly, travel to and from the Lowerworld. The bacchantes beheaded him and tossed his head into the Hebrus River. It floated to the Island of Lesbos, singing all the way. Later, it was used as an oracle. In Teutonic myths the god Mimir's head guarded a well at the base of the world tree Yggdrasil. At this well the Great Norse Shaman, Odin, received wisdom and understanding and unraveled the secrets of the runes.

Mircea Eliade notes that the Yukagir people of Central Asia preserved the skulls of shamans and revered them as sacred objects.[22] They, too, were considered to be repositories of ancient knowledge and information about the afterlife. The Yukagir consulted a shaman's skull before undertaking any important enterprise. The simplest method of divination was to note whether the skull seemed light or heavy, which indicated a yes or no answer respectively.

THE WEB OF LIFE

In *The Black Book of Camarthan*, an early Welsh work, we find a Christianization of Amergin's ancient boast, in which, according to religious writer Robert Van de Weyer, the "I am" statements are attributed to God, not the shaman/poet.[23] Some images remain the same, and some are new:

I am the wind that breathes upon the sea,
I am the wave on the ocean,
I am the murmur of leaves rustling,
I am the rays of the sun,
I am the beam of the moon and stars,
I am the power of trees growing,
I am the bud breaking into blossom, etc.

Amergin's enigmatic last line, "I can shift my shape like a god," that we have focused on as the "flame of thought" or the "fire of shamanic transformation," is here rendered:

I am the thoughts of all people
Who praise my beauty and grace.

We find here some interesting shifts in emphasis that reveal important aspects of the gradual Christianization of pagan Celtic thought. The pagan could make a bold statement concerning the power to shapeshift like a god, or to actually be the god who puts thoughts/experiences in the mind. The Christian, however, attributes this power to God alone, transcendent and existing independently of human consciousness. For the shaman, the thoughts/experiences of all creation can manifest in the human mind because he or she knows the techniques of ecstasy that facilitate those thoughts and experiences. And in the creation of thoughts and experiences, the shaman becomes a god or shares in God's power. The Christian version has two possible interpretations. Either God puts the thoughts of praise in the human mind, or by praising God's beauty and grace, a person can experience God within his or her mind. In spite of the different emphasis, we are still dealing with a unity and coherence of mental energy between the Divine and the human, as is contained in the earlier pagan version of the poem.

The lines immediately following this verse attributed to God are, in Van de Weyer's account, expressions of the soul. Again, many of them are the same images as in the pagan version. Immediately apparent here is that the soul does not claim to be one with creation in its raw, elemental state, but in conjunction with some human or divine attribute.

I am a flame of fire, blazing with passionate love,
I am a spark of light, illuminating the deepest truth,
I am a rough ocean, heaving with righteous anger,
I am a calm lake, comforting the troubled breast,
I am a wild storm, raging at human sins,
I am a gentle breeze, blowing hope in the saddened heart,
I am dry dust, choking worldly ambition,
I am wet earth, bearing rich fruits of grace.

Retaining the pagan imagery of the classic Celtic shapeshifter's boast, the Christian writer makes the haunting beauty of the images acceptable to Christian readers by implying that the soul can participate in creation (and in the Divine spirit) only by expressing a noble or ethical quality such as passionate love, deepest truth, righteous anger, spiritual comfort, rage against sin, hope for a sad heart, and so on. Whether these statements are flowing from the human soul or from God, they have acquired a moral gloss absent in the older pagan versions.

In spite of these subtle changes, the pagan belief in the "continuity of existence," or Web of Life, has been preserved. If both God and the human soul are to be found in the ocean, a lake, a flame, a spark of light, the Celtic mind was still viewing creation from a shamanic perspective, namely, every-thing in the universe is alive, conscious, accessible, and power-filled. The Creator/Spirit and the human soul are ultimately one, made of the same substance, the same divine energy.

Celticists Alwyn and Brinley Rees point out that the similarities between druids and monks, such as we find in the variations of this poem, derive from an even older heritage.[24] The role of the saints as "controllers of nature and fertility is comparable in many ways with that of the pre-Christian druids," but, as the Reeses correctly remind us, the druids were considered to be "the peers of the Tuatha de Danann [the ancient Irish gods] as masters of wizardry." Thus we find a direct lineage for the "I am" boasts of Celtic shapeshifters. There is an unbroken line of shamanic experience from the Danann deities through the druidic priesthood right down to the Christian monks. This shamanic heritage did not end there but continued into the Middle Ages and beyond in European witchcraft, which retained the same sense of close identification with the elements of nature and the ability to control them. When we consider that this same spirit is still considered to be alive and afoot in Ireland as the faery folk, the people of the sidhe, we see a continuity of shamanic belief from mythological times to the present.

Celtic scholar Christopher Bamford explains that the Celtic interpretation of the divine savior's mission was to be "all in all," and reconcile humanity and nature in God.[25] He says, "Christianity and the act of Christ was never an end in itself" but a "divine means" to achieve that state of harmony "for which creation was intended, [and which] was always in Ireland." It is a common belief among the Irish, even today, that Ireland enjoys a special immunity to the Fall of Creation. As Bamford puts it, in Ireland, and particularly in the early Irish church, one finds a potent union of ecology and holiness, a deep understanding that nature and spirit are one, and that to live in harmony with this union is the means of achieving holiness. It is mankind's duty, therefore, to become aware of, and live within, this network of divine power and natural phenomena. Traditional shamans would explain this as their duty and privilege to *journey* into that network of divine power and natural phenomena in order to experience it and make it immediate and accessible for themselves and others.

To the Celtic mind, heaven and earth are interdependent and wondrously interactive. The worlds of spirit and matter enjoy a sacred intimacy. This is the way it had been in pagan times, and even the new religion of Christianity could not change Celtic thinking on the matter. The ancient nature worship thus survived into Christian times guaranteeing that the holy union of heaven and earth would continue to be the bedrock of Celtic spirituality.

We can look to traditional shamans for a more precise expression of this concept of spirit in matter. Among the Eskimo, there is a divine power known as Sila, "a power . . . not to be explained in simple words. A great spirit, supporting the world and the weather and all life on earth."[26] Sila speaks, not through words, "but by storm and snow and rain and the fury of the sea; all the forces of nature that men fear." But Sila also contains nature's gentleness, and speaks "by sunlight and calm of the sea, and little children innocently at play." The Eskimo shaman Najagneq explains that children hear his voice as "soft and gentle . . . almost like that of a woman." Sila is "at once among us and infinitely far away," with a voice "so fine and gentle that even children cannot become afraid. What it says is, 'Be not afraid of the universe.'"

The net of divine power described as Sila parallels the divine power in other native cultures. It is similar to the divine power the Polynesians call *mana,* the Algonquin *manitou,* the Lakota *wakanda,* the Iroquoi *orenda,* the Pawnee *tirawa,* and the !Kung *ntum.* It is very much the same idea expressed as *brahman* in India and the *tao* in China and Japan. In the European esoteric tradition, it is often called *magick.* It is the God-Without-Form, the great spirit or wondrous mystery behind all that is and, in fact, it *is* All-That-Is. In many cultures, the shaman is the person who most directly penetrates this mystery and interprets its wisdom and power for humanity.

Celtic thinkers in the Christian era called this Web of Divine Power "grace" or "Christ," and in the early Irish church this concept included the earthiness of creation, the divine gift of nature in all its physicality. In Roman Catholicism and in later Protestant forms of Christianity, however, the sacred was divorced from the secular and spirit was dissociated from matter, until finally nature was not only unholy, it was demonized. "The world, the flesh, and the devil" was a popular way of phrasing it. Thus the Western world lost the older Celtic vision of the unity of nature and divinity, of matter and spirit. The world was disenchanted; the magic of life was gone.

Among the earlier Celts the Web of Life is explicitly implied in the nature of reality, in the druidic doctrine of the immortality of the soul and in the widespread belief that human and animal life can shapeshift. In countless myths, legends, and folktales, even inanimate objects are transformed into other shapes; and physical objects, such as swords, shields, cups, cauldrons, jewelry, and clothing, contain power and produce magical effects upon those who use them. Thus for example, Arthur's sword Excaliber contains power and is in its own way a protective spirit, similar to the drum, rattle, sacred pipe, smoking herbs, and even commonplace tools and weapons that have their own helping spirits in other native and ancient cultures.

The Celts appreciated the shamanic view that energy or magic resides in everything, and that any object or thing can be a protective spirit. Thus the vital essence of the universe interconnects all created things. Behind these concepts is an unspoken sense that the nature of the universe is fluid, and that our personal identity is not bounded by skin and ego, but is holographically present in all of creation. We actually persist through all time and space and can manifest in physical forms other than the one in which we currently dwell. We can be a hawk circling overhead, the sharp point of a sword, or the lure beyond the ends of the earth.

For the shaman, human consciousness is not limited to one particular body, or one particular head. Decapitation, like dismemberment, is a process of shamanic transformation. In fact, in dismemberment journeys the shaman's head might be reforged on an anvil, boiled in a cauldron, or stuffed with crystals. But the ordeal is worth it. The reconstituted shaman returns to ordinary reality with perceptive powers that have no boundaries.

In ecstatic encounters with the Otherworld, the Celtic adventurer, whether druid, bard, monk, or average man or woman, is transformed into animals, birds, or other people and returns with new knowledge and understanding of the great Web of Life. If the adventurer has a touch of the poet (and what Celt does not), he or she can sing, like Amergin, the great mesmerizing litany of all that one has been, is, and could be again, provided, of course, one has the head for it.

3

THE EDGES
OF TWILIGHT

For Irish poets, the edge of water —where bank meets river or shore meets sea—is a place of wisdom, enlightenment, and mystical knowledge. Water, fog, mist, and dew have long fascinated the Irish, possibly because the island nation is surrounded by the sea and prone to spectacular displays of fog, mist, and cloud. But any edge or border between elemental realms, any liminal zone between two complementary terrains, or a place where opposites meet is, in the Celtic imagination, a place filled with magic.

In *The Celtic Twilight*, a collection of essays on Irish mysticism, W. B. Yeats recalls a walk along the seashore with a young girl who could see faery lights in the fields.[1]

They wandered along "a far western sandy shore" and came to a "notable (faery) haunt . . . a shallow cave amidst black rocks, with its reflection under it in the wet sea sand." Predictably, the young girl gazed at the cave and its reflection for a few minutes and fell into a trance. Shortly thereafter, she began to hear faery music, voices laughing and singing, and then she saw the Good People themselves, dancing on a brilliant light shining from the mouth of the cave. W. B. Yeats himself fell into "a kind of trance, in which what we call the unreal had begun to take upon itself a masterful reality." In the next moment, he saw the faeries "in four bands" and a "gleaming woman" he recognized as the faery queen. Yeats and the queen chatted about changelings, whether Yeats knew any humans who were faeries before their births (she said he did, but would not identify them), and whether this cave above the sea-soaked sand was the "greatest faery haunt" (she said it was not). And so there, on a western shore, standing before a cave with its reflection in the wet sand, W. B. Yeats and a young girl found a threshold to the Otherworld.

In this chapter we will look closely at the shaman's understanding of reality as composed of borderlands and ambiguities. As a "walker between the worlds," a shaman is at home in places "betwixt and between," regions that are "neither this, nor that," concepts that resonate strongly with Celtic sensibilities. We will examine specifically the neophyte shaman's psychic/spiritual crisis and how the shaman's new vision of reality has striking parallels with important aspects of Celtic lore. Among these are the seminal myth of the Irish gods, the Celtic concept of time, the ambiguity of gender, the elusive roles of the minstrel and Fool, and the Celtic love of triplicates.

THE SHAMAN'S INITIATION

The Celts have a special love for places and things that are "betwixt and between," conditions best described as "neither this, nor that" such as twilight, mist, dawn and dusk, fogs and bogs, the fragile and ephemeral dew. As with W. B. Yeats and the young girl, such phenomena easily trigger spontaneous shamanic experiences, especially the altered state of consciousness that is the tip of the shamanic iceberg. Beneath it lies the shaman's journey to the Otherworld, leading through thresholds of dream and reverie, exploring the passage between ordinary and nonordinary reality, discovering the space betwixt our everyday world and the world of dream and vision. For the new shaman, initiation into the mysteries and practices of soul journey involves a dramatic encounter with these realities, usually a shattering ordeal that unravels the candidate's view of the cosmos.

This plunge into the twilight of the psyche obliterates the normal categories of perception, replacing them with a vision that is unique and personal. The shamanic candidate, led by elders, encounters spirits that are part animal and part human, men dressed as women and vice versa, and monstrous shapes and forms that represent the ambiguous forces of the universe that are frightening to the human ego. From that moment on, the universe will be wider and grander, more mysterious, and yet (and this is the point of being a shaman) more manageable. The old social boundaries and mental constructs that the new shaman formerly accepted as immovable and inviolable are revealed to be socially conditioned, arbitary structures. Like a mask, the everyday world of family and clan conceals amorphous realms of spirit, nature, beauty, and terror that defy categorization. And during the perils of initiation, the new shaman learns how to remove this mask.

The shaman develops a fluid, malleable worldview that is not as brittle as most people's. Shamans know that the *real* and the *unreal* are merely opposite ends of a continuum on which reality can be stretched to include what is normally considered unreal. Even better, the continuum, like a flexible rod, can be bent, curved, and shaped into a circle where the end points of reality and unreality meet and become the same point. To the shaman, the universe is truly the Uroborous, the serpent holding its own tail in its mouth, uniting what appears to be the beginning and end. Depending on your point of view, the serpent is either devouring or disgorging the universe of its own body. To the shaman, it may appear to be doing both at once; and the shaman is not confused by this.

The shamanic initiation is a journey into chaos, a plunge into the primal realm where things are not what they seem, where rules and guidelines governing conduct and belief fail and are no longer appropriate. The shaman-to-be is initially terrified of what appear to be hostile spirits, even while being conducted safely through the ordeal by friendly spirits who may appear as ancestors or animal powers. In the process, shamans acquire a new self. Their mental universe is unraveled and rewoven, their physical bodies are dismembered and reintegrated or replaced with spiritual bodies. Finally the shaman re-enters ordinary reality as a "wise woman" or a "man of knowledge," an interpreter of the spirit world, one who has seen reality demolished and reconstructed. The shaman begins to understand the ambiguous nature of the universe and the unending law of change by which it operates.

As shamans gain confidence in their spirit allies and learn the geography of the Otherworld, they acquire a sense of balance that will, in time, become their source of power. As one who maintains a balance between the worlds of oppositional forces, the shaman becomes a witness to the true nature of the cosmos: the unity and interdependence of all creation with the Creator.

A strong belief in nonordinary reality is second-nature to the Celts, often appearing as a strange blend of fear and longing for nonordinary realms of existence and a fascination with the paradox of good and evil. The danger and the beauty of the Celtic Otherworld are always immanently present, lying just above, below, beyond, or within the immediate center of the present moment. To appreciate the shamanic structure of Celtic thinking, let us examine a seminal Irish myth in which we find, since the beginning of time, the key elements of light and darkness that produce the twilight structure of Celtic consciousness.

The Dananns and Fomorians

Two warring tribes of spirits, the Fomorians and Dananns, are responsible for the rivalries and conflicting influences of the Irish Otherworld. Since they are primordial spiritual forces, we can think of them as the creators of the metaphysical and moral landscape, if not the physical. The Dananns and Fomorians are similar to the primordial spirits of the shaman's Otherworld, and they are the ancestral forms of the spirits and faeries that people modern folklore. In these ancient rivalries we find the explanation for good and evil, fortune and misfortune, good luck and bad luck, the true and the false, love and war, and the forces of life and death.

The Fomorians dwelt in Ireland before the arrival of the Dananns. They seem to have been present always, if not on the land itself, then lurking in their strongholds offshore in the northern seas. They were thought to be more ancient than the gods. Huge, hideous, misshapen beings, they were the powers of darkness, night, chaos, monstrous births, the antithesis of day, light, order, and human beauty. Deformed creatures, they appeared to have only one leg and one arm. Their chieftain, Balor of the Evil Eye, had a gigantic eye that burned to ashes whatever it gazed upon. Usually he kept it closed beneath a mercifully heavy lid that required several men to lift open. Balor's Eye was a powerful weapon against their adversaries.

Although the Fomorians are often portrayed as cosmic evil, a more sympathetic interpretation depicts them as the nonhuman deities who control fertility, the untamed spirits of the land, and the destructive forces of nature, such as storms, quakes, blight, and drought. As such, they cannot be totally destroyed nor viewed as totally evil, since even the natural forces that harm human society play a vital role in the grander scheme of things. Celtic scholar Alexi Kondratiev argues persuasively, "If the Fomorian forces are not defeated, the Tribe cannot get its necessary sustenance from the Land; and yet if the Fomorians are destroyed, the principle of fertility is destroyed along with them, and the result is the same."[2] It is this paradox that shamans in every culture understand and know how to manipulate in order to assure the survival of the Tribe and the continued fecundity of the Land.

In contrast to the Fomorians are the Dananns. Tradition tells us they were beautiful, handsome beings who arrived in Ireland from the sky on magical sailing ships on the first of May. Children of the Goddess Dana, the Dananns represent order, goodness, law, and the safety and comfort of a well-run tribal society. They excel at magic, healing, crafts, and cultural activities. The Dananns and Fomorians are continually at odds, often at war, and yet a strange symbiotic relationship arises as one would expect if, in fact, the Fomorians are the spirits of fertility whom the Dananns need to cultivate the land and provide food. Mythologically, the balance that both groups seek finds expression in several intermarriages. One alliance produces Lugh the Shining One, the Irish sun god, the Danann champion who defeats Balor and banishes the Fomorians to the nether regions beneath the sea, leaving Ireland to be ruled by the enlightened Dananns. In later legends and folklore, and in much contemporary fantasy fiction, these shapeless monsters of evil return in various guises to raid Faeryland and even the world of mortals.

Evil spirits like the Fomorians can be found in most cultures. Michael Harner discovered them in his own initiatory experiences with shamans in the Amazon.[3] On returning from his first journey to the Otherworld, he told his mentor that he had met hideous beings who threatened him and claimed to be the "true masters of the world." Harner describes them as "large, shiney, black creatures with stubby pterodactyl-like wings and huge whale-like bodies." He was terrified of them. When he told his native teacher about their insidious claim to control the universe, the shaman laughed it off. "Oh, they're always saying that," the old man assured Harner. "But they are only the Masters of the Outer Darkness."

After the Dananns banished the Fomorians to the outer darkness, they ruled over Ireland until they, in turn, were defeated in a war with human settlers, the Milesians, who came from across the seas. Beaten but not broken, the Dananns retreated into the Hollow Hills, leaving the physical landscape to mortals. And so it remains to this day. Human society dominates the land; the Otherworld is populated by spirits such as faeries, the dead, angelic beings, and primordial forces once known as the Dananns and Fomorians. As Celtic mythologist T. W. Rolleston describes it, "Where the human eye can see but green mounds and ramparts, the relics of ruined fortresses or sepulchres, there rise the fairy palaces of the defeated divinities; there they hold their revels in eternal sunshine, nourished by the magic meat and ale that give them undying youth and beauty; and thence they come forth at times to mingle with mortal men in love or in war."[4]

TIME OUTSIDE OF TIME

The two great feast days in the Celtic calendar, November 1 and May 1, are occasions for intense mingling between mortals and immortals and for the greatest faery reveling. They are the two days of the year most fraught with magic and mystery. They are times of fear, laughter, merriment, and danger—a complex of emotions and activities that defies neatly distinct categories of human experience. These nights are betwixting times steeped in paradox and confusion, the twilit edges of perception where more goes on than meets the eye.

Samhain (pronounced *sow-en*), the Celtic New Year, now celebrated as Halloween, is a night that falls in neither the old year nor the new one. It is a "time outside of time," when the veils between the worlds are lifted and much trafficking takes place between spirits and mortals. Boundaries are eliminated, spirits are afoot. In Scotland it is called a "night of mischief and confusion." Although the threat may seem tame compared to the deadly battles of Fomorians and Dananns, the fear is still the same. Modern celebrants, especially children, keenly sense that the normal laws are suspended. Property can be damaged, food and treats can be demanded, hospitality overrules the locked door and gated fence, boundaries between what is mine and yours are temporarily repealed. Tricksters seek admittance to others' homes, even as spirits from the Otherworld seek entry into this world. On Samhain we are reminded that doorways are open, thresholds are bridgeable, and the ordinary and nonordinary intermingle. It is also reassuring to be reminded at the start of winter that neighbors are hospitable and that food is available for sharing.

Traditionally Samhain is a night for divination, to discover who will die in the coming year, and for young women to learn the identity of their future husbands. The reason divinatory practices are so successful on this night is that the boundaries between time are lifted. On November's Eve the present and the future merge, and what lies ahead can be foreseen in the present moment. We usually seek knowledge about transitions from one stage of life into another. Who will die and enter the spirit world? Who will marry and bring new life into the physical world? It is fitting that we glean knowledge of transitions between the worlds on this night when the worlds themselves tumble into each other.

Samhain is celebrated in an ancient village ritual of extinguishing all the lights in the home and relighting them from a central bonfire, lit especially for this occasion. For a brief time, the home, the center of human community and the hearthside of comfort and safety, is dark, plunged into a chaos mirroring the original chaos of the Fomorian realm. Then human life is recreated from the central fire, symbolized by the bringing of new light into the home.

The characteristics we have come to expect of Halloween are, in fact, versions of the same initiatory experiences of the neophyte shaman. Animals, spirits, and humans intermingle; creatures are part animal and human; the sex roles are reversed or confused, with one's actual gender artfully concealed; the future and the past meet; and ancestral spirits return for a night of revel. The hospitality that has come to characterize Halloween also mirrors the underlying supposition of the shamanic journey, namely that the two worlds are open and hospitable to each other and that denizens of one world can, if they choose, seek and find entry into the other. In spite of the frightening and disorienting creatures that threaten and seem to block the way, there are friendly, helpful beings with gifts or tokens of power.

The feast of Beltane, May 1, marks the other half of the Celtic year. On this day winter ends and summer begins. It, too, is a time of spirit revels and human merrymaking, but the tone is much different from Samhain, which introduces the somber season of winter. Beltane celebrates the end of winter, the returning flowers and warmer days that are the harbingers of the fertile summer. Young people sleep outdoors overnight, make love, arise to drink water from a well before dawn, and return to the village with flowers and leaves twined through their hair. They also carry back a young sapling that will become the Maypole later in the day.

The Maypole Dance itself reflects shamanic principles. A circle of dancers rings the pole, each person holding the end of a ribbon attached to the top of the pole. Often every other dancer is either a boy or a girl, the boys dancing in one direction, the girls in the other, suggesting the great polarities of life—death and resurrection. The double-spiral dance braids the ribbon around the pole in a design that colorfully reflects the interwoven nature of dancers and directions, and the turning wheel of the universe itself. The Maypole is the World Tree, the cosmic shaft or axis connecting earth and sky. Similar trees, stripped of branches, have been found in Celtic wells and numerous neolithic shafts dug into the ground to be receptacles for sacred offerings to ancient Celtic gods. Even today it is a custom in the British Isles to "dress" wells on May Day with bouquets of flowers.

At Beltane, the ordinary laws of morality are suspended. It is a time for sexual license. It is a time to ignore restrictions and previous commitments, and in the exuberant transition into summer, fall in love. For centuries May was considered an unlucky month in which to get married; it was the month for illicit romance, not marriage, and couples who wished to marry waited until June, thus making that month the traditional wedding month. (But any child conceived at Beltane was considered sacred, an offspring of the God of Fertility and the Goddess of Spring.)

As at Samhain, spirits, faeries, and witches were active, and people expected much mischief. Divination was also practiced, again to see who a potential marriage partner might be. But since this was not the impending season of death and darkness, people did not divine for knowledge of approaching death. Instead they sought weather forecasts and advice on the proper rituals to assure a warm growing season and healthy crops.

The turning points of the year are always paradoxical. The transitional days that initiate the seasons do not belong comfortably in either of the periods of time that they separate. On these days we may feel disoriented and experience a strange suspension of time, bred in the confusion of not knowing in which season we stand at the moment. We are at both the beginning and the end. At the turning points, anything might happen.

In 1897 near Bourg in France a calendar was discovered that shed some light on the ancient Celts' method of marking and dividing time. Although the Coligny Calendar, as it is called, can be interpreted in different ways, it seems the Celts divided each month into two halves, or fortnights, corresponding to the phases of the moon. One half of the month was light, the other dark. The Druids held the sixth night of the waxing moon to be especially sacred, for this was the moon-between-the-halves—the half moon. On this night of the "Druid Moon," the brighter half of the month begins. This night may have been considered to be the actual first night of the month.

Like tribal peoples in other parts of the world (and as Jews and Moslems continue to do), the Celts reckoned a day from sunset to sunset, and the custom of feastday eves such as November Eve, May Eve, and Midsummer Eve have continued down to our modern celebrations of Christmas Eve and New Year's Eve. In this way the Celts honored the dark night of chaos from which creation sprung, the primordial "time before time" when only spirits and divine forces peopled the cosmos. Night is the time for spirits, for divination, for mischief by trickster deities, and for storytelling and dreaming. It is a time for mortals to retreat to the safety of our hearths and beds and allow unseen inhabitants to do what they will. Beginning the new year on November Eve rather than May Eve, at the onset of the dark months rather than at the beginning of summer, is yet another way of honoring the original darkness from which human life emerged. Clearly there are psychological reasons for perceiving time as beginning with the dark, since human life begins during nine months of darkness in the womb, a period that plays a subtle, if unappreciated role in our earliest memories.

The Androgynous Shaman

At Samhain, the boundaries between the sexes are also confusing for it is acceptable for revelers and trick-or-treaters to crossdress. The dissolution of genders and the blending of what we normally think of as opposites returns us, in consciousness, to the primordial unity, expressed in many creation myths by an androgynous or bisexual creator. In some accounts the original deity or human is split in two, thus creating the two sexes. On November Eve we are reminded of this original unity as we recreate it, perhaps unconsciously, in our crossdressing revels.

Shamans frequently encounter androgynous and bisexual beings and spirit guides in their initiation journeys. They play a key role in the drastic reorganization of categories that shatters the shaman's old perception of reality and opens him or her to the multiple dimensions of existence. Along these same lines, gender ambiguity frequently characterizes many shamans themselves who were gay or lesbian. Homosexuality and androgyny create a liminal status that helps to legitimize the shaman as an interpreter and go-between on both social and spiritual levels.

In Siberia a gay male shaman was called "a soft man being." In Native American communities, a young man who showed an interest in women's activities, crossdressed, and adopted feminine behavior often became a spiritual leader or healer, his decision reinforced by encouraging dreams and vision quests. It was assumed the spirits had touched him with some special magic, power, or wisdom that would be valuable for the community. This *berdache* tradition among American Indians (after the term used by French explorers, meaning someone who blends the masculine and feminine) is currently being restored by contemporary gay men in the Native American community to the honored and valued position it held before Christian missionaries discredited it.

A similar custom among lesbians in tribal societies encouraged young women, who felt called by the spirit, to crossdress, become hunters or warriors, and adopt masculine behavior. They too became exceptionally valued spiritual members of their people. Lesbian shamans have been found from the Arctic circle to the Amazon, indicating the widespread nature of this custom that recognizes in people who can bridge the social worlds of men and women a talent that renders them interpreters and go-betweens for the Otherworld as well. The strong female warrior and hunter is found in early Celtic societies. Although not always lesbians, powerful Celtic women trained male heroes in the arts of war and the hunt.

Homosexual relations seem to have been common among Celtic men, suggesting yet another way in which Celtic thinking was open to ambiguity and transcended rigid boundaries. In the first century B.C., the Roman historian Diodorus Siculus wrote, "Although they [Celtic males] have good-looking women, they pay very little attention to them, but are really crazy about having sex with men. They are accustomed to sleep on the ground on animal skins and roll around with male bed-mates on both sides."[5] Apparently incapable of appreciating homosexual activity among friends, Diodorus goes on to express first his disgust for such practices and then a bewildered shock that "the most incredible thing is that they don't think this is shameful." In fact, as the Roman notes, Celtic men "proposition someone . . . [and] . . . consider it dishonorable if he doesn't accept the offer"!

In a very unshamanic way, Diodorus seems to have stumbled into a world he does not understand.

THE SHAMAN AS TRICKSTER AND FOOL

Halloween is the night of the Trickster, the culture hero found the world over. A twilight figure, the Trickster is half comic, half serious, both harmful and playful, creative and destructive, a friend and a foe. In mythical accounts, he is often a culture bearer, and the tribesfolk honor him for the creation of what is noblest in their society (law, arts, language). But people also fear his lawless side, for since he bestows law, he can also operate outside the law. The Trickster is the original outlaw. The Greek Trickster Hermes steals Apollo's cattle shortly after escaping from his cradle. When giants try to steal treasures from the gods, the German Trickster god Loki is always an accomplice, even to the point of stealing Thor's hammer. And there is hardly a North American tale about Coyote in which he is not stealing, or attempting to steal, something from someone.

The Trickster or Foolish God teaches us that we often deceive ourselves. Beneath the ego and its mask of order and reason lies an untamed, wilder, lawless self as genuine as the masks of respectability we present to society. By embarrassing us, the Trickster teaches us deeper truths about ourselves. Not only does the Trickster confront us with the multiple nature of the universe, he shows us the multiple nature of ourselves, a truth the shaman learns through the tricks and deceptions of his initiating spirits. Indeed, trickery is part of the shaman's craft, for he or she understands that often the mind has to be tricked for the body to heal. Some shamans relied so heavily on trickery and sleight-of-hand that Western observers misunderstood their motives and dismissed them as mere charlatans. They failed to appreciate the purpose of trickery and illusion as a means of "performing" in ordinary reality the transformations that were occurring on the psychic or spiritual plane.

People who slip into the realms of Faerie, or who simply see the faeries, are thought to be somewhat "touched" in the head, either fools or idiots. (There is also a Christian tradition that the mentally retarded have been touched by the hand of God in some special way.) Western anthropologists often mistook the tribal shaman for someone crazy or insane. A common misdiagnosis was schizophrenia. Fortunately, that description of the shaman has been discredited, as Western observers more accurately note the differences between schizophrenia and shamanism. A major difference is that the shaman has control over his or her states of consciousness and is able to induce those states or return from them at will. The schizophrenic cannot. Shamans can also consciously recognize different categories of reality, even though in their casual conversation they may not distinguish between these different realities as carefully as some listeners might wish!

Undoubtedly, a person who engaged in shamanic practices in Western Europe was often considered the village idiot, but we should not assume that every village idiot was a shaman. Similarly, not everyone taken by the faeries or who saw the faeries became a shaman. Nevertheless, there is something shamanic in any encounter with the Otherworld or otherworldy spirits since that is the heart of shamanism.

Throughout Europe there are festivals in which the Fool or jester plays an important role, and invariably they contain strongly shamanic elements. In fact, the role of the Fool as a sacred clown possibly derives from the antics of the primal shamans dating back to the earliest stages of European history. At Mardi Gras, Carnival, New Year's Eve, May Eve, Midsummer Eve, and Halloween, the Fool delights in the scheduled chaos that celebrates these times of misrule. On almost all these occasions there are mock battles, sometimes acted out in folk plays, depicting the struggle of good and evil, with the former temporarily triumphing over the latter. Interestingly, the evil king, the black knight, the fire-breathing dragon, or the rival team is often ritually revived and brought back to life after the battle, since the older spirituality honored the dark as a necessary player in the drama of creation. Even the energies of the dark seasons must be revived to live and fight another day. Thus the festivities commemorate a tenuous victory over the forces of darkness, but they also suggest that the dark will be reborn, after a temporary sojourn into the Land of the Dead.

In conjunction with the death motifs of these yearly festivals, Trickster deities and shamans share the important role of psychopomp; they lead the souls of the recently departed into the Land of the Dead. In fact, trickery seems to be an integral feature of death in several respects. Death cheats or robs a person of life, and a psychopomp often needs to trick a soul into leaving the Land of the Living and departing for the Land of the Dead. Shamans trick even Death itself, for they cheat Death of its authority over the Otherworld by journeying into the Land of the Dead before their physical deaths and returning (although not always unscathed). A common shamanic service is soul retrieval, in which the shaman may have to trick the departed soul to return from the spirit world and re-enter the body of the sick or dying person. The Fool and shaman are ambiguous characters because of their ability to operate in the nether regions of human existence, the twilight borderline between life and death, between ordinary and nonordinary realities.

In whatever festival, the Fool always played an indeterminate role, somewhere between good and evil, and somewhere between the actors in the battle and the audience, often burlesquing the activity of the actors, as well as the emotional reaction of the audience. He was an interpreter, a shamanic character who moved between the worlds of the stage and the audience. He identified with both sides, and yet belonged to neither.

Visually the Fool conjured up a figure who belonged to no specific world. His costume often included some animal trappings such as fur, feathers, a tail, or horns. In some societies he wore foxskins, thus identifying himself with Reynard the Fox, who, like Coyote in North America, was the premier Trickster animal in Western Europe. As we reflect on the Fool's costume, the ambiguous nature of his character becomes clearer, since the fox and the coyote are considered to be extremely sly and deviously cunning animals. Here again opposites are blended, creating the archetype of the wise Fool, a character firmly embedded in human consciousness.

The traditional Fool was recognized by four characteristics: a pointed hat, a crazy pattern on his costume, bells, and bauble. Each of these have origins in shamanism. The bauble can be viewed as a mock sceptre or an imitation phallus, or both. The Fool is the King of Misrule, and a perennially favorite form of misrule (then as now) is sexual. The scepter announced the season of licentious revelry when the Fool ordered conventional moral standards to be temporarily suspended. Throughout history most Fools were men, but they often played their roles with an androgynous flair, burlesquing both masculine and feminine traits, which undoubtedly provided men and women a chance to re-examine the sex roles and gender stereotypes that dominate our thinking about how men and women should act in ordinary reality. The Fool, like the shaman, breaks through those stereotypes to reveal other possibilities that transcend the polarities of male and female.

The inflated pig's bladder on the end of the rod may have functioned like a balloon, allowing the Fool to hit his fellow rowdies or the audience without hurting them. The bladder was sometimes filled with dried beans to make a rattle, thus suggesting a more shamanic use. In some areas the shaman uses the rattle to summon spirits or to "shake" power over the sick. Like drumming, prolonged rattling induces a nonordinary state of consciousness for shamanic activity.

In addition to being part animal, the Fool's costume was often the traditional motley or pied pattern: a robe of many colors and patterns, sometimes arranged in a crazy-quilt fashion. Obviously, the Fool has a slippery sense of fashion not squarely rooted in any particular world, time, class, or status; this is precisely what the Fool-as-shaman wants to convey. Curiously, the parti-colored cloak crops up in other thinly veiled shamanic contexts. In the Hebrew Scripture, for example, Joseph owned a coat of many colors, spent time in a well (a form of Lower World incarceration), and was reknowned for dream interpretation, a classic shamanic service. The Pied Piper of Hamlin (minstrels and Fools shared many traditions) had shamanic power over the rodents of that town, and his musical talent created a trancelike state in the children of the village, which lured them into an opening into the earth. The piper as a shamanic figure with knowledge of entries into the Lower World is a very Celtic tradition.

The Fool's face and costume were sometimes painted one color on the left and another on the right. Some of the earliest depictions of the Fool show him wearing a tunic of two different colors, or stockings that are mismatched. The bifurcated look conveyed the image of someone who yoked opposites, someone blessed or cursed with two natures, or the ability to move into two different states of consciousness. In parades or plays, the Fool could portray two people just by spinning around. He was a person with a foot in more than one world.

The Fool wore a pointed hat, like a dunce cap, which is still suggestive of a stupid or foolish person who lacks social graces and mental stability. Again we are reminded of the crazy behavior of the shaman and the unpredictable, sometimes socially unacceptable activities of those who have been taken by the faeries. Always, however, there is a strong hint of method behind the madness, and the individual is not as lost as he or she might seem. From another perspective, the pointed cap is an exaggerated hood. The magical hood has an interesting history. It was originally a vital part of the shaman's regalia, later appearing in the stylized wizard's cap associated with Merlin, the shaman-magician of Arthurian lore, and eventually in the stereotyped witch's hat of fable and folklore. The term "hood" in American English still refers to someone who operates outside the law, a criminal who conceals his identity, a denizen of the nether regions of society.

Some Fools wear three-pointed hats that may have grown out of an earlier costume that had horns or long animal ears. The long ears may have been those of a rabbit, also a European Trickster figure. The middle ear, or prong, could have been a cock's comb, conjuring up images of the lusty rooster, long associated in European culture with sexual immorality and the cuckolded husband, who is portrayed as a fooled and/or foolish fellow. Or possibly the long ears were those of a donkey, an animal that stands for stubborn foolishness and sexual prowess in folklore. Fred Fuller, a contemporary American morris dancer and writer, points out that two slang terms that are now semitaboo—"cock" for rooster and "ass" for donkey—have been long associated with the Fool because of his exaggerated sexuality.[6]

Bells were often hung on the end of the Fool's three-pronged hat or attached to his costume in other ways. In Celtic tradition, the poet carried a branch with bells upon it when he made his entrance into a court or hall to announce his performance. Many shamanic elements are found in the training and role of the bards and poets. In other cultures, too, shamans wore or carried bells or bright, tingling objects. Siberian shamans adorned their costumes with bells, mirrors, and pieces of metal.

The wise fool, as we know him from Shakespeare's plays, had precedents in the poets and seers who served Celtic chieftains. Enid Welsford, in her study *The Fool: His Social and Literary History*, points out that in ancient Celtic tales the poets and seers were often called fools.[7] Like their later counterparts in royal courts, the chieftains valued the poet's insights and respected his ability to satirize (satire is a "twilight" literary form, somewhere between truth and falsehood, seriousness and silliness). Like the shaman, poets were respected for more than their storytelling talents or their ability to entertain. They had special vision and wisdom; they had magical powers. Welsford notes that "the Fool is a creator not of beauty but of spiritual freedom." The same is true of the poet.

By means of masks, makeup, costume, and especially behavior, the Fool presents a split personality. He is there to remind us of our own splits, our hidden selves, the shadow, the repressed aspects of our nature. He confronts us with the side of consciousness that dwells partially in the Otherworld and may only appear in dreams, the part of us we might call (to paraphrase Michael Harner's native teacher) our *inner* outer darkness. The resulting whole personality may be pictured as a person with three faces: the conscious face on the right, the unconscious on the left, and the self that combines the two in a healthy, life-affirming manner in the middle.

THE MINSTREL AS SHAMAN

Bands of wandering minstrels, jugglers, illusionists, and fortune-tellers seem to have crisscrossed Europe since the time before recorded history. Modern-day Gypsies are the latest players in a long, colorful heritage, their place of origin, like their predecessors, lost in the mists of the past. Settled communities have always looked upon these "people without a country" as magical folk who possess special, occult powers of divination, dream interpretation, and healing. Like shamans, Gypsies and wandering entertainers can pass from one reality into another. Their skills are both feared and respected. In the British Isles wandering minstrels were known as *gleemen*. In Germany they were called *spielmanner* (gamesmen). In Latin the term was *ioculatores*, which in time became *jongleur* in French and *juggler* or *joker* in English. Collectively, these terms imply a sense of fooling, joking, juggling, and misleading. The wanderers themselves exuded an air of mystery and romance, born on their travels to exotic lands, and bred in adventures denied to average men and women.

We get some insight into the exciting, unorthodox, and subversive role played by minstrels from a church regulation of 789 that forbade bishops, abbots, and abbotesses from employing or keeping *jongleurs*. There were further prohibitions in succeeding centuries. Undoubtedly these prohibitions involved many ecclesiastical worries such as church leaders indulging in frivolity; the minstrels' profane, bawdy stories and songs; and the minstrels' own reputations for licentiousness. But equally suspect was the spiritual freedom the minstrels represented. By the twelfth century the French troubadours had become key players in the Cathar heresy that, among other things, seems to have involved a form of soul travel or heavenly ascent, a somatic visionary practice with definite shamanic implications. The unfortunate results of the heresy was the Church's bloody crusade that caused over a million deaths and the creation of the Inquisition that became a mainstay in Catholic authoritarianism for several centuries.

The shamanic vision of spiritual reality is always highly personal and charged with mystical insights that are threatening to church orthodoxy. The average church administrator is either not mystically inclined, or learns early in his or her career to suppress private visions in order to toe the party line, and (perversely) to be able to brand other mystics as heretics. It is interesting that Francis of Assisi was initially considered a heretic for his mystical relationship with nature and animals, his espousal of actual poverty (as opposed to the ideal of poverty preached by the Church, but practiced by very few of the upper hierarchy), and his presenting himself as a *jongleur de Dieu*. Many of the songs and stories told by wandering minstrels in the early years of the Middle Ages are lost. It would appear, however, that if minstrels carried on the traditions of their shamanic forebearers, their entertainments bordered on fantastical, visionary material that would have been quickly perceived by church authorities as heretical and dangerous. As with the later witch hysteria, the Church would have demonized these stories and banned them.

In *The Celtic Twilight*, W. B. Yeats offers a portrait of a man he calls "the last gleeman" in Ireland.[8] Michael Moran, born in Dublin in 1794, was struck blind a fortnight after his birth, thus fueling the perennial Irish worry that newborns were particularly susceptible to malign faery influences. The boy's blindness, like other shamanic initiatory sicknesses, may have encouraged him to pursue a more eccentric way of life. Moran's mental universe may have been more creative, more resilient, more imaginative as he had to grapple with a way of being in the world that was very different from men and women with sight. W. B. Yeats notes that Moran was acknowledged as "the rector of all the balad-mongers" in his district, and that he displayed a rare "mixture of ragamuffin and of genius." In other words, Moran was perceived as a wise fool.

Michael Moran was "poet, jester, and newsman of the people." In addition to songs and silliness, the gleeman was the news reporter of his day, learning the current news from a newspaper in the morning and then incorporating it into his routine. Moran referred to the news as the material for his "meditations," from which would come, according to Yeats, his "day's store of jest and rhyme." Like the shaman, Moran was an interpreter for his people. His meditations undoubtedly drew on his personal interior and imaginative experience to find deeper moral meanings to educate and enlighten his listeners.

TRIPLES AND TRIPLICITIES

The fascination with threes is widespread in Celtic art and literature, both on the continent and in the British Isles. Celtic sculptors often group figures in threes, or sculpt one figure with three heads, or one head with three faces. From a shamanic point of view, the tricephalic figure may represent the alternative point of view that one derives from the shamanic initiation. The two-headed Janus head is traditionally interpreted as a person who can see both ahead and behind, or into both past and future. But the three-headed person, or the head with three faces as many of them are, suggests not only vision into two different worlds or time periods, but *the resulting composite vision*, the shamanic vision of a person-between-the-worlds.

The twilight vision of the shaman is in neither this world nor the other, but incorporates a little of both.

Celtic deities appear in much the same manner. With a profound and enduring love of threes, the Celts imagined their gods and goddesses in three-somes. The three Brigids, the three Mothers, the three war goddesses—Morrigan, Macha, and Bodb (collectively called the Morrigan)—are important Celtic goddesses. On the male side, gods and heroes often travel in threes. Common literary motifs include three brothers; three knights adventuring together; and three attempts to reach some goal, each requiring some different strength or virture from the hero. There are also numerous legends about a god born at the same time as two others with the same name.

The threefold gods and goddesses, while sometimes expressing three distinct aspects or functions of one deity (i.e., the goddess who is maiden, mother, crone) can also be interpreted as a single deity whose power extends beyond the ordinary limits of the god's or goddess's domain. Again the two-plus-the-one strongly implies the synthesizing figure of the shaman who can incorporate two opposing views and reconcile them.

A fascination with the number three is widespread and prevalent in both archaic and modern thinking. Various theories about its potency are based on mathematics, philosophy, aesthetics, physics, and other disciplines. A shamanic perspective may offer additional insight into the potency of this number. As we have seen, vital to shamanism is the concept of liminality. The shaman stands on the threshold, the doorway between two worlds. While the two worlds remain distinct for most people, they overlap and merge in the shaman's imagination. His or her worldview, or consciousness, is different from either the ordinary consciousness of nonshamans, as it is different from the consciousness of the spirits and otherworldly entities with whom the shaman has an ongoing relationship. Looked at from yet another angle, as one who is twice-born, the shaman shares both the experience of the living and the dead, and as such is different from both the living and the dead. However we look at it, the shaman enjoys a third mode of existence, a way of being that incorporates both the living and the dead, the mortal and the immortal, the human and the divine.

◆

Just as twilight is neither light nor dark, but a bit of each, so is the middle head, face, or person representative of that magical blend of two opposing energies. The shaman is the twilight child, born from the union of the masculine world of light and conscious awareness and the feminine world of darkness and unconscious awareness. Shamans are at home in both worlds: in that magical space and time shimmering between these worlds, that point of consciousness "betwixt and between" and "neither this, nor that," flickering at the edge of twilight.

THE MUSIC
OF ENCHANTMENT

The sounds of nature, spirit songs, the shaman's personal power chant, and faery melodies are integral parts of shamanism. From Siberia to the American Southwest, from Japan to Polynesia, the shaman's journey to the Otherworld and his or her relationship with the powers of nature are accompanied by songs of power, spirit songs rising mysteriously from the Otherworld or human songs springing spontaneously from the shaman's heart.

The Eskimo shaman, Aua, says that in his attempts to become a shaman he would often grow melancholy and depressed. But one day "for no reason . . . I felt a great, inexplicable joy, a joy so powerful that I could not restrain it, but had to break into song, a mighty song, with only room for the one word: joy, joy!"[1] Another Eskimo shaman in Greenland relates, "One day, up among the rocks, I heard someone begin to sing; I looked, but could see no one." The next day he heard it again. This time two men appeared to him and they became his "first helping spirits."[2] William Barber, an Irishman who lived during the turn of the last century, had a similar, spontaneous shamanic experience. "One dark night, about one o'clock, myself and another young man were passing along the road up there round Ben Bulben, when we heard the finest kind of music. All sorts of music seemed to be playing. We could see nothing at all, though we thought we heard voices like children's. It was the music of the *gentry* [faeries] we heard."[3]

The Papago Indians of southern Arizona, near the Mexican border, work their magic by singing. Every activity and mood has a corresponding song; if it is sung well and in the proper manner, the song casts a spell, the singer's wish comes true, and the people prosper. In a trancelike state or in a natural sleep, the Papago hear songs, and they know whether it is the hawk singing, the gulls over the ocean, a cloud, the voice of the wind, or perhaps the red spider that brings the rains. From nature and the spirits of nature, the Papago learn their songs.[4] The Huichol Indians of northwestern Mexico also hear songs in the fire or the rain. These are translated into human speech and become the people's songs of power.[5]

A Yakut shaman in Siberia describes it this way: "Mysterious noises are audible, sometimes from above, sometimes from below, sometimes in front of, sometimes behind the shaman . . . the plaintive call of the lapwing mingled with the croaking of the falcon interrupted by the whistle of the woodcock, all this is the voice of the shaman."[6]

Often shamans will say that they received their songs from the spirits. A Gitksan shaman on the Pacific coast named Isaac Tens recalled that when he once fell into trance, his body began to quiver, and he started to sing uncontrollably and had visions of huge birds and animals. He explained that "the songs force themselves out complete, without any attempt to compose them."[7] Among the Ainu of Hokkaido in Japan, the shamans sing epic songs, and although each shaman sings in her own voice, her use of the first person refers to the gods themselves who are thought to be the actual singers.

For the Celts, both pagan and Christian, the encounter with Faerie is often heralded by ethereal music, usually described as "the most beautiful music" ever heard or "like no human music." Indeed, sweet, faery music is an essential component of the Otherworld. It can lull mortals into an enchanted sleep or a shamanic state of consciousness. Like William Barber's experience, the music is often heard on lonely roads, late at night, or in the forests, emerging from the Hollow Hills or from deep within the earth. William Cain, who lived on the Isle of Man a century ago was known as Willy-the-Faery because (according to a friend), "he often hears the faeries singing and playing up the Glen o' nights. I have heard him sing airs which he said he had thus learned from the *Little People*."[8]

Both the singer and the song are powerful, and in some traditions the link between song and spirit is expressed in the language. Eliade points out that in many places terms for magic and song, especially songs related to birds, are the same word. The old German *galdr*, for example, meaning a magical spell, derives from *galan*, which means to sing and is associated with birdsong.[9] In North America the Klamath Indians use the same word for song and spirit. The English word *enchantment* is often encountered in Celtic faery lore and derives from *chant*. Most dictionaries point out its linguistic links with other terms that refer to magical-spiritual power such as *allure*, *charm*, *fascinate*, and *bewitch*.

TRUTH AND THE FITNESS OF THINGS

The poet or storyteller in pagan societies was respected and revered for the wisdom and truth the people found in the songs or tales. Poets and singers were thought to have acquired their knowledge and wisdom directly from the gods or spirits. Most cultural mythologies contain an account of how poetry was a gift from the gods, or sometimes from a single god or goddess of poetry and inspiration. The Norse tradition, for example, describes how the god Odin hung on the ash tree for nine days and nights (surely in a trance), during which time he discovered the runes, the divinatory alphabet, the secrets of wisdom. The Norse god also drank the sacred mead of poetry, a potent drink brewed from the blood of the wise and all-knowing sage, Kvasir, and mixed with honey. Similarly, we have seen that three drops from Cerridwen's Cauldron of Inspiration bestowed on Taliesin far-ranging knowledge and poetic insights. In the case of shamans, poetic truth comes from journeys to the Otherworld and the intimate relationship with helping spirits.

It was a fundamental assumption among the Celts that the poet sings the truth, and that truth derives from the gods. Divine truth, and the universal order that springs from it, create what Anne Ross calls the Celtic sense of "the fitness of things," a key concept in Celtic thinking and a concept at the heart of shamanism.[10] The "fitness of things" can be found in nature, social relationships, art, and one's personal life. It is similar to what the Navajo call *hozro*, usually translated as simply *beauty*, but with much broader, more mystical significance; it is the beauty of cosmic order, the pattern of perfection woven into the fabric of the universe at the creation. *Hozro* is a combination of beauty and harmony, and the truth we find in the blending of the two.

Living in a cynical age we have come to mistrust the spoken and written word through advertising hype, failed political promises, and the calculated, manipulative use of language in the media, not the least of which is heard in popular song lyrics. In more innocent times truth was divine. "A man is as good as his word" was an aphorism that was taken seriously. The need to "save face" before one's family, village, or tribal associates was paramount to a meaningful life. Loss of face implied loss of faith, and someone who violated his or her word could never be trusted again.

One of the most striking legends of the poet's responsibilities as a teller of truth is the story of Thomas the Rhymer, a medieval ballad set in Scotland and recorded in different versions over the centuries. One day a young poet and harper named Thomas was sitting under the Eildon tree when a beautiful woman rode up on horseback. She was the Queen of Elfland, and she enchanted Thomas with her beauty, luring him into the faery realm where he remained for seven years, enjoying her sexual favors but always longing to return to mortal life. In time she released him and he returned to ordinary reality, but the queen's farewell to him was a gift that would render him forever a stranger among mortals: the inability to speak anything but the truth. For the rest of his life Thomas the Rhymer lived with the burden of truth; he could neither utter a falsehood, nor overlook deception.

Depending on how you look at it, Thomas the Rhymer was either blessed or cursed with the responsibility of telling the truth. Shamans typically acquire this burden from their journeys into mystical reality. In the case of Black Elk, the Sioux shaman, his momentous vision on Harney Mountain gave him a personal insight into the "fitness of things." He claimed, "I saw more than I can tell, and I understood more than I saw; for I was seeing in a sacred manner the shapes of all things in the spirit, and the shape of all shapes as they must live together like one being."[11] The Eskimo shaman Aua was also able to see the reality of existence without the veils of deception, with the darkness lifted. When Aua became a shaman, he remembers, "I could see and hear in a totally different way . . . [I could] see through the darkness of life."[12] However phrased, shamans realize their responsibility as messengers of truth once they have seen behind and into the divine order of existence.

When a shaman returns from the Otherworld, he or she always brings back something in the way of vision or power, a heightened sense of reality, the ability to spot falsehood, or the burning need to call others' attention to the truth. The shaman, like Thomas the Rhymer, returns from the Otherworld with the power to see through the deceptions that separate us from each other and prevent our living together honestly "like one being."

The power of truth was the basis for a curious ritual by which the ancient Irish selected their kings. A bull was slain and its flesh prepared as a feast for an individual designated as the Truth Teller. After eating the bull's meat and drinking the broth, he went to bed, and a spell was chanted over him, so that whomever he would dream of during the night would become the next rightful high king of Ireland. It was assumed that the dreamer would speak the truth about his vision the next day, for if he did not, he would perish. We do not know why the combination of bull-feast, spell, and dreaming worked, or why the ancient Celts believed that such magic worked, but we can assume that confidence in the process originated in a deeper stratum of consciousness shaped by shamanic practices. The ancient Celts valued the information gleaned from dreams and visionary experiences, and the men and women who engaged in these practices were recognized as people who would speak the truth. To not speak the truth was fraught with peril.

TABOOS: FORMS OF TRUTH

A corollary to the power of truth was the necessity of honoring one's personal *geis* (pronounced *gaysh*) or taboo. Legendary heroes and mythological figures often came into the world with a particular taboo, or received one or more early in life. A taboo might have been something the hero had to do or do in a special way, or it might have been a prohibition against a particular act. Violating a taboo was not taken lightly; it could lead to death. For example, the warrior-hero Cuchulain could not eat the flesh of a dog, since the dog was a type of power animal for him as well as his name-sake; his name means "Chulain's hound." King Conaire's *geis* prohibited him from killing birds. The Finian warrior Diarmaid could not hunt swine. Some Christian saints had taboos to honor certain animals. St. Ailbe, for instance, claimed a kinship with wolves since he was suckled on wolf's milk as a baby. St. Ciwa was also nursed on wolf's milk, had a wolf's claw on one of her fingers, and acquired the nickname "Wolf Girl."

The *geis* to honor an animal companion or an animal that has played an important role in one's life has parallels among shamans in other cultures. Most shamans have a profound respect for their power animals, and some refuse to eat the flesh of those animals. Lame Deer, a Sioux shaman, relates how on his vision quest he heard a voice speaking for the birds. It said, "We are the fowl people, the winged ones, the eagles and the owls. We are a nation and you shall be our brother. You will never kill or harm any one of us."[13]

Some taboos create a catch-22 whereby an individual, caught in an ambiguous situation, is forced to choose between two alternatives, either of which would violate the *geis*. Cuchulain, for example, in addition to not eating the flesh of a dog, was under another taboo not to pass by a cooking hearth without eating of the meal that was being prepared. Obviously he was trapped in a dilemma when he passed three crones cooking a dead dog on a spit. When they invited him to join them in their meal, he could not refuse. When he ate the flesh of his namesake, the hand that held it was stricken, and the weakness spread up his entire arm to his shoulder. Shortly thereafter he fought his final battle.

The restrictions surrounding the Celtic hero have parallels with sha-mans everywhere. They gird the shaman's life with power and reinforce the connection with the Otherworld and the helping spirits. Taboos play a vital role as structures of truth, focal points reminding the shaman of the more encompassing truth of his or her personal vision. Charms, spells, and daily rituals often appear foolish and nonsensical to the uninitiated, but to those living a magical, visionary life they have real meaning and power. Without them the shaman's life would revert to a normalcy typical of other men and women.

Consider the following beliefs and practices. Eskimo shamans give away at once any gifts they receive because they believe that if they keep the things for themselves, they or their children will die. This practice keenly reflects the shaman's vision of the interdependence of all living things and the exchange of power and energy across the Web of Life. Matsuwa, a Huichol shaman, teaches the need for solitude in the wilderness. He says that if you want "to learn to see, to learn to hear, you must . . . go into the wilderness alone. For it is not I who teach you the ways of the gods. Such things are learned only in solitude."[14] The need for solitude, for personal vision questing, is endemic to shamanism. Dick Mahwee, a Paviotso shaman who grew up in Nevada, explains that a native doctor "gets his power from the spirit of the night. This spirit is everywhere. It has no name . . . Eagle and owl do not give a shaman power. They are just messengers that bring instructions from the spirit of the night."[15] Understanding the night as a nameless spirit who is everywhere, giving away gifts as soon as they receive them, retreating into the wilderness solitude to confront being alone with nature, these and similar practices can be found among shamans in all cultures. Equally prevalent is the sincere belief that should they fail to honor these customs, they would either lose their power as shamans or possibly die.

MUSIC WITH A FAERY TWANG

There is a strong tradition among the Celts that exceptionally brilliant musicians learned their skills from the faeries. Flannery, an old piper in County Galway in the last century, was praised by a fellow piper for his musical abilities. According to the friend, Flannery studied in the sidhe. "The *good people* took him to Fairyland to learn his profession. He studied music with them for a long time, and when he returned he was as great a piper as any in Ireland."[16] Flannery "died young, for the *good people* wanted him to play for them."

This tradition of studying in Faerie goes back a long way. In early Christian times, St. Patrick and his companions were resting on a hillside when they saw a man approaching with a harp slung over his shoulder. When asked who he was and where he came from, the stranger said he came from a sidhe of the Dananns and that his name was Cascorach, a piper for the old gods. He began to play, and his music emitted such wonderful magic that the Christians were lulled into a dreamy sleep. Later, St. Patrick, like a reluctant music critic, gave Cascorach's playing a mixed review. He said "it resemble[s] Heaven's harmony" except for an unfortunate "twang of the faery spell that infests it."[17] In the early years of the twentieth century, Evans-Wentz, a tireless student of Celtic folkways, pointed out that although there is an air of myth and legend about the story, Cascorach might actually have been "a mortal like one of the many Irish pipers and musicians who used to go, *or even go yet*, to the fairy-folk to be educated in the musical profession, and then come back as the most marvellous players that ever were in Ireland." (Italics mine.) Evans-Wentz's phrase, "or even go yet," shows how persistently the tradition survives and colors modern thinking about the influence of the Otherworld upon everyday matters.

One of the truly great Irish pipers, whose music continues to be popular both in the British Isles and America, is Turlough O'Carolan. Like other pipers, he was considered to be faery-taught, but the circumstances of his life are remarkable in the details associated with the essential archetype of shamanism. In a more traditional shamanic society, Carolan would probably have been recognized as a full-fledged shaman.

Born in 1670, Carolan showed little interest in music until he was struck blind by a severe bout of smallpox when he was eighteen years old. His father had been a blacksmith, and after the boy's illness, he studied music with a harper named Mac Dermott Roe until he was twenty-one. The Mac Dermott Roe family owned an iron foundry. Thus we see two strongly shamanic characteristics: the initiatory illness and the training with smiths. At age twenty-one Carolan became an itinerant harper.

Even before he was deprived of his sight, Carolan frequented the top of "a moat or rath," which was known in the community as a faery haunt. Later, when blind, he asked family members or neighbors to lead him up there on nice days. On the hilltop he would lay "for hours stretched before the sun and was often observed to suddenly start up in an ecstasy."[18] On one such occasion, he sat up and asked his companion to take him home immediately, where he composed one of his most highly esteemed pieces, a song for Bridget Cruise. Later Carolan was said to have related that vision to friends and confirmed that he had indeed gone among the "good people." Peasant admirers of the harper claimed that Carolan had been inspired by the Queen of the Faeries herself. At any rate, Carolan could never again be persuaded to talk about his vision.

Other shamanic qualities cling to Carolan's reputation. He was reputed to have had psychic powers. On one occasion he foretold the death of a young girl. On another he recognized the same Bridget Cruise, with whom he had once been in love, from the touch of her hand as he helped her on board a boat. He also made a pilgrimage to St. Patrick's Purgatory, a famed island retreat reknowned for the otherworldly visions it induced in people who visited it, a Christian holy place with roots in the pagan past. We will look more closely at this sacred site in the next chapter.

People who knew Carolan confirm his character to be the type we might easily associate with the shaman. One acquaintance described him as "absolutely the child of nature, he was governed by the indulgences, and at times the caprices, of that mother."[19] He was known to have had "a mind undisciplined through the defect or rather absence of cultivation," suggesting that his talents were instinctual and primal, compared to the more orthodox standards of his day. Carolan was often described in terms frequently associated with the Celtic Otherworld of Faerie, such as playful, imaginative, graceful, sportive, gay, ingenius, unpredictable, and whimsical. Often the same terms were used to describe Carolan's music. Had he not been blind, Carolan's talent to entertain might have extended to the playacting and showmanship of a more traditional trickster figure.

If St. Patrick could have heard Carolan's music, he would have probably noticed a strong "faery twang" about it. Carolan even felt compelled to coin a word, *planxty*, to describe the original, nonordinary style of harp tune he was fond of composing. Musicologists note that a planxty is not suitable for either singing or dancing, due to its erratic sequencing.

It is not bound by repeatable measures like the traditional jig. The irregularity of its cadences and the extreme range in its scale make it difficult to write lyrics for it. Even the word *planxty* itself is mysterious. Scholars cannot decide if it is an Irish or English word. Perhaps it is neither; perhaps it is a faery word.

A planxty is characterized by a circularity of construction. One commentator explains that its pleasing quality is achieved by having "the conclusion of a phrase so framed as to produce the idea of a beginning; and again, having the beginning or the middle of a phrase so constructed as to seem for a moment the notes of a passage about to close."[20] We are reminded in this of the continuous ring, without beginning, middle, or end, formed by the Uroborous, a symbol of the ambiguous and unending nature of reality that the shaman knows from direct experiences in nonordinary realms. There also seems to be a strong hint that, although mortals have trouble dancing or singing to it, the planxty might very well be suitable for faery dancing, judging from descriptions of the kaleidescopic quality of faery dances—rings upon rings of faeries performing the most intricate dance steps. Perhaps faery dancing, like faery music and the planxty itself, exists in a timeless-spaceless dimension in which it is truly impossible for ordinary mortals to "keep time" or "take positions" as they would in our ordinary space-time dance floor.

The Musical Branch

The musical branch is as central to ancient Celtic spirituality as the severed head. The branch, laden with bells, magical birds, blossoms, apples, nuts, or acorns, produced a faery music that could lull listeners into a pleasant sleep or a dream-filled reverie in which they forgot their sorrows. In some cases, the music produced a healing sleep from which the sick and wounded awoke to find themselves recovered. The musical branch was a hallmark of the Celtic poet. Master poets carried a golden branch, lesser poets had a silver branch, and all others carried a bronze branch. Poets carried their branches, adorned with bells, as they entered formal performance areas, letting the music announce their presence and alter the mood of the room.

The silver branch had the added importance of being a passport into the Otherworld, a talisman usually given by the Queen of the Otherworld to the sojourner to carry for protection and safe travel. In some respects the silver branch is similar to the Golden Bough of classical Greek legends, sacred to Proserpine, Queen of the Underworld, which she presented to all initiates who entered her subterranean realms to begin the deep journey into the mysteries of the human soul. In Vergil's *Aeneid,* the Sybil instructs Aeneas to pluck the sacred bough near the entrance to the cavern leading to the Underworld. Later the ferryman Charon refuses to transport Aeneas across the Stygian lake until he is shown the sacred branch.

In a Celtic legend, a haunting, otherworldly music lulls Bran, the son of Febal, into a trance from which he awakens to find a silver branch covered with blossoms lying by his side. He carries the branch back to his stronghold where he discovers a strange woman wearing beautiful, unearthly clothing. No one at court knows where she came from or how she got in. The faery woman sings a song to Bran, and then disappears as mysteriously as she had appeared. Before she vanishes, however, the silver branch leaps from Bran's hand into hers, and she carries it away with her. And the spell is cast. The next day Bran departs on his famous voyage toward the setting sun where he encounters the mystic islands of the Celtic Otherworld.

The Sacred Branch is a symbol of a larger shamanic concept: the World Tree. Most religions have some notion of the Center of the World, and in archaic or primitive societies this world center is often represented as a tree (sometimes a pillar, pole, or mountain). The World Tree is a universal symbol uniting the three spatial realms of experience: its branches spread high into the upper world or heaven; its trunk is accessible from the middle world or surface of the earth; and its root system grows deep into the lower world or underworld. As human beings living in a three-dimensional, physical universe, and walking upright upon the earth, we logically divide the environment around us into these three realms, for we are aware of the dome of the sky overhead, the landscape upon which we live, and the deeper regions beneath the earth accessible through caves, gorges, wells, and canyons. The tree unites all three worlds. Trees also command respect as the largest of plants and some of the oldest living things. Even ancient peoples had a sense of the longevity and sacredness of certain trees, seeing in them cosmic links between the past and the future.

In some cultures, shamans climb the sacred tree and sit in its branches as part of the soul's ascent into the upper worlds. In Siberia the World Tree was thought to contain nests in which there were eggs holding the souls of future shamans. The greatest shamans' souls were highest in the tree. Ritual tree climbing is also found in the initiation of shamans in North America. While some tribal peoples had an actual tree that was revered as the Center of the World, the more common notion was that any tree could function in this sacred manner. People who conceive of the universe as holographi- cally structured, as archaic cultures seem to have done, can locate the Cen- ter of the World in any tree or spot so designated. In a holographic universe, the part incorporates the whole; every detail contains the totality; within the microcosm we find the entire macrocosm. Thus the World Tree, and by extension the Sacred Branch, becomes a link in the mystic union of creation.

Frequently in Celtic folklore we come across a magical branch with an assortment of fruit, nuts, and blossoms (often out of season) that is able to produce faery music. Some branches contain nuts, apples, and acorns. The Irish king, Cormac, was given a silver branch with three golden apples. When he shook it, the branch emitted ethereal music that healed the sick and wounded and brought a restful sleep to the worried. A mystical branch bearing nuts, apples, and acorns all at once taps into three strains of Celtic magic: hazelnuts that bestow wisdom on those who eat them; apples that are tokens of the Otherworld, often referred to as the Land of Apples; and acorns that grow into the sacred oak that plays such a prominent role in the Celts' spiritual imagination. Whether adorned with bells or nature's bounty, the magical branch is as important to Celtic spirituality as it is to the birds who sit in it and sing.

MAGICAL BIRDS AND THE POWER OF FLIGHT

The link between birds, soul flight, and shamanism can be traced back to the paleolithic cave paintings at Lascaux, where we find a human fig- ure, most likely a shaman, lying on his back, wearing a bird mask, and

possessing clawlike fingers. Lying next to him is a staff with a bird on top
of it. It is possible that the artist was not depicting a mask or costume, but
the shapeshifted state the shaman was in. The stone-age artist was drawing a representation of a state of consciousness. Good evidence for this
is that the shaman is lying down and has an erection, typical of the dream
or trance state in males. If the artist was indeed depicting a state of consciousness, we are obviously dealing with a high level of sophistication and
awareness.

Birds and trance states can be found in the South African rock drawings of flying deer with graceful, swept-back wings. Joseph Campbell points
out that these figures represent either the souls of the dead, which were
believed to fly through the air, or trance dancers.[21] Nearby on the rock
wall are very similar dancing figures, only depicted as more human, with
the same swept-back arms and forward-thrusted torsos as the winged bucks.
Here, too, we see the connection between winged animal spirits and the
trance state of shamanic dancers.

In New Zealand, Maori shamans wear feathered outfits. In Siberia, the
Samoyed and Altaians wear caps decorated with bird feathers. In Ireland,
poets wore a *tugan*, or feathered cloak, as part of their performance regalia.
Descriptions of the Irish poet's bird mantle vary. Some say they were made
from the feathers of songbirds, appropriately enough since the poet was a
singer and shared with birds the magical power to lull listeners into a dreamlike state with music and song. Other accounts say the poet's feathers were
white, which is in keeping with the white or colorless (albino) faery animal
that often lures unsuspecting hunters and wayfarers into the Otherworld.
The poet's mantle may have also contained swan feathers, always a magical
bird in Celtic lore due to its great beauty and grace, and its ability, like other
water birds, to transcend the various realms of water, air, and land.

Mircea Eliade notes that the shaman's costume, like the poet's regalia,
was meant "to give the shaman a new, magical body in animal form . . .
(and) to don it is to return to the mystical state revealed and established during the protracted experiences and ceremonies of the shaman's initiation."[22] Special costumes, magical paraphernalia, and power objects are

mnemonic devices to trigger the shamanic vision or activate what the Australian shamans call "the strong eye." Bird regalia appears to be among the most common devices for this, since bird imagery and symbolism are highly consistent with the spirit work and soul activities of shamanism almost everywhere.

It is possible that the Celtic poet/druid's animal or bird costume functioned in a similar fashion. Poets and druids were initiated through long years of trancework and shapeshifting experiences. They, too, may have used their costumes as mnemonic devices to trigger trance states in which they could more easily recall their songs and tales.

Certain birds have long been associated with shamans. The eagle is frequently one of the major power animals in shamanic cultures, since it is the most powerful bird and has a reputation for flying the highest and seeing the farthest. Like the shaman, the eagle can journey where others cannot go and see things that others cannot see. Many native peoples regard the eagle as a solar figure having powers traditionally attributed to sun gods. Among the Buryat people in Siberia, for example, the eagle was revered as the first shaman sent by the gods to assist human beings. The Gilyaks, a coastal people on the Sea of Okhostk, have the same word for both eagle and shaman, while another Eurasian people, the Ostyaks, claim that the first shaman was a two-headed eagle.

Birds are found more extensively in Celtic religious art than other natural creatures, but the eagle does not play as prominent a role among the Celts as we might expect. The Celtic sun gods were associated with waterbirds, rather than eagles. As Anne Ross records, waterbirds of every kind were part of the cult of the sun, especially in its healing aspect.[23] There are depictions of the sun being drawn by waterbirds, such as a cormorant, a duck, or a goose. Sculpted figures of deities sometimes are seated in chariots to which waterbirds are harnessed. This fascination with waterbirds aligns the Celtic tribes with North American tribal artists who frequently celebrate waterbirds and other amphibious creatures, such as the frog, because they have the ability to transform themselves by evolving through very different physical forms in their natural development. Birds and animals that display the ability to live in more than one medium, such as the otter, beaver, frogs, and waterbirds, are fitting symbols and allies for the shaman who also undergoes a series of transformations and is able to journey in and between the worlds of air, water, and earth.

It is a widespread spiritual belief that all humans were able to fly in primordial times, *in illo tempore*, before the fall from original grace, when the first people shared much in common with supernatural beings. In later times, only the spiritually gifted, such as wizards, yogis, witches, saints, and shamans, were believed to fly or levitate. Two ideas related to flight appear in religious thought around the world: first, that the human soul has the form of a bird, and second, that birds function as psychopomps, leading the souls of the dead into the next life. Associated with bird and soul imagery is a widespread notion that at death the human soul becomes discarnate, leaves the body, and flies like a bird. Flight, therefore, is a strong symbol of the soul's autonomy, transcendence, and ultimate destiny after death. People capable of either physical flight or soul flight during their lifetimes are considered to have transcended the human condition and re-entered the original time; they enjoy supernatural privileges, denied most people until death. The shaman is revered, and sometimes feared, precisely on these terms: He or she has the power to leave our ordinary condition and pass the boundaries into the spirit world; to be able to fly and visit the land of the dead; and to enjoy the friendship of discarnate beings, the helping spirits.

In the Christian era the shamanic association of birds, flight, and the Otherworld continued to color the Celtic imagination. Birds were still seen as messengers, informants, and servants, but their allegiance was now restricted to the "kingdom of heaven." Legends indicate that "Christian birds" occasionally sang the Mass and that angels hovered around the heavenly throne as flocks of birds. One early convert accepted Christianity after an intense vision in which (he later relates) "I was borne away to look upon heaven, and I looked upon the Lord himself on His throne and a bird-flock of angels making music to Him. Then I saw a bright bird, and sweeter than all music his singing. [St.] Michael moreover . . . was in bird form in the presence of the Creator."[24]

A Christian poem addressed to the "King of the Tree of Life" says:

The blossoms on the branches are your people,
The singing birds are your angels,
The whispering breeze is your Spirit."[25]

The poem goes on to pray that the blossoms bring forth sweet fruit, the birds sing the highest praise, and the "Spirit cover[s] all with his gentle breath." Thus the poet's magical branch and the shaman's World Tree are transformed into Christian symbology, becoming a nexus for human life and the Spirit of God.

The druids found omens in birds. The flight of birds, their calls, and erratic behavior all indicated the wishes of the gods and goddesses. This practice did not immediately die out as Christian monks replaced druids in Irish society. St. Columba, for example, could hear the blessing of God in the screech of gulls that welcomed his boat to shore. In his words, "the joyous shrieks of the swooping gulls" indicated that nature resounded to the monk's successful voyage.[26]

Winged creatures in all cultures are natural symbols for the soul's flight, and birds are obvious forms for the shamanic imagination. Joan Halifax suggests the "winged angels and demons flying through mythologies of cultures everywhere" have "their seed form" in "the psyche of the shaman."[27] If the shamanic archetype is a natural part of the human psyche, then it should not be unusual to discover certain power animals repeated across cultures and through the centuries. Mircea Eliade even speaks about "the nostalgia for flight" being an essential element in human consciousness.[28] Certainly the "seed form" of heavenly birds and angelic counselors found in the tales of Irish monks can be traced back to earlier beliefs and images in the psyche of the druids and poets, thus indicating a continuity of spiritual expression from pagan times to the Christian era.

Songs of Protection

A prayer to St. Brigid reads:

Every day I pray to St. Brigid that . . .
No fire, no flame shall burn me,

No lake, no sea shall drown me,
No sword, no spear shall wound me,
No king, no chief insult me.
All the birds shall sing for me,
All the cattle low for me,
All the insects buzz for me,
God's angels shall protect me.[29]

We've seen this shamanic summons of the elements before. Among other places, it can be found in the pagan Celts' loyalty oath, a monkish poem about Christ's crucifixion, and the sentimental Irish blessing on contemporary greeting cards. Celts, then and now, seem preoccupied with the need for protection by means of spells and chants to summon the powers of God or nature. To this end the Irish developed a singularly focused protection spell called a *lorica* or *breastplate*. In the lorica the supplicant calls upon transpersonal powers for protection, often including images that reflect the four elements: earth, air, fire, and water. Safe within one's verbal armor, the Celt can face whatever dangers lurk ahead.

Often the primary motif of the lorica is to literally wrap oneself with power. In St. Patrick's "Deer's Cry," one of the most celebrated Christian poems of Celtic heritage, we find Patrick invoking the power of Christ to surround him.

Christ with me, Christ before me, Christ behind me,
Christ in me, Christ beneath me, Christ above me,
Christ when I lie down, Christ when I sit down,
Christ when I rise . . .[30]

The flavor and structure of this invocation has deep roots in pagan spirituality. We find it among the Navajo, for example, in many of their *sings*. In the "Night Chant," a song sung by Dawn Boy contains this passage.

Beauty before me, with it I wander.
Beauty behind me, with it I wander.
Beauty below me, with it I wander.
Beauty above me, with it I wander.[31]

A lyric structure such as this stirs something deep within us. Whether we call upon Christ to surround and protect us or we ask for "Beauty," we recreate the great Wheel of Life, placing ourselves in its center. This invocation of the four directions is central to many earth-rites, whether it be casting a circle for ceremonial purposes, laying out standing stones, or constructing a Native American medicine wheel. We can assume that since sacred sites utilizing the circle and marking the four quarters enjoy such great antiquity, this geometric figure, whether created visually or verbally, taps something intrinsic to the human soul, some primal understanding of ourselves as material beings walking upright on this three-dimensional planet. Shamanically speaking, invoking the directions creates a timeless-spaceless realm that transcends physical reality, even as it uses the elements and directions of physical reality. By creating a circle that is both present and not present, both here and not here, we put our consciousness in a framework that is both temporal and eternal, similar to the shaman's trance consciousness.

An Irish medieval manuscript applies the "protective power-wrap" of the lorica to the individual days of the week by invoking a particular angel to guard each specific day. The following is the invocation for Thursday:

> **Sariel on Thursday I speak of, against the swift waves of the sea,**
> **Against every evil that comes to a man, against every disease that**
> **seizes him.**[32]

The angel Sariel may not be familiar to those steeped in Roman Catholicism. This Irish prayer of protection reveals that the apocryphal sources of Christianity still held some sway in Celtic literature. Similar prayers beseech Catholic saints in the same manner, assigning a particular saint to each day of the week.

St. Patrick's lorica is a Christian variation for older magic, typical of the druids. Patrick composed it on a trek to Tara fraught with enemy ambushes. Before the saint and his eight young clerics departed, he cast a spell over them to make them invisible. As they passed, the enemy soldiers saw only eight deer. As an enchantment of invisibility or as a shapeshifting feat, Patrick's spell succeeded, and he sang triumphantly the hymn that became known, appropriately, as the "Deer's Cry."

The hymn also includes "Patrick's Breastplate," translated in numerous ways over the years to emphasize either the poetry or the prayer. In the version below with its lean, unembellished imagery, the lorica could be uttered convincingly by any pagan priest or shaman.

> I arise today
> Through the strength of heaven:
> Light of sun,
> Radiance of moon,
> Splendour of fire,
> Speed of lightning,
> Swiftness of wind,
> Depth of sea,
> Stability of earth,
> Firmness of rock.[33]

A considerably expanded version of the lorica survives as the *Rune of St. Patrick*. The elements of nature are the same as in pre-Christian spells, but the final invocation is for God's help to protect the spellcaster from evil.

> At Tara today in this fateful hour
> I place all Heaven with its power,
> And the Sun with its brightness,
> And the snow with its whiteness,
> And Fire with all the strength it hath,
> And lightning with its rapid wrath,
> And the winds with their swiftness along the path,
> And the sea with its deepness,
> And the rocks with their steepness,
> And the Earth with its starkness:
> All these I place
> By God's almighty help and grace,
> Between myself and the powers of Darkness.[34]

THE POWER OF SATIRE

In the prayer above to St. Brigid, we hear a curious request: not to be insulted by a king or chief. The malicious insult enjoys a distinguished history in Celtic society. Among the poet's magical powers was the ability to compose a satire that would bring ruin upon the subject, reshape the landscape, control the elements, and influence animals. Kings especially feared the poet's satire for it could cause them to lose their right to rule. An early Irish tradition claims that highly trained poets had once been judges, and were therefore experts on the rights and duties of kings.

The very first recorded satire in Irish history was directed at Bres the Beautiful, the Danann king, who, in spite of his good looks, proved to be an insensitive ruler and broke the Dananns' code of hospitality. It happened this way. The poet Copry arrived at Bres's court and was ushered into a small, dark, unheated chamber with no furniture. After a considerable wait, he was finally served three dry, miserable cakes and, most notably, no ale. In revenge he spoke a satire against Bres.

> Without food quickly served,
> Without a cow's milk, whereon a calf can grow,
> Without a dwelling fit for a man under the gloomy night,
> Without means to entertain a bardic company—
> Let such be the condition of Bres.[35]

And so it was. Poetic satire had magical power to create the conditions about which it spoke. Once "be-rhymed," Bres had to surrender his sovereignty.

Another incident in Irish legend concerns King Caier whose wife was in love with the poet Nede. She asked that Nede compose a satire to cause blisters to break out on Caier's face, since according to Celtic tradition, a blemished or crippled king could not reign. Blisters would do the trick. Nede's satire says:

> Evil, death, and a short life to Caier;
> May spears of battle slay Caier;
> The rejected of the land and the earth is Caier;
> Beneath the mounds and the rocks be Caier.[36]

The next morning the hoped-for blotches appeared on Caier's face, and he fled into exile.

The corollary to the poet's satire, the song of praise, was also a form of magic. Kings and powerful families welcomed favorable songs because they spoke of and created protection, happiness, and successful endeavors. In these tribal customs were the origins of the current office of poet laureate, whose talents still have a hint of magic. Official poems are written to honor the nation and in so doing assure its prosperity. Were a poet laureate to write a poem highly critical of his or her country, some citizens would no doubt see it as at least an ill omen, if not an outright baneful spell, putting the nation in jeopardy.

Belief in the power of the poet's words can be found in many societies and among strongly shamanic cultures. The shaman-poet was both loved and feared, depending on whose side he was. For example, Igjugarjuk, the Eskimo shaman, told Rasmussen that one always ought to proceed with caution around shamans because they are "skillful in magic" and "able to kill through words and thoughts."[37]

THE WOUNDED FOOT

There is a fascinating parallel between an old Celtic formula for casting a spell and a key element of shamanism, as well as another link between what might have been the original Celtic shamans and the classic shamans of Siberia. In a curious episode, Lugh, the multiskilled Irish sun god, exhorts the Danann army before a battle by singing a chant while hopping on one foot and keeping one eye closed. This contorted pose seems unbecoming for high-command military officers and powerful sun gods. What is going on here?

In *Celtic Heritage*, Alwyn and Brinley Rees point out that this bizarre behavior resonated in the Celtic imagination with the dreaded Fomorians.[38] In effect, Lugh was contorting his body to resemble those primal spirits of evil and destruction. In another tale, Cuchulain's enemies, the sons of Calatin, who had practiced sorcery for seventeen years, were mutilated in an odd fashion; the sons had their right feet and left hands cut off, and the daughters were blinded in the left eye. The Rees's comment is, "In short they had been given a Fomorian aspect."[39] It would appear from these examples that spells to do harm, such as battle spells and baneful sorcery, are connected with the "evil spirits" of the cosmos, the Fomorians.

Casting a spell on one foot with one hand behind the back and one eye closed is a typical (albeit uncomfortable) posture in many magical traditions. Whatever association it has with evildoing is, like so much connected with magic, a result of the modern scientific and Christian prejudice against personal power that cannot be rationally explained or attributed to divine intervention. Casting spells and working magic was not always considered evil, but it was always considered beyond the natural abilities of ordinary men and women. The roots of this strange posture can be traced directly to shamanic concepts of magic, the power to cast spells, and the assistance of helping spirits from the Otherworld.

Carlo Ginzburg, in his intriguing study, *Ecstasies: Deciphering the Witches' Sabbath*, argues persuasively that one-footedness and peculiarities connected with walking found in European myths and folklore indicate that the afflicted person has been a visitor to the Otherworld or in some way enjoys the favor of otherworldly allies.[40] The themes of one-footedness, monosandalism, and an inability to walk due to a wound in the foot, leg, or thigh form a constellation of mythically consistent images that reveal a form of physical asymmetry in the hero after contact with the Otherworld, and often a contact reminiscent of the shamanic initiation adventure.

Ginzburg catalogues popular myths and folktales that point to this phenomenon. Oedipus has his feet pierced in an attempt to kill him as a baby; Jason fulfills a prophecy by wearing one sandal when he appears before his uncle Pelias; Perseus receives one sandal from Hermes before he fights the Gorgon; Telephus is wounded in the left leg by Achilles who himself has a vulnerable heel; Theseus finds the gilded sandals that will help others recognize him when he returns home; the monster Typhon cuts off Zeus's hands and feet and hides them in a cave. Ginzburg maintains that the clumsiness related to walking is, in each case, part of the hero's initiation rite, either an initiation into a role or power he will assume or an initiation into self-discovery (often the two are the same).

A more accessible tale for contemporary people is that of Cinderella, a heroine who loses a slipper after a magical night at the ball (the Otherworld). Modern versions of the Cinderella story often omit a key subplot (to make it more appropriate for young children); the two hateful stepsisters cut off parts of their own feet so they will fit into the lost slipper. They hope their amputated feet will qualify them for entry into the otherworldly mysteries of the royal court. They miscalculate horribly. Other fascinating shamanic features of the tale are that Cinderella's helping spirit is a faery godmother, who, in some versions, is the spirit of Cinderella's deceased mother; the heroine enjoys the friendship of animals; and she is forced to live a smithlike existence in the lower chambers of the house, tending the subterranean fireplace.

Regarding physical asymmetry, Ginzburg says that "the physical imbalance that characterizes divinities like Hermes or Dionysos, or heroes like Jason or Perseus . . . [symbolizes] a permanent or temporary connection with the realm of the dead."[41] In other words, an imbalance of gait, such as limping, having a vulnerable heel, dragging one foot, walking with one foot unshod, stumbling, or hopping on one foot, suggests that the person has been marked by Otherworld experiences. It implies that contact with the Otherworld requires us to become less of a human being in terms of what we usually associate with normalcy, namely, symmetry of bodily proportion. The shaman who is crippled in one foot, blinded in one eye, or missing an arm is free from the duality of the human body, just as his or her thinking is freed from dualistic thought patterns as a result of the initiatory journeys to the Otherworld. In both physical and mental ways, they have learned how to transcend polarities.

It is not surprising that physically deformed individuals have often been shunned throughout history, possibly because the healthy-bodied intuitively recognize a maimed or severed body as being either more or less than human. The crippled are not like others, and in a way that goes beyond physical deformity. *They are not in the world as we who have a whole body are in the world.* They see and experience things differently, and we who lack that deformity do not share their vision. It is alien to us. In some societies, especially tribal and shamanic cultures, deformity can be construed as a sign that one has been singled out by supernatual beings for some special purpose, often to play a spiritual role such as shaman.

There are many variations on this theme of the wounded foot in Celtic literature. We have already seen that Bran the Blessed was wounded in the foot on a military expedition to Ireland, and recognized in the accident that his reign as king was over. Thereupon he requests that his head be severed from his body, and he returns to the Otherworld (or at least his head does, as a guide). Ossian, the Irish bard, returns from Faerie with the *geis* not to let his foot touch Irish soil. As long as he stays on horseback, he is safe, but as soon as he dismounts, he ages rapidly (all the years in Faerie catching up with him) and he dies. We have also noted the connection between shamans and smiths who are traditionally lame (Hephaestus, Vulcan, Wayland) and whose skill and practice involves subterranean fire handling and transformation of ores into precious metals. In the treasury of Arthurian romance, we meet a man with a leg made of silver, gold, and precious stones. The man is a gatekeeper at the entrance to a castle surrounded by flames. The otherworldly nature of the castle is clear in that it has a reputation for housing the dead. W. B. Yeats knew of a woman in western Ireland, at the turn of the last century, who had been spirited off by the faeries for seven years. When she returned, Yeats recounts, "she had no toes left. She had danced them off."[42] Further examples could be cited, but the point is that visits to the Otherworld, even pleasant ones, can be harmful to your health!

There are children's games found all over the world that involve hopping on one foot. Many games, as children's writer Jack Maguire points out, were originally played by both children and adults. "For most of human history, the young and the old enjoyed the same pastimes, just as they shared the same labors."[43] Maguire continues, "Codified in many of the . . . games kids now play . . . are ancient incantations and movements originally designed to impose some order on the mysteries of the universe." Some games and dances were rituals; they were formulas for casting protection spells, or their sing-song rhymes were instructions to ward off evil. For example, in Ring-Around-the-Rosy, the "ring" referred to the red circular body rash of the Great Plague of London that killed 70,000 people in the 1660s. The "pocket full of posies" referred to the magical herbs thought to protect one against the disease. "Ashes, ashes, we all fall down" has two interpretations: People who died of the plague were cremated; "ashes, ashes" is a variant pronunciation of the sneezing sound "achoo, achoo," implying sickness. The dancing players spin around and around (creating an altered state of consciousness), grow weak and dizzy, and finally fall down as if dead.

In Siberia we find some of the clearest expressions of this ancient shamanic motif, linking one-footedness with travel through the Otherworld. A Samoyed tale relates how the hero is killed four times by an enemy, but each time is helped back to life by an old man with one leg, one hand, and one eye. The old man, clearly a practitioner of shamanic arts, leads the hero deep into the earth where an old woman restores life to the dead by sleeping on their bones. Such a tale could have logically sprung from the shamanic imagination, or even from actual journey accounts by shamans, for death and rebirth, the reduction of the body to bones, the subterranean chamber of healing, all have classic shamanic implications. We might also consider in this context a Siberian tradition that the Mother of All Animals entrusts newborn shamans to Burgestez-Udagan, a spirit with one leg, one hand, and one eye.

Carlo Ginzburg relates a tale from the Caucasus, recorded a half century ago, but with much older roots, about a hero named Amirani who is remarkably similar to the Greek hero Prometheus.[44] At one point Amirani is without fire and learns that the nine brothers who live in the underworld are the only ones who possess fire. Now one of them is lame. Amirani journeys to the Lower World and fights the healthy brothers, steals the fire, and departs. He does not assault the lame brother, suggesting several possibilities for the original significance of this tale. Either the lame brother is a friendly spirit who helped Amirani (the way a helping spirit assists the neo-shaman through the initiation crisis) or the lame spirit is the primary smith, the shaman firekeeper who is to be treated with respect (since one may steal physical fire but should not harm the guardian or the spirit of fire). It is also possible that Amirani feels no need to attack one who is crippled because he is no threat, or because the hero feels compassion for the disabled brother. In the shamanic imagination all these interpretations make sense. The lame firekeeper/smith is no threat; he is the shaman's ally.

Like Prometheus, who steals fire from the lame smith Hephaestus and is eventually chained to a rock where an eagle eats away at his liver, Amirani also feeds an eagle with his flesh. But the situation is much different. After stealing the fire, Amirani falls into a series of adventures that include being devoured by a dragon who takes him deep into the earth. He manages to escape and meets an eagle who agrees to fly him to the surface of the earth in exchange for food. On the flight Amirani runs out of food, so he cuts off a piece of his own flesh to feed his rescuer. The eagle enjoys Amirani's flesh more than the previous food, and when they arrive safely, he gives Amirani a piece of his wing to rub on the wound, which heals it immediately.

The Caucasus tale does not tell us from which part of his body Amirani took his flesh. But Ginzburg, ever eager to connect myths, traces this theme of feeding an eagle with part of one's body through another related legend, and concludes that the piece of flesh was a slice of Amirani's heel. Thus, if Ginzburg is correct, Amirani returns from the Otherworld with the expected affliction.

What is interesting in our search for the Celtic shaman is again the Scythian link between Celtic spiritual motifs and the shamanic practices of Central Asia. The archeological record shows that the Scythians penetrated deep into the Caucasus between the seventh and fourth centuries B.C. They may have been the link between Asiatic beliefs relating one-footedness to shamanic journeys into the Otherworld and similar Celtic themes. If so, the theme has had a long, fascinating, and circuitous history, from the primeval fire-wielding shamans of Siberia through the mythological fire-stealing heroes of Greece and the Caucasus to the Celtic descriptions of casting spells by assuming the stance and condition of the Fomorians, the original inhabitants of the spirit world.

THE AMBIVALENT CRANE

A game played during Dionysian festivals in Delos and Crete involved balancing and hopping on one foot. The Greek name of this game refers to a crane, a water bird noted for standing for great lengths of time on one foot, apparently in a trancelike state, and staring into the water. The game, and related dance, dramatized the winding paths of the labyrinth where Theseus hunted the minotaur, an obvious otherworldly domain, symbolizing the realm of the dead. We can find the same type of association on the other side of the globe in China, where female shamans cover their face with handkerchiefs and dance on one foot until they go into trance and fall over.

The contemporary Huichol shaman Ramon Medina Silva demonstrated to an anthropologist the shaman's need for balance. He removed his sandals at the edge of a waterfall and proceded to scamper up the slippery rocks. As he leaped from rock to rock, he spread his arms, threw his head back, bent his body forward, and balanced himself on one foot. Later the anthropologist admitted that when Silva first spoke about balance, she interpreted it in a metaphysical way: that the shaman had to balance polarities, be a mediator between opposites, and so on, as we have discussed. The next day Silva explained to her in no uncertain terms that the shaman must have physical balance as well. The shaman must have "superb equilibrium" or "he will not reach his destination and will fall this way or that." He then spoke of the abyss the shaman must cross and how narrow it is. "Without balance, one is eaten by the animals below," he warned.[45]

In addition to being a bird of exquisite balance and trancelike demeanor, the crane has played, and continues to play, an ambivalent role in Celtic spirituality. In pagan times the crane-bag (a bag made from the skin of a crane) was a revered object. Taliesin sings, "I have been a well-filled crane-bag, a sight to behold." Celtic scholar John Matthews describes this mysterious symbol as "a repository for the Poetic Tradition itself, containing like the shaman's pouch, the magical tools of Creation."[46] The origins of the crane-bag can be found with Mananan, the Celtic sea god and lord of the Underworld. Into the crane-bag he placed all his secrets of magic and power. Coincidentally, three cranes guard Mananan's stronghold.

The crane is associated with the supernatural in other ways too. The Irish hero Finn, for example, is rescued by his grandmother, the goddess, who transforms herself into a crane and catches him in midair as he falls off a cliff. In the Scottish Highlands, there is a taboo against eating crane meat because the crane's flesh is believed to be unclean. While at first glance this may suggest that the crane is an evil bird, we must keep in mind that often a prohibition against eating a certain bird or animal is an indication that the bird or animal was once (or is still) held sacred. The association of the crane with uncleanliness and evil, however, is strong. In Ireland, mean women are called cranes, often a euphemism for "witch," a term that in the popular mind continues to denote a woman who uses magical powers to do harm. In the Christian era this association of the crane with evil women most likely developed from an earlier association of the crane with the goddess and other supernatural beings.

A verse in modern Scottish Gaelic calls upon St. Columba to protect the supplicant against the nastiness of cranes (as well as faeries and all the wickedness of the world).

> The fine armour of Columba
> is protecting you from the fairy arrows
> against the screeching cranes
> against the gnawing cranes
> against the temptation of the present world
> against the wickedness of the world beyond.[47]

Gone was the crane as a sacred bird, as the goddess, as a keeper of the secrets of the poetic arts. Christian propagandists consciously linked surviving goddess worshippers with evildoers and used the term *witch* to refer to these holdovers from the Old Religion. Hence the transition from the crane-as-goddess to the crane-as-witch.

THE STORYTELLER'S CHARM

Mythopoetic language, specifically metaphor, has the ability to heal mental and emotional pain because the metaphor mediates the contradictions of life, thus providing a solution that appeals to our deepest hope that it is possible to transcend the human condition. Shamans use mythopoetic language to relate their exploits into nonordinary realms. We have seen that the shaman is a Trickster who often tricks the mind of a patient into healing itself by costumes, songs, dances, drama, sleight of hand, and not the least of which is the ability to spin fantastical tales of magic and mystery.

As a storyteller, the shaman leads listeners back into the primordial chaos, or perhaps to the brink of that chaos, to the edge of twilight, where the original unity existed. Here the shaman and his or her patient/listener get a glimpse of the supernatural state in which opposites are reconciled and the anguish of life can be alleviated by magic. The storyteller who can induce even a slight trance in his or her audience often achieves the same shamanic trick. And when we consider that it was not unusual for some Irish storytellers to tell unbelievably lengthy tales, some lasting for six hours or more, we should probably assume that the tales did indeed put audiences into some type of a trance state.

The Irish and Welsh storytellers of modern times preserve this healing tradition. An Irish text notes that the listeners to a story will be protected from harm for a year. "Nothing sorrowful shall be heard by anyone who has heard [the story]; it will be a year's protection to them."[48] Specifically the text promises that a newly married couple who hears it will produce a child and be free from hunger or want. If it is told in a new house, no one will die in that house, nor will the inhabitants go without food or clothing, nor will it catch fire. A king who hears it before battle will return victorious. Clearly, something magical takes place beyond mere entertainment. The Celtic storytelling tradition emphatically states that certain tales should be told only at certain times of the year, on special occasions, and in a reverential manner because the act of storytelling is a sacred act. Storytelling is a sacramental act in that it allows the sacred mysteries to break through into ordinary consciousness, stirring the mind and firing the imagination with the possibilities of nonordinary worlds.

In medieval times Celtic storytellers were eccentrics who had studied for many years to memorize the hundreds of tales in their repertoires. Their immense learning and skill was akin to that of the druids and bards, and they were often held in the same respect as a learned class of individuals. This reputation continued into more modern times as we have seen in the Irish gleeman Michael Moran, who lived in the early nineteenth century. Such individuals, like the poets and druids before them, were considered to have otherworldly skills as well as the ability to spin a good yarn. They were sought out for divination, prophecy, and spiritual advice.

Alwyn and Brinley Rees note that the Latin word *historia*, from which the word *story* derives, is also the root for the word *history*, a term originally meaning "knowing," "learned," and "wise."[49] In old Welsh the word for story meant "guidance," "direction," and "instruction." The stem for the Welsh term meant "sign," "symbol," "omen," and "miracle." The Rees's conclusion to this etymological puzzle is that the ancient Welsh storyteller was indeed a seer and teacher "who guided the souls of his hearers through the world of 'mystery'." Thus we find the Celtic storytellers fulfilling one of the important roles played by classical shamans, the guider and instructor of souls.

In the storytellers' repertoire were riddles—formulaic questions that placed the listener into the heart of ambiguity. The impact of Celtic riddles is similar to that derived from the Zen koan: initial confusion, resulting in the stretching of mental limits, which in turn increases the elasticity of the imagination. The effect is the breakdown of the rational categories that limit our perception to ordinary, everyday reality. Ultimately, of course, one cannot force a solution to a koan. It must spring into awareness spontaneously. It is a moment of enlightenment, often occurring when we are distracted by some monotonous task. Koans and Celtic riddles defy consciously arrived-at solutions; they require a suspension of belief in the rational parameters of existence. To solve them we must have faith in ambiguity and enigma, and learn to be comfortable in the twilight state where all things are possible. We must adopt the shaman's worldview and see the hidden mysteries behind the natural world in which we live. We must break the spell of ordinary reality.

The classic formula for the riddle was to ask for something that was both "this" and "not this," something that "was" and "was not" at the same time. The answer required something that exemplified both "being" and "nonbeing." A riddle concerning the birth of the Irish hero Cuchulain asked for the following:

"A dog that was not a dog, born of a woman that was not a woman, in a house that wasn't there; he was begotten by a man that was not a man; his father was reared by his mother as a child, a child which died and did not die; his mother swallowed a worm that was not a worm—and his father was also his uncle."[50]

It is not our task here to unravel the details of this riddle, but to appreciate the fact that ambiguity is at the heart of mythology. It is also the essence of the shaman's vision, for the shaman's worldview is by its very nature both ambiguous and mythological since it incorporates and blends together elements from more than one reality, more than one context of space and time.

A favorite Celtic motif, and one found in many European faery tales, is the requirement for the hero to perform some impossible task before he can marry the woman of his dreams. Usually the task is assigned by the woman's father and is a variation of the riddle, which at first glance also seems impossible. In the faery tale, the purpose of the impossible task is to keep separated two opposing worlds, or worldviews, symbolized by the young man and his intended bride, just as we are accustomed to keeping ordinary and nonordinary realities separate in daily life. But mystical insight and enlightenment occur when the veil between the worlds is lifted, the worlds are bridged, the gap closes, and we cross over.

In the love story of Diarmaid and Grainne, Diarmaid tells Grainne that he will not accept her unless she comes to him under certain, nigh impossible conditions. Different texts present variations on Diarmaid's riddle, but the specifics generally include the following: "I will not take you either by day or by night, clothed or unclothed, on foot or on horseback, neither within nor without." Grainne seeks the help of a faery woman who gives her clothing made from mountain flowers. She appears at dusk riding a goat. When she is in the doorway, she announces herself, "I am not without, nor within; I am not on foot, nor on horseback; I am not clothed, nor unclothed; it is neither day nor night." She had answered the riddle and won.

In the Welsh tale of Llyn y Fan, the hero sees a faery woman on a lake who refuses his gift of baked bread. So he resorts to giving her dough. This, too, she refuses. Finally, he offers a loaf that is half-baked—bread that is both "baked and not baked." Then she accepts him, and his world of ordinary reality and her realm of enchantment are united.

The Celtic poet was a master of spiritual innuendo and mind-stretching allusions. In a celebrated duel between two Irish poets/seers, Nede and Ferchertne, we see this display of verbal sparring, proving that each man was a virtuoso of imagistic spellcasting. Each asks the other a series of questions that evoke mysterious replies.[51] For example, each asks the other where he comes from. Nede answers:

> From a confluence of wisdom,
> From perfection of goodness,
> From the brightness of the sunrise,
> From the nine hazels of poetic art.

In his answer to the same question, Ferchertne states that he comes from

> Along the streams of Leinster,
> From the elfmound of Nechtan's wife,
> Down the forearm of Nuada's wife,
> From the land of the sun,
> From the dwelling of the moon.

When asked his name, Nede answers:

> Very-small, Very-great, Very-bright, Very-hard.
> Angriness of fire,
> Fire of speech,
> Noise of knowledge,
> Well of wisdom,
> Sword of song.

To the question of "what path have you walked," Nede replies:

> On the plain of knowledge,
> On a king's beard,
> On a wood of age,
> On the back of a ploughing ox,
> On the light of a summer's moon,
> On rich mast and food,
> On the corn and milk of a goddess,
> On thin corn,
> On a narrow ford,
> On my own strong thighs.

In some respects, these boasts are similar to Amergin's and Taliesin's claims to have been in all things and to have experienced the oneness of the

universe and the shapeshifting nature of reality, yet we have in these lines
a sense of riddle. They are not simply shapeshifting statements. Because
they are answers to rather straightforward questions ("Where do you come
from?", "What is your name?"), they require the listener to reflect, ponder,
stretch the imagination, and yet ultimately surrender to the burst of insight
that will come in its own good time, if it comes at all. In some cases it will
not come, and we must resign ourselves to living with an unanswerable
question and a questionable answer.

An indication that the purpose of these poems may transcend what we
think of as normal analysis is the repetitive cadences of their structure.
Undoubtedly, listeners in an oral culture would find the rhythm mesmerizing, the images working their subtle magic on the imagination, rather than
on the rational faculty. Indeed, when listened to, there would be no time
to "make sense" of each line. The audience would be caught up in the flow
of imagery; the verses would create a pleasant intuitive state of consciousness, satisfying in its own way, without the need for rational understanding.
The mesmerizing effect might be analogous to that of a shamanic drumbeat
or chant.

A popular Welsh literary form, the *gnome*, is a brief, almost haikulike
verse that juxtaposes images in much the same manner as these longer lists.
The impact of these poems comes not from making a rational connection
between the apparently unrelated images, but letting the mystery of their
union work its subtle influence over the imagination. If they leave the listener feeling unsettled and intellectually unsatisfied, it is because their
meaning is not meant to be fully comprehended on the first encounter. Like
the koan with its inscrutability and the haiku with its disarming simplicity,
the full significance of the gnome may come only gradually, if at all. The
following gnomes come from the Christian era, hence their strong moraliz-
ing quality.[52]

Red is the cock's comb, and loud his voice. God praises man when
man praises God.

Quarrelsome are the geese in the farmyard, and fearsome their wings.
The generous man feels richer than the miser.

White are the wings of a dove, and plump its body.

The greedy man feeds his greed each time he eats.

Delightful are the tops of apple trees; their flowers turn into sweetest fruit. Those who are too contented grow lazy and sleepy.

Delightful are the tops of bracken; the leaves give protection to wild animals. Prayer for one who is not loved will have no effect.

◆

The shaman was traditionally the teller of tales, the maker of riddles, the shapeshifting figure who mediated between otherworldly realities and ordinary daily life where the tales and riddles were told. The shaman feels comfortable in that state of ambiguity and trickery, for the shaman has helping spirits, and after many journeys, the shaman knows the "territory" and the "rules" of the Otherworld. If the modern world is bereft of full-time shamans, the initiation into nonordinary reality may still occur (although on a considerably reduced scale) in the form of spellbinding tales by a master storyteller that are woven with magic, riddles, and enchantments. Throughout the centuries the Celts have preserved these stories, riddles, and songs in their love of language. And these primitive folk-forms of entertainment and enlightenment can still work their magic around a fire, for the shamanic archetype is still active even in contemporary listeners. There is still a rush of excitement when we hear about other worlds and the mortals, like us, who travel there.

5

THE SOUL OF NATURE

Shamans develop a personal, mystical relationship with the land and the forces of nature, whether they live in the desert, tropical rain forests, by the sea, or on the ice banks of the Arctic. The landscape figures prominently in the shaman's magic and in his or her visionary experiences because the land, its features, and the animal life it nurtures reflect important truths about the human soul. Nature is not just a backdrop but a living, intelligent being, worthy of respect. It has personality, spirit, and human qualities. It contains secret places that invite the shaman to enter and explore. Not everyone enters the woods with the eyes and sensibilities of a shaman, however.

The Roman historian Lucan described a sacred woodland near present-day Marseilles that Caesar violated and destroyed on his campaign into Gaul. "And there were many dark springs running there, and grim-faced figures of gods uncouthly hewn by the axe from the untrimmed tree-trunk, rotted to whiteness."[1] We can almost hear the Roman's disgust as his artistic and religious prejudices seep through this poetic description of a Celtic sanctuary. The gods were "grim-faced," the artist sculpted crudely with an axe into wood that had not been properly stripped and prepared, and the ungrateful worshippers had undoubtedly allowed the weather and the elements to rot the holy faces. What an outrage! As so often happens, strangers to a culture are blinded by their own values and assumptions, and fail to appreciate what the native population holds dear. It is easy to destroy what we either misunderstand or do not understand.

The springs rising deep in the thick groves of trees, the shady darkness, the images amateurly carved into the trunks of trees, the effects of wind and rain upon the sculpture, all reflect some of the most important themes of pagan Celtic spirituality. Nature occupied a special place in the Celtic imagination, and this chapter will trace its importance as both a sacred place and a mystical experience in traditional Celtic thought from earliest times to the present.

NATURE ENSOULED

A Chukchee shaman in Siberia told the anthropologist Waldemar Bogoras, "All that exists lives."[2] In Native America there is an age-old belief that everything in nature is alive and wants to communicate. The Ainu shamans of northern Japan believe that all things that are not human (that is, all the rest of nature) are gods. D. L. Philippi, who has studied the Ainu, explains this notion. The gods are "non-human beings with supernatural attributes who live in thoroughly anthropomorphic fashion in their own god-worlds, where they are invisible to human eyes, but who also share a common territory with humans and pay frequent visits to them in disguise. Animals are such gods in disguise."[3] Philippi could have been describing the Celtic belief in the faery folk who are also perceived as non-human, supernatural beings with godlike qualities, living anthropomorphically in a magical realm where both humans and faeries can meet.

The natural world is alive with power, information, counsel, and wisdom. The Divine Power behind creation can, and does, communicate to us through natural phenomena such as animals, weather patterns, plants, landscapes, and the spirits of these things. The faces carved in the rotting trunks of ancient trees were the Celts' attempts to portray and honor this intelligence behind and within creation. It was their sacred effort to draw out from nature the Spirit they perceived in human terms.

The consciousness of nature is not solely a primitive concept. In the mystical literature of all peoples, regardless of religion or century, we find vestiges of the belief that the natural landscape is spiritually alive and that an indwelling spirit animates each living or created thing. Understandably, we think of these spirits in human terms because the imagination works best with familiarity. Anthropomorphic visions of the spirit behind and within nature make it easier for the human mind to process unknowable mysteries. We see ourselves in nature, and nature in ourselves. As Stephen Larsen puts it in *The Mythic Imagination*, "Everywhere, and throughout history, images of psyche have become entangled with the physical environment."[4] Larsen quotes philosopher Robert Avens who explains that "the world of the primitive is fully alive because it is neither purely subjective nor purely objective, neither spiritual nor material, but *ensouled.*" Thus the world exhibits to the archaic imagination a transcendent blend of opposites central to the shaman's way of thinking.

The Four Ancient Books of Wales, a fourteenth-century Welsh manuscript, contains a poem that expresses well this notion of the ensouled universe, of nature entwined with the human psyche. The poem is addressed to the Creator

> Who infused through my head
> A soul to direct me.
> Who has made for me in perception,
> My seven faculties:
> Of fire and earth,
> And water and air,
> And mist and flowers,
> And southerly wind.[5]

The verse is remarkable on two counts. First, it clearly associates the soul, which resides in the head, and its powers of perception with the external elements of nature. Second, it adds to the traditional four elements three unexpected candidates: mist, flowers, and southerly wind. When we reflect on these three, we find that they combine the original four. Mist is a combination of air and water; the warm wind is air and fire; the flower is a product of these three plus earth. Here, as in other contexts, we find once again the Celtic love of things that are "neither this, nor that," things "betwixt and between," things that are blends of opposites. Mist, southerly breeze, and the fragile flower are also ephemeral, suggesting the transient state of the soul (consciousness) ever poised to evolve into something else.

Irish mystic A. E. captured the spirit of this passage in describing modern Celts. "During all these centuries the Celt has kept in his heart some affinity with the mighty beings ruling in the Unseen . . . His legends and faery tales have connected his soul with the inner lives of air and water and earth, and they in turn have kept his heart sweet with hidden influence."[6] A. E.'s vision contains strong shamanic resonance. We find the same sentiments expressed in shamans from other cultures. For example, Matsuwa, a contemporary Huichol shaman, laments the fact that many people are so caught up "in their own little lives" that they do not send "their love up to the sun, out to the ocean, and into the earth."[7] He advises that we devise ceremonies to send our love into the five directions, because doing so "brings life force into you . . . since human history began, people are wrapped up in their little worlds, and they forget the elements, forget the source of life." Being connected with the inner lives of the elements brings that life force into us; it keeps our hearts sweet with divine influence.

To view nature as imbued with soul, and each creature in the universe as alive and communicative, is a form of animism consistent with the earliest spiritual framework of the ancient Celts. But it has survived into Christian and even post-Christian times. After extensive fieldwork interviewing modern Celts in the six Celtic nations, Evans-Wentz concluded that modern Celts' belief in the spirits of nature are similar to the *Alcheringa* of the Australian Aboriginees. They are "a spirit race inhabiting an invisible or fairy world."[8] He notes that both cultures view these spirits as "haunt[ing] inanimate objects such as stones and trees" and "frequent[ing] totem centres, as in Ireland demons are believed to frequent certain places known to have been anciently dedicated to the religious rites of the pre-Christian Celts." He also points out that, like the Australians, both "ancient and modern Celts" see themselves as "incarnations or reincarnations of ancestors and of [these] fairy beings."

In this same discussion, Evans-Wentz also calls attention to an important implication in our kinship with nature and nature's gods. The "Celts think of fairies as real invisible entities who must be propitiated if men wish to secure their goodwill; and as beneficent and protecting beings when not offended, who may attach themselves to individuals as guardian spirits." From pagan times to modern times, the Celts have woven into their lives ceremonies and rituals to acknowledge and honor the spirits of nature. Celtic scholar Barry Cunliffe suggests that offerings to the woodland gods and the spirits of the fields and forests is "the essence of Celtic religion."[9] Cunliffe says that in the Celtic imagination "to be whole a man has to be in communion with the gods through the medium of sacrifice and offerings." This is also the essence of the shaman's spirituality: communion and communication with the spirits by offering one's self to the Otherworld, by being a mediator between the world of spirit and the physical world of daily life.

The Clearing in the Woods

All across Europe, from Britain to Asia Minor, there are place names derived from the Celtic word *nemeton*. For the Celts a nemeton was a sacred grove. The Latin word *nemus* means simply a clearing in the woods. A similar Greek term, *tenemos*, referred to land dedicated to a god. The old Irish word, *nemed*, meant a shrine, and *fidnemed* referred specifically to a forest shrine. The Roman historian Tacitus, noting the Celts' enduring and widespread love of sacred groves and clearings, concluded that "The grove is the center of their whole religion. It is regarded as the cradle of the race and the dwelling-place of the supreme god to whom all things are subject and obedient."[10]

The Celts could not escape the forests of ancient Europe, anymore than Polynesians could escape the sea or the Arctic peoples the snow and ice. The forest colored their thinking, their perceptions of the spirit world, their sense of home. Some Celtic tribes identified so closely with the forests they adopted trees as clan totems. They were known as "Sons of the Oak," "a Son of the Yew," or "Men of the Rowan."

The druids centered their rituals, even their identity, around dense oak forests. The Roman writer Pliny points out that the druids "perform no sacred rites without oak leaves, so that from this custom they may seem to have been called 'druids'."[11] There has been much speculation over the etymology of the word *druid*, but most scholars tend to agree with Pliny who related the word to the Greek *drus*, which meant "oak." The word *druid*, therefore, most generally means "men of the oak," or "wise in the oak," or "having knowledge of the oak."

In his study of druids, Ward Rutherford discovered that a related word in Manx, *druaight*, means "enchantment."[12] There are similar words in Irish and Scottish. Perhaps here is another candidate for the rich constellation of ideas associated with the druids. If Pliny is correct and druidic priests used oak leaves in their rituals, then their magic and enchantments would be, in some way, dependent upon these sacred leaves. The oak tree was, therefore, a primary source of druidic power.

The novice druids' training, according to the Roman Pomponius Mela, was conducted, at least in part, "in secret in a cave or *in abditis saltibus.*" The latter phrase, according to Stuart Piggot, could be translated as "remote woods or valley."[13] Since the forest clearing or secluded grove was the Celts' favorite sanctuary, this would make sense. The dark forest played a vital role in the training of druids, on two counts. First, it offered silence and solitude, the freedom from distractions needed to memorize the vast amount of poetry, law, and history typical of druidic training. Second, the dark thicket of trees provided the sensory deprivation needed to block out the human world of ordinary reality in order to concentrate on the inner world, giving the druid novices opportunity to hone the imaginal skills used in visionary experience. Since the training lasted twenty years, we can suppose the young druids spent a considerable part of their lives engaged in visionary work in the woods.

The same type of training continued for bards into the eighteenth century. In the Western Highlands, students were required to lie on their backs in a darkened room for a day or more at a time with a stone placed on their stomachs and their eyes covered. Under such ascetic conditions the young neophytes would compose their verse and develop their use of highly imagistic language. The stone may have been used to create a certain amount of discomfort so the student would not fall asleep, but it might just as likely have been a kind of mnemonic device to trigger and sustain the journey into nonordinary consciousness where the young bards found the imagery for their poetry. It is also quite possible the stone was a power object, a sacred stone such as a crystal, placed over the solar plexis.

Memorizing extensive amounts of technical information, cultivating visualization skills, and learning ritual procedures are not unrelated tasks. In an oral culture that did not have the aid of written materials, the imagination and its carefully perfected visualizing skills were needed to memorize large amounts of information. Druidic priests were famous for their wide-ranging knowledge on many diverse subjects. Celtic scholar Jean Markale has suggested that the word *druid* comes from *dru-wid-es* meaning "far-seeing ones," or "deep-seeing ones," or "very learned," a definition that reinforces the druids' reputation for having an immense scope of knowledge and information.[14] It also strongly suggests that their "seeing" went deeper than the merely physical. Their vision also penetrated metaphysical realms, invisible to ordinary men and women.

What appears to be unfolding here is a complex of terms and ideas long associated with shamanism in various forms around the world. The shaman derives knowledge and power from nature because the natural world is to a great extent the container of the Spirit. Paradoxically, in the physical world, we encounter the metaphysical. Only in modern times have we lost this vision of nature ensouled and enchanted with both divine and human attributes. To earlier tribal peoples it was more evident, and the men and women who cultivated a close relationship with nature also developed intense familiarity with the spirits of nature, precisely because they learned to view the spirits and the energy of nature in human terms.

There is a great wisdom in personalizing the physical world. Relationship requires a sense of respect and equality for the other, and to cultivate a relationship with the Divine demands that we treat with respect and equality the natural world that contains the Divine. This is one of the shaman's great insights; we can approach the Divine Mystery of the Universe through nature, and our relationship with the Divine evolves from our partnership with nature. Shamans also demonstrate that we cannot launch an undifferentiated relationship with "nature as a whole." We must begin on a smaller, more personal level—with one special animal spirit, or power animal—and progress from there to other animals, plants, rivers, hills, trees, and sacred places. Eventually our familiarity with the individual aspects of nature leads us to nature's gods and goddesses, and finally to the Divine Creator behind creation.

The forest, therefore, is not just the realm of the natural, but also the supernatural. In Celtic legends the notion of the enchanted forest preserves this archaic belief. Celtic scholar and modern druidic practitioner Kaledon Naddair reminds us that the old Celtic words for oak include *"dur," "daroch," "der,"* and *"derwen."*[15] These appear to be related to the Sanskrit and Gaelic term *duir* meaning "door." Naddair finds it exciting that the concepts of "door" and "oak" are related in the Celtic language. This connection, he claims, explains the term "secret oaken doors" that feature prominently in Celtic mythology and in the poems of Taliesin. The "oaken door" is an entry into the realm of Faerie. It is also a clear metaphor for the entries into the spirit world that one would find in the oak forest.

In the early 1990s a member of the Foundation for Shamanic Studies interviewed an Irish expatriate in America who had been taught shamanic practices by her grandmother. When asked about the importance of the oak tree, she replied, "That is the center. The oak is the doorway between the worlds. It's the tree of life, the oak. That is a part of our culture and the tree is something you climb up to go to another world."[16]

DOORWAYS OF STONE

Throughout Celtic lands stand imposing megalithic structures, the most famous being those at Stonehenge and Avebury. Many of these enormous stone clusters are circular in shape, thus suggesting a type of clearing made of stone similar to the clearing in the oak forest where the largest oaks would have ringed the central area. Over a thousand stone circles have been discovered in Britain and Ireland alone, not to mention the many others on the continent. At many of these sites are dolmens, composed of two or more massive, upright stones with a lintel stone placed across them, thus forming mysteriously vacant doorways. Such a portal seems to lead nowhere, but for the initiate into Celtic mysteries, it is an entry into the Otherworld.

For centuries it was believed that the druids built these structures for ceremonial purposes. Today we know that the megaliths are much older, predating the arrival of the Celts in Western Europe and the British Isles. They are pre-Celtic and were built before 1000 B.C. None seem to have been constructed after that date. Consequently, their construction cannot be attributed to the druidic priesthood. Nevertheless, given the Celts' metaphysical-spiritual sensibilities, the megaliths must have exerted the same haunting and otherworldly influence over their imaginations as they continue to exert over our own in the present century. The old druidic adage that "truth is written in the stones" may have come from the druids recognizing in these ancient stoneworks the same type of spiritual energy as they found in ancient oaks. Although the etymology of their name would not suggest it, druids also may have been "men of the stones." Certainly, tradition attests to their utilizing the stones for ceremonies and sacred events, just as modern druids and neo-pagans continue to do.

Legendary accounts claim that Merlin constructed Stonehenge with megaliths he magically imported from Ireland. Modern research claims (along with the earlier date of construction) that the stones came from Wales. Several interesting themes intersect in this legend. The Celts posited that one important approach to the Otherworld, especially the Land of Promise, was by a sea journey to a far western island. Ireland, like other islands to the west, represented the Land of Enchantment from the perspective of England and Wales. In this view the stones at Stonehenge are emissaries from the Otherworld, even as they create sacred space and sacred portals into that world. The circular enclosure sets off an area of nonordinary reality, a power spot in the local terrain filled with myth and magic.

Furthermore, as an astronomer, Merlin ordered an observatory to be built with seventy doors and seventy windows for viewing the heavens at night. The significance of the number seventy is not clear, except that the number may have something to do with the seven known planets in the

Middle Ages. Be that as it may, many interpreters and scholars believe that ancient architects (not Merlin) constructed Stonehenge to be a celestial observatory, aligned with the rising or setting of important stars, constellations, or planets. Its calendrical role is to mark key points on the Wheel of the Year. Thus Merlin's activities as astronomer, always associated with divination and spiritual knowledge, lend a shamanic quality to the legends that connect him and other druids with the stonehenges of Celtic lands.

It is difficult to imagine that the shamanic practices that survived into medieval times were not influenced by the presence of these magnificent stone structures. Like Merlin, and the pre-Celtic astronomers who built the henges and the mysterious doorways long before him, the shaman recognizes in the natural world entries to and manifestations of the nonordinary (or spirit) realms in which human life concurrently exists. Entering stone circles, passing through dolmens, journeying into the forests to find the clearings for sacred rituals re-enacts on the physical plane the shamanic journey into invisible realms.

THE WOODLAND GODS

Among the many Celtic words derived from the prolific root *dru* are Manx and Irish words for the "wild man of the oak woods."[17] The idea of a wild, hairy man or woman living deep in the forest is a popular motif in European literature, and even in European art dating back to antiquity. The theme also has deep religious roots in ancient shamanism. In one of his incarnations, the Wild Man is the Green Man of the Forest, his foliated head covered with vines, grass, and leaves sprouting from mouth, nose, and ears, or growing wildly as a tangled beard or mane of hair. As a fertility god, the Green Man expresses an ancient spiritual view of our relationship with nature, a oneness with the earth, a belief that within the wooded groves and fields live humanlike presences that are in fact divine. A corollary to the belief is that we, like the natural world we live in, follow nature's same cyclic patterns of birth, growth, maturity, decay, and death, followed by rebirth. It is an idea that shamans understood thoroughly as they hunted for power in the spirit world with animal guides and shapeshifted into animal forms to share their power, found medicinal remedies in herbs and plants, and summoned the large herds that sustained the life of their communities.

The sacramental function of nature and its oneness with human life were ideas the Christian church could not tolerate for very long. A twelfth-century manuscript shows a picture of a woman hacking down a tree with an ax, while two spirit heads spring from the top of the tree, horrified at her act. St. Amand, a Catholic bishop, is shown blessing her with approval. The woman is a pagan and blind, as obviously the two are meant to be related. According to the legend, her willingness to destroy a sacred tree, home to the two woodland spirits rising from the branches, restored her sight and demonstrated her conversion to Christianity. Missionary priests, like St. Amand, successfully launched what has been called the greatest psychic revolution in the history of the West, namely, the conversion of pagan Europe to Christianity, which (strengthened by the Scientific Revolution of the seventeenth century) would effectively remove any sense of spirit or divinity from nature.

With the new religion came a radically different way of viewing the organic world. What once had been holy now became demonized. The fertile, life-giving spirits of nature were now portrayed as evil. The sacred groves were cut down, the healing springs were polluted, and the Green Men were turned into devils. Where pagan devotions continued unabated in the face of Christian opposition, the Church co-opted the sacred sites, turning them into Christian sanctuaries dedicated to a saint of the Church. But the objective was the same everywhere: to destroy or transform the natural places where Europeans had for centuries met and honored their gods and goddesses.

The Church could neither destroy nor deny the beauty of nature, but it demythologized that beauty into a shallow materiality that reflected or symbolized the glory of God but was in no way Divinity Itself or even a container of the Divine. What formerly had been religion for the Celtic peoples became mere aesthetics. In the Celtic imagination, the forest was not just beautiful; it was divine. For the Christian it was merely woods, haunted by demons, wild animals, and wild people. As the shaman faded into obscurity and shamanic skills disappeared among the people, many converts to the new faith forgot that nature had once been a source of healing power and spiritual wisdom. Men and women, versed in shamanic practices, who formerly journeyed into the spiritual landscape of nature to make contact with the Divine, were now suspected of trafficking with evil spirits or demons.

In spite of Christian apologists, many people, both Celt and non-Celt, kept alive the ancient practices to the woodland deities and spirits of nature. Even today formerly pagan practices continue, sometimes surreptitiously and artfully disguised as "old folk customs." People "dress wells" in May with flowers and ribbons, toss coins or pins into wells and springs, leave pieces of cloth tied to branches of a tree over a spring as prayer offerings to the spirits of the waters, pledge their lovers' vows at certain aged oak trees, and make pilgrimages to special stones thought to have powers to ensure fertility, love, and long life.

The ancient Celts did not feel at one with the universe if they did not make offerings to the gods and goddesses of their local regions. A great quantity of pagan Celtic art and artifacts have been discovered in the bottom of wells, ritual shafts, and bogs. In some cases the disposed of items were expensive and well-crafted, and it appears that some very valuable works were created specifically to be thrown into the bogs as votive offerings. The sacrificed object might have been a symbol of something that was needed by the suppliant. From the wealth of carved, wooden objects depicting various parts of the human body, it appears that the Celts offered a symbolic representation of the body part that was afflicted and needed healing.

Images of the Green Man and the rotting wooden faces carved into the tree trunks that disgusted Lucan in Roman times are attempts to anthropomorphize the spirits of vegetation. As William Anderson puts it in his study of the Green Man, it is a natural human desire "to draw out the hidden intelligence in plant forms and to give them human forms and faces."[18] Perhaps the desire is part of the human psyche and an aspect of the shamanic archetype that nurtures in each person the hope that the intelligence behind the universe—perceived as spirits, faeries, or Green Men—is not totally hidden from human view, and that there are people trained in ecstatic techniques who know how to journey to invisible places to contact that woodland intelligence and tap into its fertile power and energy.

THE HORNED ONE

Among the classic images in shamanic spirituality is the horned figure known as the Animal Master or the Lord of the Animals. Traditionally, the shaman wearing horns and antlers becomes the Animal Master, the member of the tribe who summons the great herds at hunting time, and whose magic extends over the weather, even the plants and foliage that people depend on for food and medicine. The shaman's counterpart in the spirit world is the Lord of the Animals or Spirit of the Animals, often depicted as a deity. In some shamanic traditions, the shaman becomes the god while in trance.

Horns and antlers are common headgear for shamans living in the presence of large herds of deer, elk, or bison. Two paleolithic figures drawn on the cave wall at Trois Freres in the French Pyrenees wear horns and antlers. Both appear to be humans but with impressive animal parts. Whether they are anthropomorphic gods or animal-clad shamans we can only speculate. As we noted earlier, they may be representations of the shaman's altered state of consciousness in which he perceives himself as a horned beast.

A Celtic figure who shares the dual role of god and shaman is the Horned God, the antlered figure sitting cross-legged, holding a ram-headed serpent in one hand and a torque in the other, his eyes either closed, half-closed, or fixated in a glassy stare. This is how he appears on the Gundestrup cauldron, a Celtic artifact dating from the first century B.C. The actual name of the Horned God, Cernunnos, has been found in only one location, an altar stone in Gaul with an inscription translated as the "horned" or "peaked" one. But images of him appear throughout the Celtic world with remarkable consistency in description and attributes. The Celtic tribes may have known him under various names, or with some variation of

Cernunnos (Cern, Herne, Corn), but he is undeniably the same god-form wherever he appears.

The figure on the Gundestrup cauldron might also be a shaman dressed as a Horned Man. The entranced gaze in the figure's eyes (whether they be open or closed) strongly suggests that the Horned One is looking into nonordinary reality. There is a striking similarity between the figure's cross-legged position and that of the classic Buddhist pose used in meditation. There are other Celtic figures sculpted in this pose, even the full-lotus position with two feet resting on the thighs, each hand grasping one foot. The Gundestrup figure may also be a slight optical illusion, making it look like he is sitting, when in fact he may be balancing himself on one toe, a form of levitation, confirming his yogic or shamanic training.

An equally plausible explanation is that the shaman is merely sitting on the ground as the Celts were fond of doing, similar to Native Americans. Both peoples eschewed the use of chairs or stools for a long time after they had been introduced by their (supposedly) more civilized conquerors. Anne Ross calls this the "national sitting posture of the Celts," so it might have nothing to do with a shamanic trance or yogic meditation.[19]

Recently archeologist Timothy Taylor questioned Cernunnos's gender.[20] Taylor points out that on the cauldron, the males are bearded and breastless, and the females are beardless and breasted. He suggests that the beardless and breastless Cernunnos is of "ambiguous gender." If such is the case, Taylor also provides another fascinating link between the Celts and the Scythians. He notes that the Enares, a type of soothsayer/judge who interpreted omens and settled disputes among upper-class Scythians, were described in the fifth century by Herodotus and Hippocrates as biologically male but who dressed as women. Taylor then relates the Enares to other spiritual specialists of the Iron Age such as "the shamans of Scythia and the yogis of India, . . . the seers of Thrace, the druids of Gaul, and a few centuries later, the bards of Ireland." In Ireland the male bard, who sang praises for the chieftain, was referred to as female, in contrast to (and perhaps to highlight) the chief's masculinity. If the Cernunnos figure is, among other things, a Celtic shaman, this may explain his ambiguous gender, since homosexuality was often a characteristic of the shaman, indicative of the many ways he or she stood "between the worlds."

Whether god or shaman, Cernunnos is an Animal Master. He appears throughout Celtic lands, depicted in the company of a stag, wolf, boar, or other animal. He holds the mysterious horned serpent in one hand, a beast respected for its ability to travel quickly and silently between the worlds, slipping into the earth, gliding across a lake, or slithering up a tree to coil around a branch. In some representations, Cernunnos has vegetation growing from his head like the Green Man. On the Gundestrup cauldron a stylized tendril of leaves sprouts from one antler. Some images show his hair looking like grass. An aura of quiet dignity surrounds him, suggesting self-possession and inner personal power, in addition to whatever power he has over the animals and vegetation.

There is a brief period in the early Christian era when the Irish saints were intimately familiar with animals and exercised authority over them. To cite but one example among many, St. Gall, who came with St. Columbanus from Bangor to establish a monastery in Burgundy, had mastery over a wild bear. While St. Gall was praying, a bear wandered into his camp and began eating the crumbs from the evening meal. Gall commanded in the name of God that the bear grab a log and toss it on the fire. It obeyed, and St. Gall, "drawing forth a loaf [of bread] yet untouched from his scanty store, gave it to his servitor, saying, 'In the name of the Lord Jesus Christ, depart from this valley: thou art free to range the hills and mountains around at will so long as thou doest no harm to man or beast in this spot.'" One of Gall's companions witnessed this and declared that "the Lord is with thee, since even the beasts of the wilderness obey thee."[21]

It is difficult for the modern mind to truly appreciate the moment in Celtic Christianity when nature and sanctity were so closely intertwined. Religious historian Christopher Bamford suggests that not only is this heritage "shrouded in mystery, [it] is quintessentially mysterious," and that because in this era "the spiritual is so closely and clearly involved with the phenomenal . . . all of [our] usual means of understanding are wanting."[22] We have lost the ability to even *imagine* a culture that lives by the belief that human consciousness can participate in the natural world and that the natural world responds to the will of human consciousness. This is the con-sciousness of the shaman, and I might add, the *ordinary consciousness of the shaman*, for even in a nontrance state of mind, the shaman saw and under-stood a different reality than we do today.

It is this participatory consciousness that is represented in images of figures that are part animal, part human, the most spectacular and awe-inspiring being that of the Horned Man. There are also representations of Horned Women, but these are not as prevalent. The concept of the Horned One flows through Celtic folklore so strongly that medieval church fathers took great pains to portray this archaic figure as the Christian Satan. During the witch-hunts in the late Middle Ages and Renaissance, the Horned God continued to excite the European imagination, but in a demonic sense. In spite of the tremendous pressures to eliminate all conceptions of a horned deity, pressures leading to unspeakable torture and execution by church and state authorities, many brave people continued to practice the Old Religion, holding fast to the belief in the Horned One as the Lord of the Wild Things, the Animal Master, a close kin to the Green Man, the Lord of the Forests.

The Church's animosity toward horns on humans began much earlier. In the fourth century St. Augustine lambasted what he called "that most filthy habit of dressing up as a horse or stag."[23] Church admonitions against such costumes continued into modern times. In our own century people in Corn-wall still sing at Beltane, the First of May, "Take no scorn to wear the horns, they were a sign ere you were born/Your father's father wore them, and your father wore them too." The Church still does not approve.

Some of the earliest legends about Merlin depict him as a type of wild man of the forest, sometimes wearing antlers. In a Welsh poem Merlin speaks to a pig, expounding his mystical insights about life to this animal who was considered sacred to the Celts and whose meat was thought to be a choice delicacy. Merlin respects the pig and honors its knowledge and wis-dom. He says, "You lived in these woods before I did and age has whitened your hairs first."[24] During one of his periods of "madness" in the forest, Merlin collects a herd of stags, mounts one of them, and drives them, along with deer and she-goats, to his sister's wedding where he disrupts the intended marriage by ripping antlers off a stag and hurling them at the despised brother-in-law-to-be. The antlers smash the bridegroom's head and kill him. Merlin then tries to escape back to the forest but is captured. The onlookers may have been aghast at Merlin's extreme solution to the problem of an unwanted brother-in-law, but they were considerably impressed with his power over the wild animals.

The shaman's association with animals was both magical and religious in nature; it was a source of personal power and a basis for worship. Judging from the testimony of tribal peoples who practice their traditional spirituality today, this magico-religious kinship with animals is typical of all members of the tribe, not just shamans. Eliade points out that "a mystical solidarity between man and animal" was common among paleolithic hunting peoples, shamans and nonshamans.[25] Among Native American cultures in our own time, it is assumed that the majority of men and women are capable of "crying for a vision" and thus establishing their own personal relationship with individual animal powers and helping spirits. What distinguishes the shaman from other tribal members is the degree to which the shaman perfects this relationship; it becomes the basis for a life of community service.

In pagan Celtic societies, druids and bards nurtured an intensely magical, mystical life with nature, similarly grounding their public work in the community. With the arrival of Christianity, the early Irish monks continued this tradition, but explained it within the Christian worldview. The responsiveness of animals and natural elements to human desires was the working of God rather than an expression of the monk's personal power, as it would be understood in shamanic cultures. The tradition of animals as spirit guides survived also in European folk and faery lore, where the hero is often led into the enchanted forest or the Otherworld by following a mystical animal who then becomes the hero's guide for returning to ordinary life.

The Horned God and the Green Man continue to vanish and reappear throughout Western history. Like vegetation itself, these images are born, thrive, decline, and die out, only to be reborn in slightly altered guises. If indeed the Horned God and Green Man are part of the human psyche, an "archetype of our oneness with the Earth" as William Anderson puts it, they are undoubtedly linked to the essential archetype of shamanism.[26] Depending on our beliefs in the goodness or corruptness of nature, we will see these godlike figures as divine or demonic. In Shakespeare's *Merry Wives of Windsor*, for example, Mistress Page says:

> There is an old tale goes that Herne the Hunter,
> Sometime a keeper here in Windsor forest,
> Doth all the winter-time, at still midnight,
> Walk round about an oak, with great ragg'd horns'
> And there he blasts the tree, and takes the cattle
> And makes milch-kine yield blood, and shakes a chain
> In a most hideous and dreadful manner.
> (Act 4, scene 3)

From a shamanic point of view, it is hard to dredge up the horror that Mistress Page hopes to instill in her listeners. Old Herne is not "hideous and dreadful" at all. Herne's midnight raid on the trees and cattle is open to a more favorable interpretation; it reflects the natural cycle of life and death. Here we find another example of the paradox known to shamans. Behind the mysteries of nature sits an intelligence who is sometimes fierce, sometimes gentle, but to those who know how to speak the secret language of the animals, is always attentive and eager to communicate. Like the Eskimo spirit Sila, Herne may say to us, "Be not afraid of the universe."

THE HOLLOW HILLS

On the River Boyne in Ireland is a prehistoric tumulus, or mound, 338 feet in diameter and 30 feet high, covering one acre. Its entrance opens toward the southeast. The stones at the entrance to the mound and on the structures within are carved with a mysterious triple-spiral design. After passing through the entrance, you proceed down a sixty-two-foot-long corridor that varies from about five feet to eight feet in height and is about three feet wide. At the end you are standing in a chamber with a corbelled ceiling about twenty feet high. At the winter solstice, the shortest day of the year, light from the rising sun would beam down the entry corridor and shine in your eyes.

On each of the three sides of the central room is a smaller recess containing a stone with a shallow oval basin. What they were used for is a mystery. The shallow, bowl-like stones might have been sarcophagi or coffins. The entire mound at New Grange, like similar ones found in Western Europe, might have been used for burial purposes, initiation ceremonies into pagan religious mysteries, or something else altogether.

Even though the magnificent Bronze-age structure at New Grange was built in the third millennium B.C., long before the Celts arrived in Ireland, it played a vital role in Celtic spirituality. In Irish literature the tumulus is frequently associated with the Dananns as one of their primary faery palaces. The area around it is the famous burial site of the kings of Tara. King Cormac, who was supposed to have received the new faith even before Patrick came to Ireland, refused to be buried there because of its pagan associations. Clearly, the area around New Grange with its forty prehistoric monuments has had a long history of spiritual activities and associations, and even today the neolithic tumulus is an awe-inspiring monument to modern pilgrims and sightseers.

We can only imagine how the chambers were used in Celtic and pre-Celtic religious rites. But literary and historical evidence regarding the mounds on the Boyne and the hundreds in similar places, holy to both pagans and Christians, allows us to reconstruct a possible scenario for how these underground chambers were used. What we discover is that they were places where humans could meet the faery folk and taste the riches of the immortal worlds that lie beneath the landscape of ordinary consciousness.

In a fifteenth-century manuscript copied from older documents is a tale concerning the three sons of one of Ireland's kings who hoped to acquire lands and riches for themselves by fasting at the Dananns' sidhe on the Boyne. The three noble youths entered the faery palace in the sidhe to fast, while the gods met in council to evaluate their requests. Eventually the divine decision was to let them marry three daughters of Midhir, a Danann god. The young men then stayed in the sidhe for three more days and nights. As they left they were given three apple trees, one in full bloom, one shedding its blossoms, and the third ripe with apples.

Here several shamanic themes are veiled in typical Celtic imagery. First, mortal men seek power, although in this case, material power, from faery folk or spirits. Since the kings of Ireland believed themselves to be descended from the older gods, the Dananns, this story is an account of men seeking power from ancestral spirits. To achieve their desires, they must endure physical suffering and temporary dissociation from ordinary reality. In the Celtic scheme of things, a king is married to the goddess of the land and enjoys sovereignty only through her, so the three princes must legitimate their authority by marrying goddesses. And finally they leave with apple trees, the Celtic symbol of youth and power, a fruit sacred to the goddess and associated with the Otherworld.

The three trees in various stages of growth reflect the Celtic love of threes, but the trees symbolize much more. They demonstrate the transformative stages of life; the sweet-scented blossoms must die for the tree to bear fruit, which itself, in time, ripens and dies. Shamanic initiation accounts consistently deal with this same mystery of regeneration, the ever-turning Wheel of Life and Death, although the details differ depending on culture. Shamans themselves undergo a psychic death and rebirth to experience this transformation in themselves.

THE RITES OF INITIATION

Over 200 caves have been discovered in Western Europe, similar to Lascaux in the Pyrenees, elaborately designed with paleolithic drawings of animals, shamans, handprints, and other esoteric symbols. These and others not yet found may have functioned as places of initiation into the most important mysteries concerning life and death. Archeologist John E. Pfeiffer presents intriguing evidence concerning this in his provocative work *The Creative Explosion: An Inquiry into the Origins of Art and Religion*. Pfeiffer suggests that the cathedral-like chambers at the end of dark, narrow, suffocating passageways were utilized for extravagant rites and ceremonies of initiation and instruction.[27] He argues that "images, painted and engraved on cave walls, and sacred objects served a most important function in prehistoric ceremonies," allowing the initiates to witness strange, hallucinatory effects on the walls, ceilings, and all around them. Elaborate lighting and sound effects, produced by elders concealed in the shadows and side chambers, caused the animal figures on the walls to shimmer and appear to move in the flickering lights. Then the initiates and the presiding shamans would dance and crawl to imitate the animals.

The experience must have produced a profound and disturbing impression on the psyches of the young initiates. In a ritual sense, they were plunged into a dark, frightening chaos, the primal void where their assumptions about ordinary reality were shattered. Forced to confront their own deaths and the animal spirits that inhabit the Otherworld, the experience would have radically transformed their understanding of human existence. Something in them would die, and something new would be born. They would never be the same again.

In the early Christian era Irish pilgrims spent the night lying in stone coffins or sarcophagi in sacred underground sites to simulate death and rebirth experiences. Some scholars believe that this may have been one of the uses for the stone basins at New Grange and other Celtic sites. The ancient pagans, like the saints and pilgrims who came after them, laid down on stone beds or troughs to sleep, perhaps to dream, or simply keep vigil, awaiting the otherworldly visions that would visit them in the night.

St. Patrick's Purgatory in County Donegal in Ireland is just such a place. It lies on an island in Logh Derg, or Red Lake. From the Middle Ages to the present it has been a popular destination for Christian pilgrims. Even before Patrick's time it was considered "a strange and mysterious place, apparently an Otherworld preserve."[28] Two legends tell us about its origins. One maintains that its name, Red Lake, refers to the blood of a water monster slain by St. Patrick. Another legend claims that the island was the druids' last stronghold, implying that Patrick drove the "snakes" into the water and they sought refuge on the island.

On the island is a cave. It may have had an ancient reputation as a place of visions and otherworldly initiations since it continued to be used for visionary retreats into Christian times. The following instructions, attributed to Patrick, describe how someone applied for acceptance at the site. The procedure may have been based on older pagan practices. First, a pilgrim must receive permission from the bishop after stating that he came of his own free will and was not being coerced into the pilgrimage. The bishop tried to dissuade the would-be pilgrim by describing the perils to body and soul that awaited him. If the pilgrim persisted, he received a letter from the bishop addressed to the prior of the island, who also attempted to talk the pilgrim out of the ordeal. If the pilgrim still wished to continue, he was then required to fast and pray for fifteen days, after which he attended mass, received communion, and was sprinkled with holy water. At this point the authorities tried a third time to discourage him.

A candidate who made it this far was then blessed by the priests, led into the cave, and the doorway was sealed. The next morning the door was reopened. If the pilgrim was still there, the ordeal was considered successful, and the cleansed pilgrim was led away for another fifteen days of observation, prayer, and ceremony. If, however, the pilgrim was not found, it was assumed that he had been taken from this world and was not in the Purgatory. The door was then closed, and the candidate was never spoken of again.

In the Middle Ages a considerable body of literature on St. Patrick's Purgatory was produced in both vernacular and Latin languages. The story of Sir Owain is typical of the stories about penitents who visited the sacred place and sheds some light on what a person actually experienced in this otherworldly retreat.

Sir Owain, a medieval knight, applied and was accepted. After being locked in the cave, he began to explore the depths with his lamp that eventually went out, leaving him in total darkness. In time his eyes adjusted to the eerie twilight, and he continued his journey. He came to a hall where he found fifteen men with shaved heads clad in white robes. These clerics instructed Owain on the dangers he was about to face at the hands of evil spirits and the methods to withstand them. Then they departed, leaving Owain alone. And just as they had predicted, demons appeared and tortured the knight until he escaped by crossing a narrow bridge over a deep chasm. On the other side was a celestial city with a sweet scent that soothed his wounds, both physical and spiritual.

A procession of heavenly beings came out of the city to greet Owain and lead him to the Garden of Eden where he was given food to eat. He had no desire to leave and return to his earthly existence, but he was told that he had to suffer a mortal death and leave his physical body behind before he could begin his celestial life in earnest. So Owain began his journey back to the cavern's entrance by a shorter and less aggravating route. He met up with the fifteen clerics again who told him what his future held, and when he reached the door, he sat down until the authorities opened it the next morning. Amidst great joy and excitement, he was taken to the fifteen-day debriefing session with the priests.

The story of Owain and the tale of the three Irish princes could be duplicated again and again. Whether "fasting on the Dananns" or undergoing the preparatory fasts for Patrick's Purgatory, the physical and psychological results are similar. Sensory deprivation in a dark, underground chamber, bodily discomfort, a certain amount of terror either self-induced or carefully choreographed by clerics or elder shamans will readily produce visionary experiences. In shamanic cultures the experience prepares the candidate for becoming a new shaman. In mythological tales the seekers enter the caverns to find wives, riches, lands, and apple trees. In Christian cultures the initiate is cleansed of sins and given the grace to lead a saintly life. The details vary, but the core experience is the same. In the ancient tumuli scattered across the British Isles and Western Europe, in Christian retreat houses, or in the weirdly lit galleries of Paleolithic caves, people have hungered for visionary experiences that will transform their physical, mental, and spiritual condition.

PEOPLE OF THE WELLS

The Romans auctioned off wells and springs in Gaul to the highest bidder. In addition to being places of healing, transformation, and contact with the spirits, the sacred waters were also vast reservoirs of gold, silver, and exquisite Celtic art and craft objects. The owner of a popular well not only received the booty he could dredge up from the bottom, but with the proper resources, he could also levy taxes for visiting, bathing, or taking the water. Water rights, then as now, could be very lucrative.

The Irish had such a deep devotion to sacred waters that they were known as "People of the Wells."[29] Intense reverence for the natural sources of water, however, was not confined to the Irish. All across the former Celtic lands, we find special springs, wells, and river sources where the Celts worshipped their deities. There is something very shamanic in the Celts' respect for the spring or well as a portal into the Otherworld. The spring or river connects the shaman's three realms: the Upper Worlds of clouds, storms, and rain; the Lower Worlds of underground rivers and springs, and the vast realms beneath the sea; and the Middle World of fresh flowing water for cleansing and drinking.

At Uisnech, the mythological center of Ireland, the twelve major rivers of Ireland flowed from the Well of Life. Actually, Uisnech, in the center of County Meath and not far from the mystical Tara, is not the geographic center of Ireland, nor do the major rivers flow from this point. But historically and mythologically the area is important and corresponds to the notion of the Center of the World in shamanic cultures. The twelve major rivers flowing from Uisnech were thought to have been formed from a magical hailstorm during pagan times, or in a Christian version, created by St. Ciaran's miracle to end a drought.

From the shaman's point of view, water contains universal knowledge because its journey takes it to every corner of the physical universe; rain from the sky soaks deep into underground wells and springs, eventually feeding rivers and lakes, finally leaving the earth as mist and fog and rising to the sky, completing the circle. The fountain expresses this wholeness and completeness for its water is continually recycled. The circular dynamic of fountains (and all springs or rivers) symbolizes the reconciliation of opposites; since water flows through all arcs of the circle, it unites all polarities.

This fact was not lost on the Celts. Taliesin catalogues the major healing waters of the world, noting which polarities they resolved. For example, in Boeotia there was a fountain of forgetfulness and one of memory; in Sicily there was a fountain of fertility and one of sterility; the Garamantes fountain was cold during the day and hot at night; Lake Trogdytus has water that three times during the day is bitter and three times sweet; in some parts of the world there is water where everything sinks, and in other areas there is water where everything floats; in Thessaly sheep that drink from one river turn white, and those that drink from another turn black.

This same text from Talisein also contains a list of various streams and rivers that provide cures for specific illnesses, a folk-belief that continues today at various wells and natural springs across Europe.[30]

Central to the Celtic worship of wells was the belief in the Maiden of the Well, a term meaning, in older times, the goddess of the well or her priestess. Over the centuries these supernatural guardians of the wells were transformed from goddesses into spirits, faeries, and saints, with considerable overlap at various points. Pilgrims visited the wells for personal healing, but the wells played a larger role in the culture as a whole, for they (or the maidens) were responsible for the very health and prosperity of the land itself. In some versions of the Grail story, for example, the Well Maidens are abducted and raped, the waters run dry, and the realm becomes a Wasteland. Entwined in these beliefs and devotions are profound spiritual and psychological mysteries concerning the role of the feminine in matters of personal and ecological health, the love and respect for the earth as mother, and the need to return often to our "source" for renewal.

The Woman Beneath the Waters

At this point our search for the Celtic shaman leads us to two important archetypes in the Western psyche: the princess under the sea and the submerged city, two powerful images that haunt many popular folktales and local customs. The core of the story is rather simple. A maiden or princess guards an important well or fountain. Because of a flaw or failing, or thoughtlessness on her part, the waters flood the town and it sinks beneath the sea. The princess is then imprisoned in the town (or an underwater castle) as a kind of punishment for her folly.

What can we make of this tale of the submerged princess? Imbedded in the various legends is a strong male suspicion of the feminine as inherently rebellious of patriarchal authority. Some legends are not even subtle about this; the princess's "crime" is that she defies or interferes with the king's wishes or blatantly steals her father's key. In many of these stories we find a generalized male fear of drowning or being submerged in the feminine, never to emerge. These fears find resonance in the worldwide tales and superstitions warning sailors, and by extension all men, to be on guard against underwater maidens, mermaids, sirens, and nymphs intent on seducing men into their watery lairs. In a patriarchal culture this fear is institutionalized in many ways, all geared toward controlling, devaluing, and suppressing women.

Male paranoia regarding the power of the feminine, combined with the Christian hatred for anything pagan, especially beliefs and devotions centered around the goddess, help to explain why shamanism died out in Western Europe. In a version of the sunken-city legend from Brittany, the princess is named Dahud-Ahes, derived from the ancient term *dago-soitis*, meaning "good witch."[31] In his study of Celtic women, Jean Markale calls our attention to the fact that the good witch was considered to have, in a debased form, powers originally belonging to the gods. In Christian times, of course, supernatural powers were highly suspect, even among saints, monks, and other ecclesiastics who often performed "miracles" that resembled the feats of older deities and, of course, shamans. Over time, the male clergy appropriated the right to work this kind of magic, and intimidated women who continued to practice it, accusing them of being in league with the devil, that is, "evil witches." At some point, the general Christian attitude crystalized around the notion that *all* magic was the work of Satan and that *all* witches were bad. Then even priests were forbidden to practice it.

To the Christian apologist, and to the modern scientific rationalist, shamanism amd witchcraft are reversions to a pagan past that we have mercifully transcended. If we wonder why it has been so difficult to identify shamans in Western Europe (both past and present), we might seriously consider the blind spot created by the Christian-European superiority complex that holds that modern people of Western European civilization are superior in every way to their pagan ancestors, and especially superior to peoples in other parts of the world who do not share modern Western beliefs and European skintones. Assumptions of cultural and racial superiority blind us from recognizing shamanism in our own European heritage. Implied in this prejudice is the notion that even when Europeans *were* pagan, they were not *that* uncivilized. It was easy, therefore, for Western anthropologists to discover, study, and explain shamans in Siberia, Africa,

Polynesia, and North America without ever entertaining seriously the notion that their own forebearers once lived in strongly shamanic cultures and that shamanism is *their* heritage as well as the heritage of native peoples in other parts of the world.

BEAUTY AND THE KISS

Five young hunters, all sons of Eochaid, King of Ireland, were desperately looking for water. They encountered a hideous old woman described in one text as "black as coal from top to toe. Her bristly grey hair stood up like a wild horse's tail. Her teeth were green and reached to her ears . . . She had dark and bleary eyes, a hooked nose with cavernous nostrils. Her body was stringy, sickly and covered with boils. Her legs were twisted in all directions, her ankles thick, her shoulders wide, her knees fat, her nails green."[32] The old woman promised to give the boys a drink of water from her well in exchange for a kiss. Four of the five brothers were sickened by the thought and refused. Only Niall, the youngest and dumbest, kissed the old crone, whereupon she turned into the most beautiful girl they had ever seen. She revealed to them her true name, Flaithius, which means "royalty." And so Niall married her and became King of Ireland.

At some point in the shaman's initiation, the candidate must meet the dark side of his or her consciousness. The neophyte must take the plunge into Chaos and Old Night, the undifferentiated state of the womb where distinctions, like beautiful and ugly, have not yet emerged. In most tales about several brothers on a quest, it is always the youngest and dumbest who finds the courage to perform the impossible task, because the youngest lives from his heart, not his head. Like the shaman, or the Fool in the Tarot, he must leave society and its ways behind. The experience is terrifying, and the accounts of shamans recorded in modern times attest to the fear and reluctance many of them felt at similar encounters with beasts and demons. Some refuse and do not become shamans.

In the stories about the Irish hero Finn and his warriors is the tale of Diarmaid, the only one in his band of men who will give lodging to a disgusting old woman seeking shelter for the night. He invites her to the fire, and even allows her to share his bed. How fortunate! The crone turns into a beautiful young woman who magically creates a castle for Diarmaid and agrees to live with him, on the condition that he not hold it over her that he had pitied her in her former state. He breaks his promise, and she along with the castle disappear. Borrowing a boat that takes him under the sea, he learns that the girl is the daughter of a king. But she has grown very ill and cannot recover. He discovers a magic cup that restores her health, but she no longer interests him, so he goes back to Ireland.

Perhaps Diarmaid is the reluctant shaman, the initiate who leaves the mysteries revealed to him to return to ordinary reality where life is more predictable. We have strong hints here of the Grail story, for the magical goblet would restore the princess's health, and since the royal feminine is identical in the Celtic imagination with the land, we can also surmise that, if he were a Grail seeker, Diarmaid could have healed the land as well as the princess beneath the sea. He would have played the shaman's role as invoker and appeaser of the spirits of nature on whom human society is dependent for prosperity. But unfortunately, he does not.

Transformative tales of beauties and beasts, frogs and princes, hags and maidens all reflect the ancient shamanic concern with transformation. On the shamanic journey these kinds of changes take place as a matter of course. But changes transpiring in the spiritual realm often have a corresponding effect on the physical plane, since the shaman's work bridges the spiritual and material realms of life. Today people using shamanic journey techniques will "kiss the frog" or "slay the dragon" in nonordinary reality, knowing that the frog or the dragon is the spiritual dimension of some practical problem in their lives. By taming the beast in one reality, they begin the process of healing the unlovable, fearful, damaged parts of their lives.

Demonizing the Forests

The Church's Council of Rouen in the seventh century forbade Christians from leaving offerings at sacred wells, on the grounds that they were actually being offered to the devil. Charlemagne and other early medieval monarchs restated the prohibition over the next few centuries. But by the seventeenth century the popular practice had not abated, and the common folk's devotion to certain wells continued to aggravate church authorities. In 1628 in Scotland the Church outlawed visits to Christ's Well on May mornings. The fine was twenty pounds, and the transgressor had to appear in church wearing sackcloth for three successive Sundays. A similar law carried the penalty of one week in prison on bread and water. Curiously, these later laws concerned wells and springs that had been Christianized for centuries, but obviously the behavior was still perceived as pagan and therefore satanic.

Actually, Church authorities had reason to fret. Often the outings to sacred springs took the pilgrims into wilderness areas and deep forests where they found the freedom to practice their pagan religious devotions and escape the starchy respectability of village life. In the woods they could be as wild and "unrespectable" as they wished. Thirsty hikers carried whiskey; old feuds and new insults turned bloody. People could sing and dance to old folk tunes with pagan overtones and make love "in the greenwood" as their pagan ancestors once did. But in addition to scandalous social behavior, the treks to the sacred well also revealed that the baptism of so-called Christian pilgrims (even after generations within the Church) had not erased all vestiges of paganism. Sacred stones were still worshipped, milk was poured on the hills, and occasionally a bull was sacrificed. Many of these practices continued in remote areas, as described in the late nineteenth century by T. C. Croker in *Fairy Legends of Ireland:* "Near these wells little altars or shrines are frequently constructed, often in the rudest manner, and kneeling before them, the Irish peasant is seen offering up his prayers."[33]

In addition to prayers at the "rude" woodland altars, Celtic worshippers left flowers, festive branches, and pieces of cloth tied to trees near the water, and they tossed pins and coins into the water itself. Metal offerings to the goddess, spirit, or faeries have a long history. Originally metal goods were extremely valuable, so the offering represented a real sacrifice. There was also a magical, alchemical significance to metal, as we have already seen, since the smith had special powers and knowledge, and enjoyed a kinship with the gods and the earth spirits. In later times it was a common folk belief that the faeries, the "little people" living in the Hollow Hills, had need of metal to melt down and reshape into their own tools and weapons.

Christian missionaries, sometimes as a political statement or just out of spite, cut down sacred groves or the single oak dedicated to the god or goddess. Springs were filled up with stones, or rededicated to Christian saints after being "exorcised of demons." And yet, the reverence for trees as somehow representing more than just lumber, continued, which is to say the Celtic spirit could not be felled as easily as the oak itself. Even St. Columba, who was not hesitant to burn down an entire town and its fortifications (to descredit former authorities, both human and spiritual), called upon his own spiritual forces to prevent a conflagration from burning down a nearby grove of trees. He even ordered the chapel at Derry to be built on a north-south axis, instead of the customary east-west, in order to avoid cutting down sacred trees. He also proclaimed that trees that fell on their own or were blown down by a wind should be left alone for nine days, a sign of reverence for the life and spirit that had inhabited them. After nine days the trees were chopped up and the wood distributed to the poor.

The forest, like nature herself, was changable. Sometimes it was a safe retreat from society, a place for visions and communion with the gods and goddesses; at other times it was a frightening place, dangerous and life-threatening. But however ambivalent, the Celt always found the forest inherently spiritual and, for that reason, exciting. For as the shaman knows only too well, initiation into the mysteries of the spirit can be both comforting and frightful. Like the Green Man of the Forest, the Lord of the Animals, or the Witch of the Woods, nature takes life as well as gives it, for nature is the source of life and death. Like the goddess of the wells, nature is the lovely maiden ready to bestow kingdoms and palaces, but she is also the miserable hag with foul breath.

In spite of the Church's unrelenting efforts to stamp out paganism, the older Celtic spirit survived, sometimes underground, sometimes in thinly veiled Christian garb, sometimes nakedly pagan. The ancient spirituality and its shamanic worldview were too beautiful and alluring. To paraphrase a contemporary slogan, you could take the Celt out of the forest, but you couldn't take the forest out of the Celt.

6

FOREST FOLK

Modern shamanic practitioners sometimes debate the wisdom, even the possibility, of shamanizing in an urban environment. Serge Kalili King, teacher of Hawaiian shamanism and author of *Urban Shaman*, argues that shamanism's "application to urban environments is both natural and needed." King, emphasizing shamanism as "a distinct form of healing," emphasizes correctly that "a shaman is a healer, regardless of culture or environment."[1] Other teachers, especially those trained in Native American traditions, may wish to emphasize the source of the shaman's ability to heal: the shamanic journey and the intimate association with helping spirits who are most frequently the spirits of nature and animal spirits in particular. Such relationships may require, for some practitioners at least, periodic forays for extended periods of time into the physical wilderness to break the urban grip on their souls. Often they will complain that it is enervating to practice shamanism in a city. The debate over this is not simply an esoteric squabble between the city mouse and country mouse because the underlying assumptions and their related values render the argument worthy of serious consideration. If shamanism is a technique of ecstasy to create a visionary state of consciousness, does it matter into what *type* of visionary environment the shaman perceives himself or herself journeying? And does the visionary environment in any way depend upon the physical environment, or natural landscape, in which the shaman practices?

The nonordinary realm into which most modern shamanic practitioners journey is visually a natural setting such as forests, deserts, valleys, mountains, meadows, and occasionally gardens that indicate some human activity. In most cases, the *norscape* (nonordinary-reality-landscape) is a wilderness or quasi-wilderness, lacking the typical clutter of contemporary culture. Interestingly, when human communities do appear, they often take the form of tribal or archaic village settings, frequently with a Native American flavor. A close runner-up to the Native American norscape is a Celticized medieval setting with castles, moors, Arthurian forests, and the enchanted greenwood of medieval romance. What can we make of this? Is there some inherent natural and archaic quality to the Otherworld that reappears in shamanic journeys whether undertaken by tribal shamans of yesteryear or contemporary shamanic practitioners? Or are modern practitioners "programmed" to find the Otherworlds of traditional shamans whose descriptions of nonordinary reality are often part of the contemporary shaman's reading, training, and initiation?

As modern shamanic practitioners we can, of course, select or borrow cultural elements from the traditions that appeal to our individual sensibilities, in other words, those that "work" for us. We may consciously or semiconsciously construct and journey into a norscape that reflects our favorite natural landscape or an ethnic enclave to which we feel spiritually drawn, such as Native American, Hawaiian, Aboriginal, or Celtic.

Shamanism is about transcending the ordinary human condition, which we inevitably perceive in terms of contemporary civilization; and shamanic journeys provide opportunities to explore beyond our customary way of life and discover aspects of ourselves that are not evident in modern society or that are not culturebound. As urban shamans, we need the forest or desert to connect with a universe larger than what we know, and to discover what kind of beings we are (or become) when we leave our familiar civilized surroundings, for we are also fugitives from human civilization. This seems to be a perennial human need for the shaman, as it is for most spiritual seekers. Even in tribal societies living "close to nature," both neo-phyte and elder shamans feel the need to leave the human community and spend great lengths of time even closer to nature, closer to the Source, wrapped in the solitude of Self and the company of Spirit.

The shaman, especially the contemporary shamanic practitioner, is a spiritual renegade or outlaw who withdraws into the forest or desert or ice fields to be free of the constraints of ordinary daily life. In the Celtic tradition we find three types of spiritual outlaws who individually and collectively shed light on Celtic shamanism: the Fenian brotherhood of ancient Ireland, the outlaws of Sherwood Forest, and the witches who preserved the older shamanic practices into the modern period. In this chapter we will look at these "forest folk" as embodiments of the Celtic spirit and as models of the shaman's maverick status on the margins of orthodox belief.

The Fenians

The Fenian Cycle of Irish tales is much different from other mythological stories of ancient Ireland. The setting is unrelentingly wild and wooded, as opposed to the Ulster Cycle of tales in which the human community dominates. The stories are really about Faeryland, rather than the original Irish people. In fact, wild nature, the greenwood, mountain retreats and hideouts, friendly and intelligent animals, and mythical beasts characterize the stories. Often the magical adventure ensues as the heroes chase a stag or deer into an enchanted forest, where they meet the faery folk, the people of the sidhe, or the older Irish deities. According to Poinsias Mac Cana, the Fenians maintained "constant dialogue with the people of the sidhe."[2] These tales present a more consciously created wonderland, reminiscent of the Otherworld into which shamans journey; magic abounds, the unexpected happens, and shapeshifting is an ordinary occurrence.

In this magical environment live the Fenians (or in Irish, the *Fiana*), who were paralegal military bands of hunters and warriors whose mission was to protect Ireland from invasions. But the tales, recorded in the Late Middle Irish period, date from an earlier time than the Viking attacks of the ninth century or the Norman invasion in 1170 when such a military organization would have been most needed. The society described in the Fenian stories reflects a much older way of life, typical of the second or third century A.D.[3] Judging from the Fenians' relationships with the Dananns and other faery folk, their enemy was most likely not a human hord of foreign invaders, such as the Vikings, but the age-old cosmic foe, the Fomorians. Celtic scholars suggest that the "official purpose" of protecting Ireland from actual foreign invasion by enemy peoples was a later literary development to give the tales a political and historical basis.

The original Fenian legends concern two favorite themes of the Celtic imagination: war and magic. Indeed, the Fenians were both formidable warriors and magicians. Sorcery and poetry were requirements for initiation into the Fiana and were considered to be of equal value and importance as martial arts and wilderness survival skills. The Fenians' escapades repeatedly take these Irish warriors from ordinary reality into the Otherworld of faery magic where verbal wit, spellcasting, and magical weapons can make the difference between life and death. The Fenians were "walkers between the worlds," between human culture and the spirit realms upon which human culture, especially Celtic culture, was built. Their favorite haunt was the borderland between the worlds of human society and Faerie—the wild, trackless, and enchanted forest. Mac Cana notes that the Fiana's "freedom of movement is not confined to the actual land of Ireland, for one of the characteristics of their legend is the ease with which they pass from the natural world to the supernatural," an ease typical of the shaman.[4]

Marie-Louise Sjoestedt makes an important point in this regard, namely, that in the wilderness "the conditions of the mythological period still prevail."[5] These conditions include the close familiarity that humans, animals, and spirits enjoyed with each other. Perhaps this provides an important clue to the natural quality of the norscape recounted in the journeys of so many contemporary shamanic practitioners. In the natural norscape we experience the fluid connections between human, animal, and spirit. The wildwood bears the stamp of the earliest paradisal stages of creation, hence the earliest mark of the Creator. In contrast, an urban norscape, even when enhanced by magic and the surreal qualities of visionary experience, bears the unrelenting stamp of human activity and human creation. If the shaman's goal is to transcend the human and enter the divine realms, the natural landscape provides a more immediate connection with the spirit of creation, as opposed to the urban milieu marked by the works of humanity or the "spirit of man."

To become a Fenian, a man had to pass rigorous ordeals to prove himself warrior, hunter, poet, magicworker. Requirements for membership were arduous. A candidate had to memorize twelve books of poetry. He was buried up to his waist in the ground, from which position he had to defend himself against the spears of nine warriors with only a shield and a hazel stick. The hazel tree and its nuts had magical properties, so the stick was a magical tool rather than ordinary weaponry. While being chased through the forest by other Fenians, he was not to let a stick crack under his foot or allow a strand of his braided hair to come undone. He must also prevent his weapons from trembling in his hands when he fought against attackers. Two other tests for the candidate were to leap over a stick held at eye level and to run at full speed under a stick held at knee level. He must also be able to remove a thorn from his foot while running without slowing down. Clearly, the would-be Fenian had to be either a super-athlete or, more likely, a supermagician. As Sjoestedt remarks, the Celtic hero, especially the Fenian hero, was always a combination of professional warrior and "magician, or, if one prefers, a sorcerer (*shaman*)."[6] Like shamans who find a spiritual dimension to every problem or situation, the Celtic hero believed, in Sjoestedt's words, that "no activity can be effective unless it has an element of magic."

The Fenian enjoyed a unique legal status living outside the network of tribal responsibilities. Once a man severed all personal ties and adopted a nomadic forest life, he was clanless, and belonged to no social group except his brotherhood of quasi-outlaws. Even when he married, a Fenian was not allowed to accept a dowry with his wife. In the Celtic legal system, property was passed through the wife and would thus constitute a tie with the community. If a Fenian owned property, enemies seeking revenge could make a claim on it in legal disputes. The Fenian's only home was the forest, his only social obligations being to his fellow warrior-magicians. In summer he hunted freely; in winter he was quartered in villages as part of the payment for his services to the realm.

The Fenians were not treated as outlaws, but as outsiders. Sjoestedt suggests that the Fenians probably attracted individuals who were naturally unfit to live in society, the marginal types who might have been a burden or an embarrassment to the tribes. The Fenian tribe was their escape hatch. Here they could find a life that would accept and even find use for eccentricities which, if indulged within the tribal community, would have run them afoul of the law. The Fiana provided a needed service to the community but managed to remain quasi-independent of the community, no doubt relishing and capitalizing on the romance and mystery that surrounded their way of life. By training, lifestyle, and personal power the Fenians were both feared and respected. They were probably looked upon much like shamans in other societies, marked by some mental or behavioral irregularity— eccentrics by community standards but with personal power and a lifestyle that was admired and respected.

An enigmatic account in the Fenian literature illustrates the eccentric quality that could be found among the Fenians. Three warriors, accompanied by an enormous hound (traditionally an animal guardian of the Otherworld), approached Finn MacCool, the leader of the Fenians, and requested to be admitted to his band of men. As part of their arrangement, they discuss the particular services the men can offer the Fenians and the requirements they expect in return. They have one important and somewhat odd request: to sleep apart from the other men at night and have no one come near to watch them. Finn asks why. They answer that one of the men must "die" each night and the other two must guard him. They give no further explanation, and the story of these three men ends. We are left to draw our own conclusions.

The three men could have been shamans, masters of the "night journey," who practiced out-of-body rites. In the language of the tale, they "died," or had near-death experiences. Since the historical account of this episode seems unfinished, we could write our own. In our search for Celtic shamans, we could imagine one possible scenario: On being told of their nightly ritual, Finn breaks into a hearty laugh, throws his arms around their shoulders, and reassures the three men in words something like, "Well now, lads, you needn't worry about your nightly deaths. We've been doing that for years!"

FINN MACCOOL

The life of Finn MacCool, the most celebrated leader of the Fiana, contains the shamanic features we have come to recognize in the lives of other Celtic heroes. His mother, Murna, is of Danaan ancestry, thus making Finn a semidivine figure. After her husband's defeat, Murna takes refuge in the forest where she gives birth to Finn. Fearing attempts on his life, she gives the young boy to two witches to raise in the wildwood where he learns the secrets of magic and nature. The two women were also warriors and taught Finn the martial arts. It is a common practice in Celtic literature for the male hero to be fostered with a strong woman warrior who teaches him the martial arts and often initiates him into the mysteries of sex. Later as a young man, Finn studies poetry and science with Finegas, a wise old druid who lives on the River Boyne.

Finn's initiation as a shaman is completed when Finegas, after years of futile attempts, finally catches the Salmon of Knowledge that swims in the river. The old man gives the fish to Finn to cook, with orders not to eat it. But Finn burns his thumb while turning the salmon on the spit, much like the young boy Gwion who also botched a sacred task. He places the thumb in his mouth to cool the burn and is transformed by the salmon's power. The change is immediately apparent to Finegas who then questions the young man. When the druid hears what has just happened, he realizes that the boy has fulfilled an ancient prophecy that the salmon should only be eaten by a man named Finn. So Finegas gives Finn the entire fish, and the young hero receives universal wisdom. From that moment on, whenever Finn needed occult knowledge, he had merely to put his thumb in his mouth, and he could divine and prophesize.

Finn had two power animals, Bran and Skolawn, the faery hounds who were actually his nephews by his mother's sister (she bore them while under a faery enchantment that changed her into a dog). As Finn's companions, Bran and Skolawn led him into the faery realms, similar to the way power animals guide the shaman into the spirit world. A common scenario in the tales depicts the two dogs chasing a deer or stag into a densely forested area that is actually an entrance into the world of Faerie.

For example, on one occasion, the two dogs startle a fawn and chase it to the top of a mountain widely recognized as an important power spot and entry into the realm of Faerie. The fawn, as so often happens, disappears on the side of the mountain, and Finn, searching for it, discovers a beautiful woman crying over a golden ring she lost in the lake nearby. The woman commands him to swim to the bottom to recover the ring, which he does, only to learn when he returns that the woman too has disappeared. Weak from his swim, he collapses on the shore of the lake and sleeps. Later he awakens as a decrepid old man with silver-white hair. He is so transformed by the ordeal that not even his faithful hounds recognize him.

Unable to walk, a sign that he had visited the Otherworld beneath the waters, Finn waits until some of his men wander by. They too have difficulty recognizing their leader, but he whispers to one of them, and the man realizes who the old codger really is. They carry Finn away on a stretcher to the faery mound where the daughter of the smith Cullan dwells, for they surmise that it was she who seduced Finn into the fateful swim. The Fenians dig away at the mound, trying to rouse the spirits who live there. Eventually they penetrate its secret chamber and see a lovely woman with a red-golden drinking horn, which she gives to Finn. The drink restores Finn's strength, youth, and beauty, but his hair remains silver-white. Another swig from the horn would have restored the natural color of his hair, but Finn refused it. His hair remained white until his death, a mark of his journey into the Otherworld.

The Fenians as Animal Masters

Finn shares the shaman's triple nature: human, animal, and spirit. He is faery on his mother's side, human by his father, and animal through shamanic initiation. A prophecy concerning Finn (who is later reborn as the Irish King Mongan) claims that he will go through numerous transformations as animals.

He will be a dragon before hosts at the onset,
He will be a wolf of every great forest,
He will be a stag with horns of silver . . .
He will be a speckled salmon in a full pool,
He will be a seal, he will be a fair-white swan.[7]

Many of the Fenians had a semianimal nature. Conan Mac Morna, for example, had a black sheep's fleece instead of skin on his back and buttocks. Finn's nephews were hounds. His son Ossian was part deer. In nature-oriented cultures in which the species are not viewed as distinct and separate, humans, animals, and spirits can interact on very intimate terms. In fact, humans, animals, and spirits are not considered to be three totally separate entities, but relatives with the power to communicate with one another, live in each other's worlds, even inhabit each other's skin. The Native American refrain, "All my relations," is uttered on sacred occasions to acknowledge and honor this type of kinship with all of creation.

An episode concerning Saba, one of Finn's wives, shows this sense of kinship between animal and human. Saba had been transformed into a doe by a vengeful druid for having spurned his love. She cleverly lures Finn's dogs into chasing her, and then quickly befriends them in a playful manner. Suspecting something magical, Finn orders no one to shoot her. That night she reveals herself to Finn as the beautiful woman she really is and asks for sanctuary with him and his men. Then she explains that she knew Finn's hounds would not tear her to pieces because, being his nephews, they "have the nature of men." Finn, of course, allows Saba to stay with them, true to his pledge to welcome the oppressed. As one text records his reply, "Have no fear. We are free, and our guests and friends are free."[8]

A story about the Fenian Derg Corra offers tantalizing details about the shamanic quality of life among the woodland warriors, particularly their close relationship with animals. Derg Corra, whose full name means "the Peaked Red One," was famous for his power of leaping, especially over fires. Leaping abilities, like levitation among Hindus, is a form of flying. Some of the early Christian saints were great leapers, another indication that the ability to fly, formerly a druidic-shamanic ability, continued to inspire religious practices and the religious imagination even among the baptized Celts.

Finn, for all his sterling qualities, had a jealous streak, and Derg Corra, on one occasion, was the target of it. Finn ordered him to leave camp. But the next day Finn went looking for him in the forest and spotted a man sitting in the top of a tree. The full description is worth quoting. The man had

> a blackbird on his right shoulder and in his left hand a white vessel of bronze, filled with water in which was a skittish trout and a stag at the foot of the tree. And this was the practice of the man, cracking nuts; and he would give half the kernel of a nut to the blackbird that was on his right shoulder while he would himself eat the other half; and he would take an apple out of the bronze vessel that was in his left hand, divide it in two, throw one half to the stag that was at the foot of the tree and then eat the other half himself. And on it he would drink a sip of the bronze vessel that was in his hand so that he and the trout and the stag and the blackbird drank together. And then Finn's followers asked him who he in the tree was, for they did not recognize him on account of the hood of disguise which he wore.[9]

The man was, of course, Derg Corra.

A lot happens in this short passage. Sitting in the top of a tree is a ritual in more than one shamanic culture. The tree represents the Center of the World from which the shaman can journey upward through the branches into the sky or downward through the roots into the earth. It represents the World Tree because it nurtures many types of life; nuts, apples, a stag, a bird, and a fish all cluster around it. It is a microcosm of the world, mythically a home for all creation—plant, animal, fish, bird, and human. Derg is both Lord of the Tree (a kind of Green Man) and Lord of the Animals. Sharing his own food and water with animals attests to his kinship with them, or at the very least a strong sense of companionship.

THE MAGICAL HOOD

Derg Corra's "hood of disguise" is particularly noteworthy. If Derg's hood was red, as his name suggests, we see a strong continuity with the customs of the faerie folk who favored red or sometimes green caps. Derg is not the only hooded character in these woods. Finn also had a magic hood that gave him the power to shapeshift. Depending on how he wore it, he appeared either as a man, a dog, or a deer. The two animals, dog and deer, are logical alter egos for a warrior-hunter. It is common wisdom among hunters, even today, that success requires knowing intimately the animal you hope to kill—its moods, fears, instincts, behaviors. You must truly become both hunter and hunted to anticipate your prey's every move. Warriors make the same claim regarding their foes. They must think like the enemy to outwit him. Finn's ability to transform himself, therefore, into either the hunter's dog or the deer itself would make him a formidable huntsman, allowing him to move physically and *psychically* between the world of the hunter and the woodland world of the deer.

The close association of a magical hood and the ability to shapeshift into animal form, particularly into one's power animal, as in Finn's case, suggests that we look further into the relationship between shamans and magical head coverings. Mircea Eliade calls our attention to the magical hood or cap as being one of the Siberian shaman's chief attributes. He says that "in certain tribes . . . it is considered the most important part of the shamanic dress."[10] Rasmussen recalled that when Russian investigators asked unwilling Siberian shamans to perform a ceremony, they would do so without their caps, thus rendering the entire performance a parody of their real work. He stated their belief that "a great part of their power is hidden in these caps."[11] The caps or hoods were frequently decorated with animal figures or the parts of animals, such as horns, antlers, and feathers. A hood may be made, for example, of the entire head of a bear with other parts of the body still attached, hanging down as a kind of cloak or robe covering the shoulders. Birds, too, especially the swan, eagle, and owl, were common totemic birds. Sometimes the wings were left on, sometimes the entire head.

In her classic study, *The God of the Witches*, Margaret Murray notes that head coverings were very important among the faery folk. "The most characteristic article of attire . . . for all ranks [of faeries] was the hat, cap, or hood."[12] Faeries were known to risk their lives to reclaim lost or stolen caps because, like Siberian shamans, faery folk needed the hoods for magic and power. Typical colors were red or green, and many were conical or pointed, a style associated with witches and wizards. Legendary wisdom notes that the faeries' ability to disappear or render themselves invisible resided in the cap. Some folktales and children's stories retain this motif of the magical cap that makes the wearer invisible.

ROBIN, THE HOODED MAN

The origins of the name for the famous outlaw of Sherwood Forest, Robin Hood, are wrapped in mystery. He was also called "Robin in the Hood," "Robin the Hood," and "Robin, the Hooded Man." Whatever the original intent, Robin's hood was an important key in defining who he was. Woven through his legendary exploits is the ability to disappear into the forest when pursued by the local authorities. Was it the hood that made him invisible? Tradition tells us that Robin and his men wore green, the color of the forest, which undoubtedly helped to camouflage them, and of course Robin's disappearing act was also enhanced by a superb knowledge of the woodland trails with their secret hiding places.

But natural survival skills aside, an older theme in the Robin Hood legends, one that occasionally surfaces even in modern retellings, is Robin's skill as a worker of magic. In this light, his hood takes on special significance, paralleling its role in both Fenian mythology and Siberian shamanic lore. From a shamanic perspective, the hood, its green color, and the wearer's ability to become one with the forest make perfect sense. Any hood can conceal one's identity when pulled partly down over the face, but a magical hood could give the wearer an entirely new shape. Robin's hood may have had shapeshifting power like Finn's. As the tales were stripped of their magical qualities, Robin and his men became merely "masters of disguise," capable of passing through the gates of Nottingham undetected by the evil sheriff and his dimwitted thugs. But perhaps what became an ordinary skill of disguise was once a supernatural ability.

An old tradition suggests that Robin was the son of Herne, the Horned God and Leader of the Wild Hunt. Thus Robin, like Finn, had the shamanic heritage of man and spirit. Indeed, Robin was known by some as the "witch of Sherwood Forest" whose band of followers engaged in pagan rites deep in their forest hideout (the hard-drinking Friar Tuck nothwithstanding). His reputation as a sorcerer and magicworker may have grown out of shamanic practices, including the shamanic journey that may have been the source for episodic material that later became part of his legend.

The Robin Hood legend is not essentially Celtic, but the cult of Robin Hood is so widespread in space and time, it undoubtedly provided grist for many local traditions and fueled tales of hooded heroes, Celtic and non-Celtic. The stories were well known in both England and Scotland. The tradition's antecedents, however, lay in the Irish mythology of Finn and the Fenians.

Both brotherhoods, the Fiana and the Sherwood outlaws, made their home in the wilderness as hunters and warriors. Both societies existed outside the law and the accepted social conventions of their time. Both Robin Hood and Finn were popular heroes who gave away material goods. Legend says that "Finn gave away gold as if it were the leaves of the woodland, and silver as if it were the foam of the sea."[13] Among the Fenians, the greatest virtue was generosity. Both bands of quasi-outlaws were dedicated to righting wrongs and protecting the land, the Fenians from foreign invasion, the Merry Men from internal traitors who would overthrow the rightful king, Richard the Lion-Hearted.

What appears to lie half-buried beneath the adventures of Robin and his hooded men is evidence strongly suggesting that, in addition to whatever else it may have been, the call of the greenwood was a mystical vocation. Robin's most famous companions have names and characteristics that indicate they may have originally been deities, faeries, or shamans. John Little, for example, is renamed Little John, an obvious attempt to hide his ambiguous nature, since the man himself was taller than average, even described as a giant. Was he a giant, or one of the "Little People"? The name Alan-a-Dale means Alan of the Valley; he was a musician from "between the hills." Was he a faery piper? The name Will Scarlet may refer to his impetuous nature, his hotheaded temperament, but he was also fond of wearing red, the color most often associated with the faery folk.

Pagan and Christian mysticism converge in Marian and Friar Tuck. Marian may have been a "Maid" in the sense of "Maiden," a name that refers

to a specific coven officer. The name Marian, however, has Christian significance in that it is a form of Mary, a name that dots the Celtic landscape,
camouflaging sites sacred to older mother goddesses. Friar Tuck (formerly
Friar Michael) is an outcast from Fountains Abbey, an institution with possible older goddess associations if we take the term *fountains* to imply sacred
waters. Back in the world, Tuck builds his hermitage by a river, where he
makes a modest living by ferrying travelers across the water, echoing the
widespread tradition of the supernatural boatman who ferries the recently
deceased into the Land of the Dead.

Although the mystical vocation of Robin's outlaw gang may have been
long lost in the pages of folklore and faery tale, there seems to be a rich sub-
stratum of mystical purpose to the outlaws of Sherwood Forest.

WITCHES AND THE SHAMANIC SOUL FLIGHT

Andras Corban Arthen, writer and director of EarthSpirit, one of the
oldest neo-pagan communities in North America, has pointed out that
witchcraft shared certain key elements with what was most likely an older
form of European shamanism. These include healing, journeys to the upper
and lower worlds, spirit animals, trance work, the use of hallucinogenic
plants, and the vocational crisis.[14] If we consider these in terms of the shamanic archetype and the core elements of the shamanic journey, as does
Arthen, we find strong evidence that the men and women who were known
as witches in historical times might indeed have been practicing a form of
shamanism, rooted in the spiritual practices of the ancient Celtic tribes.

Basic to core shamanism is a visionary state of consciousness in which
the shaman perceives himself or herself as journeying into nonordinary
reality. Documents from witch trials frequently mention that the accused
went into a "great trance" or an "iron sleep." Witches are known to have
used herbal salves, sometimes called "flying ointments," made from ingre-
dients with hallucinogenic properties. These ointments were used in rituals
and ceremonies described by witnesses as frenzied and orgiastic, a good
indication that the participants had entered an altered state of consciousness. There is also evidence that witches used *amanita,* a hallucinogenic

mushroom, and *cannabis,* the hemp plant now known as marijuana. We have seen that the Celtic tribes had links with the Scythians who used hemp in sweat lodges to induce altered states of consciousness. The Celts may have even introduced the practice into Western Europe where it continued into medieval times as a practice among witches.

Not everyone who goes into an altered state is a shaman. The shamanic state of consciousness induces the experience of journeying, commonly referred to as "soul flight." One of the most common traits of European witchcraft is the night flight across the sky, a type of journey to the upper world. This tradition has much older pagan sediments, traceable to Roman rituals in northern Italy that included night flights with the goddess Diana. Interestingly, this Roman tradition is also found in the Western Alps around Lake Neuchatel, the La Tene area where major Celtic Iron Age settlements were discovered. From his studies of European witchcraft, Carlo Ginzburg concludes that in this region the Roman name Diana was superimposed over the older Celtic name Epona, the Celts' major horse goddess, and that the night ride was characteristically a Celtic phenomenon.[15]

Horses are closely associated with the night rides across the sky, giving rise to the "witch's broomstick" tradition. The "hobby horse," a stick with a wooden or straw horse's head, substituted for a real horse among poor women who did not have horses to ride to their sabbaths. In the context of ritual, riding around a fire on a stick or hobby horse recreated the ride on horseback. In any event, witch trials repeatedly refer to witches riding or flying through the sky on animals' backs or on wands and broomsticks. During times of persecution, people practicing witchcraft used simple household utensils, such as broomsticks, as magical tools to avoid being caught with special ritual paraphernalia.

There are also interesting parallels between the witches' ecstatic practices and those of a sixteenth-century Northern Italian sect, the benandanti.[16] While in trance state, the female benandanti perceived themselves leading a procession of the dead, while the male members saw themselves engaged in ritual sky battles with evil spirits intent on destroying the forces of fertility. In both cases, the ritual activity took place in a trance state, during which the individuals' spirits left their bodies in animal form. The benandanti described this nonordinary state of consciousness in terms of a temporary death. The features of the benandanti's nightly journey are remarkably similar to those that emerge in the questioning and testimony of witches during the trials.

There are also striking similarities in the trance states of the benandanti and those of Eurasian shamans. In Lapland, for example, "magicians" went into cataleptic states described this way by a sixteenth-century writer: "Twenty-four hours having passed, with the return of the spirit, as though from a deep sleep, the inanimate body awakens with a moan, almost as though called back to life from the death into which it had fallen."[17] Ginzburg compares this description with testimony given only thirty years later in Italy concerning a member of the benandanti that reads: "When he is forced to go into combat he is overcome by a very deep sleep, and sleeping belly up as the spirit issues forth, one hears him emit three moans, as often times do those who are dying." The similar descriptions of Eurasian shamans, the benandanti society of Northern Italy, and the witches' sabbaths presented during the witch trials indicate shamanic beliefs and practices survived among the common folk far longer than the official histories of the era would imply.

A curious footnote. When the benandanti were questioned about whom they fought in their ecstatic trances, they answered "evil witches." In their minds, they themselves were not practicing witchcraft or an evil form of sorcery, but saving the community from evildoing by others. The common explanation they gave in their defense was that they were called by God to defend the people *against witches*. In this testimony we see another example of how pagan ways could be incorporated into Christian ideology, and continue to shape folk spirituality, long after a given population had been "converted" to the new religion.

What is interesting to us from a shamanic point of view is how witnesses to shamanic trance states equated them with a death or near-death experience. The shamanic journey is still explained in these terms, as Holgar Kalweit has so brilliantly elucidated in his work, *Dreamtime and Inner Space*. Indeed, a common result of doing shamanic work on a regular basis and for an extended period of time, often over years, is that the practitioner loses the fear of the universe that he or she may have had at the beginning of the practice. Included in the fear of the universe is a fear of death. Time and again, witnesses to the witch executions commented on how the victims seemed to have no fear of death. Perhaps their experiences in nonordinary reality and their Old Religion beliefs, based on the cycles of nature, gave them the courage to face their own deaths with grace and dignity. Or perhaps in the final hours and minutes, even then, those about to die left their bodies willingly and purposefully.

It is common for shamanic practitioners to experience death or its equivalent on shamanic journeys in the form of "dismemberment" episodes in which their bodies are torn apart by spirits or power animals and reassembled in a lighter, more transcendent form. The close links between shamanic journeying and near-death experience help to explain why shamans and European witches could be actively involved in the deaths and dying processes of those in their communities who came to them for assistance in these last rites. They may have experienced their own deaths in trance.

Witch Holes and Faery Mounds

The witches' flight across the sky is a form of Upper World journey typical of shamanic practices worldwide. The journey to the Lower World was also attributed to witches. Some witches were believed to live underground. Andras Corban Arthen points out that, even today, holes found at the base of trees and in excessively haunted areas are called "witch houses" or "witch holes."[18] The belief was that witches either lived in these holes as permanent residences or went there to perform spells and rituals. Here we find another parallel with faeries who live in the sidhe or the Hollow Hills.

There is anthropological evidence that the "little people" dwelt beneath or in the earth. In Britain the Neolithic and Bronze Age peoples lived in circular huts made of wattle and daub, and sunk into the earth about two to three feet. These houses were then roofed with turf on which shrubs, grass, or bracken grew, thus creating the appearance of small hills or mounds. The original inhabitants in some areas, notably the Picts in Scotland, were of small stature, which fueled the belief that the faerie folk were small in size and dwelt in the Hollow Hills.[19] In the middle of the sixteenth century a man by the name of John Walsh testified that he consulted with faeries who lived inside hills; and a woodcut from the same era shows a knight visiting a faery house, the dwelling being under stones and foliage, and the inhabitants appearing smaller than the knight himself. Thus from the Neolithic era to the present we find an unbroken tradition of marginal people who practice magic living in underground dwellings, whether they be the original, diminutive residents of the British Isles, the early Celtic deities who retreated into the lower worlds to give the surface realms to mortals, the faerie folk of romance and legend, or the forest-dwelling witches.

THE WITCH'S ANIMAL POWERS

Shamans have personal relationships with certain animal helpers. In both ordinary and nonordinary reality, a shaman's special animal companions bestow power and identity upon the shaman. Frequently a shaman will have powers analogous to the animal who serves as his or her spirit guide, and the shaman may have a name or a physical trait similar to the animal. A widespread practice among shamans is to shapeshift into animals while in a visionary state of consiousness in order to experience that power and identify with it more fully. In this way shamans "become" their power animals on the shamanic journey when such transformation will assist them in the mission of the journey.

Witches also enjoyed this magical relationship with animals. The witch's "familiar" animal (cat, toad, owl, hare, crow, raven) was often accused of carrying out the witch's spells for her so that she herself would not get caught. People who feared a witch for evildoing may be equally frightened to encounter her familiar. We have already noted that witches were thought to ride to their sabbaths on the backs of flying animals, or by turning themselves into animals for the sabbath. The chronicles of the witch trials are filled with references to people believing that an animal acting suspiciously in the village or a strange animal that wandered in from the forest was really a witch who had come to town to do harm in the guise of an animal.

During the witch trials in Hungary in the late seventeenth and early eighteenth centuries, the accused men and women, called the *taltos*, exhibited remarkable shamanic features, including fertility battles and shapeshifting rituals. Carlo Ginzburg believes that their methods of shapeshifting into animals and their initiation into shamanic magic paralleled those of other European witches.[20] For example, the *taltos* are marked at birth with some physical abnormality such as six fingers or toes, full grown teeth, or a caul. As children they are withdrawn, meditative, antisocial in nature, and silent to an extent considered strange. Around age seven they begin to have visions, often of an elder *taltos* who may appear as a horse or bull and with whom the younger one must fight. Formal initiation as a *taltos* includes a three-day trance during which the neophyte experiences himself or herself being dismembered. Another test involves climbing extremely tall trees. Periodically the *taltos* must participate in a struggle for fertility in the shape of a stallion, bull, or flame, to fight off opposing figures. Victory assures a good crop and substantial harvest for the community.

Witches also honored the animal powers by worshipping the male deity in the form of the Horned God, similar to the Greek Pan and Celtic Cernunnos. As Lord of the Animals, a male witch wearing horns or antlers was often the center of a ring dance, which was a common form of religious dancing among peasant folk in the Middle Ages. The Church, however, branded such practices as satanic, assuming that the horned dancer was impersonating the Christian devil. Such sabbath rituals also gave rise to the witch's reputation for disappearing and vanishing at will. If witches danced naked around a fire or a man dressed as the Horned God, as many accounts attest, and if they ran the risk of being discovered by local authorities, then the traditional black robe would have been a necessary article of clothing for concealment. When church or civic forces approached during a ritual, witches could quickly slip into black, hooded robes and vanish into the darkness of the forest.

THE DANCE OF THE WITCHES

A common connection between witches, shamans, and faeries is the dance to raise power or induce a visionary state of consciousness. One of the most documented examples of this among contemporary tribal societies is the ritual of the !Kung people in Africa, where the women sing and the men dance until they feel the energy "boil" within them. When the men collapse from physical and emotional exhaustion, they are so filled with energy that they can heal others. The Batak people of Malaysia dance themselves into a trance, as do certain Chinese sorcerers. The Goldi shamans in Siberia dance in order to "feel" their tutelary spirits. Initiation dances among the Caribs in Dutch Guiana involved ritual animal movements. For many shamanic peoples and for modern shamanic practitioners, dancing is a method of calling, honoring, and metamorphosing into one's power animal. Eliade also calls attention to the dance's ability to "reproduce the shaman's ecstatic journey to the sky."[21]

European witches are not alone in using a broomstick, wand, or hobby horse while dancing. The Buryat shamans in Asia use a horseheaded stick in their ecstatic dances, as do the Batak of Malaysia. In Java and Bali horses are associated with the ecstatic dance, and in India the hobby horse is part of ritual dancing. Wands, or riding sticks, can serve as power objects or ritual props to raise energy for the shamanic dance ceremony.

Anthropologist John Pfeiffer in his study of paleolithic cave drawings says that a possible interpretation of some of the human figures is that they are dancing. Some field scholars think that the many footprints that have survived on the floors of the caves indicate dance movements. Some footprints are accompanied by indentations made by hands and knuckles, suggesting that the dancers may have been crawling or walking on all fours, imitating four-footed beasts.[22] Pfeiffer draws parallels between dance rituals performed by contemporary Aborigines in Australia and what may have been important ceremonial customs of prehistoric Europeans. The Aborigines' dance is an ecstatic technique to "identify completely with the spirit and journeys and adventures of [their] totemic beings."[23] The results of such dancing are purely shamanic: visionary identification with animal spirits and their journeys into nonordinary reality.

Witches danced for similar reasons. Margaret Murray claims that their "main ceremony was the sacred dance,"[24] and it would be odd if the dance did not honor or call upon the deities of the Old Religion, and the animals sacred to those gods and goddesses. The round or ring dance is clearly depicted in illustrations and woodcuts. Typical scenes show a circle of men and women dancing around a horned and phallic figure, frequently named "Robin Goodfellow," an appellation given to the King of the Faeries. The same type of circle dance is also attributed to the faeries, judging by the accounts of those who have witnessed it. In 1991 in England, large, mysterious, circular depressions in the grass and wheat fields were attributed, according to some theories, to faery dancing.

The dance of the witches, like the dance of the faeries, was considered lewd and indecent by church and civil authorities. It led to sexual improprieties, especially when performed at Beltane (May 1) or at Midsummer Eve (June 21), both fertility holidays. In 1662 in Shaftesbury, England, an agreement was reached to limit the traditional May Day dance when it fell on Sunday. A description of it calls to mind essential features of Celtic shamanism. The lead dancers carry a calf's head on a dish, the horns garlanded with seasonal flowers. The procession led out from town to a greenwood with a pool of water, and many springs and wells.[25] More ancient fertility rituals echo strongly here. According to an eyewitness whose account was published years later, the revelers were "dancing in the most ridiculous way . . . finishing the day with May Games and the greatest Festivity."[26]

Margaret Murray calls attention to a paleolithic dance scene found in Catalonia, Spain, showing women with hoods and heavy drooping breasts, dancing around a phallic male figure in the center, a dance scene not unlike those involving Robin Goodfellow and similar to the descriptions of dancing in the chronicles of the witch trials.[27] Although it is argued by farming communities that such fertility dancing is necessary for healthy crops (the same argument given for the ritual battles of the benandanti), Church authorities often view it differently. Since the Church demonized activities of this kind when it desacralized the earth, nature is now viewed simply as divine law, not the work of individual earth spirits, and not needing human participation (song, dance, sex) on a seasonal and joyful basis.

Not all pagan dancing is joyful however. In earth-centered spiritualities dancing can celebrate the darker as well as the brighter side of life. It can celebrate death. Shamans are the original psychopomps, individuals familiar with the geography of death who lead the souls of the recently departed into the next world. In some cultures shamans danced, sang, and chanted the souls to their final rest.

The "wise women" and "cunning men" accused of practicing baneful magic in the witch trials may have actually been functioning as guides to assist the dying through the gateways of death. In practical matters, they were keepers of the folk medicines that could provide speedy and painless deaths. In some villages witches were the only herbalists, and their knowledge of medicinal herbs also included the deadly ones. Among Europeans still practicing the old nature religion of their ancestors, death was viewed as a natural process on the Wheel of Life, and there would have been no stigma attached to the healers and spiritual leaders who recommended the specific herbs and potions that would facilitate a painless death for a person dying or suffering from an incurable illness.

SECRET SOCIETIES

By now we notice a curious convergence of shamanic features in the Fenian tales of ancient Ireland, the Robin Hood legends of Britain, and the fact and folklore surrounding the so-called "witch cult"[28] of the late Middle Ages and Renaissance. The magical hood or cap associated with all three groups is merely an emblem of something more deeply embedded in these traditions. But let us allow the symbol of the hood to carry our thinking a bit further. Witches, Fenians, and the Sherwood outlaws were among the "hoods" of their day, social outcasts living outside the law with a reputation for either "hoodlum" activities or "hoodwinking" unsuspecting travelers through their forest hideouts. In some sense, each of these three types of "shamanic outlaws" represents a kind of secret brotherhood or sisterhood with an initiation requirement that has noteworthy similarities to shamanic initiation procedures found in other mystical societies.

Writing about secret societies among North American Indians, Mircea Eliade points out[29] that "brotherhoods based on mysteries have a shamanic structure, in the sense that their ideology and techniques share in the great shamanic tradition." These include the initiate's symbolic death to his or her former life, the soul journeys into nonordinary reality, learning the group's secret mysteries, and so on. Paradoxically, mystical brotherhoods, even though they have what Eliade calls a "shamanic structure," harbor an inherent opposition to shamans. The crux of hostility is the notion of special privilege. Secret societies covet special privileges for their own members and them alone; independent shamans claim it for themselves. The two are fated to collide. Secret brotherhoods often claim to be fighting "evil sorcerers" in their communities, the magicworkers who do not belong to the secret society. Whether or not you view the independent magicians, witches, shamans, or sorcerers as evildoers depends, of course, on whose side you are on.

Eliade points out that the real difference between the "consecrated" members and the "profane" others in society may be only a question of degree. It is quantitative rather than qualitative. The full members may have *more* spirit power than outsiders, but everyone in the tribe has some power. In Native American communities, for example, each man or woman can seek a vision and obtain helping spirits. The medicine people, however, have stronger or more frequent visions, and, as a rule, they have more helping spirits.

Witches, the Fenians, and the Sherwood band may have been viewed with suspicion by conventional members of society partly on the grounds that they constituted in the popular mind secret societies with special, mystical privileges not shared by the population at large, or not shared to the same extent. A significant difference separating them from the dominant population may have been the greater sense of freedom with which they led their lives, including a greater mobility. The price for this privilege, however, was the initiation into a maverick lifestyle that required their dying symbolically to their former lives. Again, we confront death as the giver-of-new-life, as the shaman maker.

Courting death is part of the shamanic archetype. Shamans say that they court death on their visionary journeys where they battle malevolent spirits. We would probably do well to allow a certain amount of room for exaggeration and bombast, since a shaman's power depends to some extent on his or her reputation, and it is in the shaman's professional interest to be a bit "careless with the truth." In shamanic initiations, the death of the neophyte was allegorical, but novices did return to the village after what

seemed to them to be a scrape with death, if not the actual thing. They
suffered memory loss, an inability to walk, eat, dress, or talk in the normal
way. They often returned with knowledge of another, secret language, and
possibly with a new name. They were now different from ordinary members of the tribe or village. They had died to their former way of being in
the world.

In Celtic societies, ambivalence about the sacred creates the potential
for acute tension. If the typical Celt has a fierce strain of mysticism, and evidence strongly suggests that this is true, every Celt is a potential shaman.
Or we might say that the shamanic archetype in the Celtic unconscious is
particularly easy to activate. We can discover in this tension the roots of so
much ambivalence in the Celtic soul over the wisdom of directly confront-
ing the sacred mysteries. In more secular terms, this can be seen in the "fear
of faeries." In orthodox Christian terms, it is the fear and hatred of witchcraft, worship of the old Celtic gods and goddesses, and shamanic practices.

In numerous stories that ostensibly demonstrate the folly of visiting
faeries or witches, there runs a strong fascination for those individuals who
share a special relationship with the divine (witness the historic place of
honor and political power the parish priest has held in Irish society). This
fascination is made even stronger by the Celt's conscious or semiconscious
desire to indulge his or her own mystical or magical talents, knowing that
to do so would incur the wrath of the church.

A Gaelic-speaking, Irish expatriate, interviewed by the Foundation for
Shamanic Studies on the condition that her identity be withheld, sheds
some light on this situation even in the twentieth century.[30] She was
astounded that, in America, shamanic practitioners can drum and journey
without fear of reprisals from church and state. As she put it, "For many
centuries [my] people could not listen to this [shamanic knowledge and
practice]. They could not hear these concepts. People typically respond
with fear to a knowledge which they cannot handle, and fear breeds violence and destruction." The woman also said that her grandmother, who
had taught her shamanic techniques when she was a child, was suspected
of having moments of insanity near the end of her life. But evidentally, the
grandmother had realized even earlier in life that if her mystical knowledge

and shamanic practices were discovered, she might be "locked away in an insane asylum." Her granddaughter said, "She lived with that terror all her life."

The fear of and fascination with spiritual power has a counterpart in terms of political and social power. The Celt has been plagued with a long-standing reputation for being hot-tempered and easily provoked to violence, sometimes regarded even as a love of violence. In other words, the need to break the law, or think of oneself as outside of or above the law, is particularly strong and appealing to the Celt. One of the primary reasons for prejudice against Irish immigrants in America in the mid-nineteenth century was their reputed disregard for civil law. Renegade champions of the poor and oppressed, like the Fenians and the outlaws of Sherwood, are appealing figures, fighting against the privileged classes of society. Like masked avengers or hooded men, they are dangerously fascinating precisely because they operate outside the accepted norms and legal constraints of society.

In their own ways, shamans play similarly dangerous, yet fascinating roles, but in a spiritual context. While not totally outside the religious constraints of their societies, they have personal and unorthodox methods of contacting the divine powers. Joseph Campbell has characterized this tension as that between the shaman and the priest. The latter is the "socially initiated, ceremonially inducted member of a recognized religious organization, where he holds a certain rank and functions as the tenant of an office that was held by others before him, while the shaman is one who, as a consequence of a personal psychological crisis, has gained a certain power of his own."[31] The shaman's helping spirits are (to use the witch's term) "familiars," personal protectors known only to the shaman. To seek help from the shaman, rather than the priest, is to go outside the normally accepted routes to the sacred. It is, in our analogy, to enter the forest rather than the church, to invoke a power animal rather than a saint or a god or goddess in the culture's pantheon.

Regarding shamanic initiation, there is more than one path. In some cases, when the candidate is being enrolled into a society of shamans or after an apprenticeship with an elder shaman, initiation may be accompanied by an elaborate public ceremony for the community. But such an event is not always necessary. Initiation can, as Mircea Eliade points out, take place solely in the candidate's ecstatic experiences, such as dreams, visions, or trances.[32] Initiation can take place totally within the visionary imagination of the new shaman. We find similar arrangements for membership in our three groups of forest folk. The Fenians had elaborate procedures for membership. Joining the Sherwood gang seems to have been much looser. Judging from the tales, each newcomer had to prove himself in some way acceptable to Robin and his men.

Concerning initiation into witchcraft, there are various paths. Some men and women trained with covens, or other witches, and were formally initiated. This practice still holds among many modern traditions. But the self-initiated witch has a long respectable history as well. The vocational crisis, often paralleling the shamanic illness, undoubtedly convinces many men and women to pursue the arts of witchcraft. Indeed, there probably were individuals whose decision to be a witch was "forced" on them by their treatment in the community. They were treated like witches whether they were or not. Andras Arthen notes that "aberrant behavior was, in the minds of the witch hunters, one of the most conclusive signs that a person was a witch."[33] He points out that what are considered common neurological disorders today, such as epilepsy, palsy, stammering, or senility, could bring on accusations of witchcraft. If witch hunters saw these behaviors as signs of election to witchcraft, others probably did too, including witches themselves. Like shamans in other societies, personal illness or accidents may have been the catalyst to realizing one's call to a mystical life. Then again, some witches may have begun their practice from primarily visionary experiences, such as dreams, trances, or mystical episodes that changed their lives.

◆

To return to our initial question: Does it matter what type of visionary environment the shaman journeys into and what type of ecology makes up his or her ordinary life? The answer may ultimately hinge on something a bit more subtle. In addition to the inherent spiritual value in a natural, organic norscape, the shaman needs something in addition, namely, a strong sense of being an outsider in relation to his or her everyday culture. The reason is that shamans derive their power (vision, insight, sense of values) from their ecstatic experiences. Their power comes from time spent "standing outside" the socially accepted parameters of reality that will, most likely, always be defined by people who are *not* ecstatics. Were everyone in a society a shaman, there would probably be no need for shamans.

So the friendly rivalry between "country shamans" and "urban shamans" over the relative value of their respective norscapes should not cloud an equally important consideration: that the journey takes the shaman to a place *outside* the scope of his or her everyday life. To adopt an idea from one of the greatest shamanic stories in modern literature (and one of the most popular Hollywood films ever made), the point of nonordinary reality is not whether it is urban or woodland, but that, like the Land of Oz, it isn't Kansas anymore.

7

PERILOUS JOURNEYS

Wherever it may lead, the perilous journey is always, of course, perilous. The hero, traditionally a young man, must defend himself against beast and foe. In Celtic folktales and faery tales he often risks physical danger, bodily harm, even death, as he quests for a marvelous object that he believes will bring luck, health, or a richer life: a magical sword, a cauldron of wisdom, a cup of knowledge, or a faery lover. On the shaman's initiation journey the danger is psychic—the disintegration and reintegration of personality. The object of the quest is a "new soul," a shamanic soul with its disorienting and upsetting vision of reality. On subsequent journeys, the shaman's quest may still be for nothing less than the human soul of a patient who is sick, of someone severely depressed, or of a person recently deceased. As psychologists and symbologists note, the archetypal journey is always one of initiation and self-discovery. The physical objects sought on the quest are symbols of psychic wholeness, health, and the integrated soul, or in Jungian terms, the Self. The perilous journey, therefore, is always about soul loss and soul retrieval.

In this chapter we will look at some of the ways that the world of myth and folklore is the literary equivalent of the human soul—mysterious, unpredictable, and inherently magical. The territory of the soul is not well mapped, neither the familiar terrain, nor the secret, hidden places. And as we go through life, we continually stumble into psychic landscapes and adventures that startle us. We must always be on guard for the unexpected. In Celtic folklore the magic of deception and surprise is at the core of most tales concerning the plunder of faeryland by human heroes and the parallel invasions by faeries into the world of mortals. There is considerable pilfering in both directions, as the players trek back and forth between the worlds. Faeries steal objects or humans from our world, and mortals slip into the realm of Faerie seeking magical talismans or hoping to retrieve lost or stolen objects, sometimes to rescue someone abducted by faery raiders.

The archetypal tale of the two worlds intruding upon each other has perennial appeal. In it we recognize, either consciously or unconsciously, a symbolic parallel to the intimate ways the conscious (mortal) and unconscious (faery) interact in our ordinary lives. In every instance, the immediate problem is the attack upon our sense of balance or wholeness, and the urgent need to redress it, whether in the fields of everyday emotions or in the enchanted forests of ancient Britain.

THE GRAIL QUEST

The classic elements of shamanism converge in the most profound Celtic quest story, the Search for the Grail. Many variations on the Grail Quest appear in Western literature, from the oldest stories about Celtic warriors raiding the Otherworld for magical cauldrons to more recent versions about the search for the cup Jesus was believed to have used at the Last Supper or the cup Joseph of Arimethea used to catch the blood of Christ while he hung on the cross. We will look first at the core story, keeping in mind that many conflicting variations of the tale have been developed over the centuries since it was first written down in 1185. This "first" written account was based on earlier versions that have been lost, and they in turn were based on even older oral accounts. We may never know who, if any single individual, first told the tale. And judging from the popularity of Grail themes in contemporary fiction and Hollywood films, there will probably never be a final version. The Grail Quest is a timeless story about the Search for a Magical Vessel that holds the "Secret of Life." It is a human story, archetypal and universal in its significance and importance. It will always haunt us.

The basic outline of the story is this: A young, innocent knight sets out to find the Grail. On the way he has many adventures, some of them perilous, some filled with wonders and delights. He stumbles upon the Grail King, sometimes referred to as the Fisher King, who is wounded in the thigh or loins. His kingdom is a vast Waste Land, caused by the wound that will not heal. In his castle is the mysterious Grail, brought out at a glorious banquet, sometimes with an equally mysterious bleeding Lance. The young knight is awestruck by the spectacle, but he fails to ask three crucial questions: "Whom does the Grail serve?", "Why does the Lance bleed?", and "What do these Wonders mean?" Had he asked these questions, the Maimed King would have been healed and his barren land restored to prosperity. But because of a lack of will or courage, or out of fear, the young knight remains silent. The next morning he awakens to discover that he is alone. The castle has disappeared, and he must begin the quest again.

The story of the Grail Quest contains brilliant insights into classic shamanic experiences. On a more subtle level, it is the story about how Western civilization forsook its rich shamanic heritage. For these reasons, the tale is doubly sad and disturbing. It is not only about the unsuccessful search for the Grail, but the consequences of deshamanizing the Western psyche. The story of the Grail illuminates the problem Europeans have had in accepting and practicing shamanism in the Christian era. The "Grail Problem" is the intellectual, spiritual, and psychic "block" that Christianized Europeans developed on their own journey to modernity, a journey mapped by a rational, scientific worldview in which there was increasingly little room for mystical and magical experience.

What obscures the shamanic structure of the Grail Quest is the fact that there are two shamans: the young knight and the old king. Both are caught in the reluctance or refusal to accept the shamanic vocation. Let us begin with the Wounded King.

THE FISHER KING AS A DYSFUNCTIONAL SHAMAN

There is little agreement on how the king was wounded. In some versions the wound is never explained; in one account the wound is delivered by the king's evil brother, the Invisible Knight. Nor is it clear exactly where the wound is on the king's body. "Thigh" can be a euphemism for the loins, in which case he has been maimed in the genitals. Suffice it to say, the wound from the Dolorous Blow of the lance will not heal, and the king is too weak to walk (or walk well). For all practical purposes, he is crippled, and spends his days reclining on a couch in the castle or by a stream fishing. What is important here is what he *cannot* do; he cannot journey. Were he a young and vigorous king, the foremost hero of his realm, he would be a hunter and a warrior setting out on perilous journeys to defend his people, hunt the large game, or (in psychological and shamanic terms) save his soul. We have seen that in Celtic mythology, the hunt or the expedition against an enemy is frequently the naturalistic prelude to the supernatural adventure in the Otherworld where the real quest takes place. But the wounded Grail King cannot leave the realm of ordinary reality, daily routine, and psychological inertia. He cannot fulfill his duties as king. Instead, he fishes.

Psychologically the Fisher King sits above the waters of the unconscious hoping for whatever wisdom or understanding will rise sufficiently to the surface to be caught. Like all fishermen, he is dependent upon luck. He cannot forsake ordinary reality and plunge into the Otherworld of the unconscious to pursue his quarry as a vigorous shaman/king would do. Instead, he sits at the edge of water (a traditional place of enlightenment for Irish poets and seers), but without the physical stamina or the moral fortitude to be either a good king or a good shaman. He cannot benefit from the Grail that already resides in the spiritual realm of his kingdom, the hidden "kingdom within the kingdom." Ironically he is the Grail's guardian, but its wisdom and power lie beyond his grasp because he suffers a spiritual malaise, a psychic lethargy, that brings all life and growth, both physical and spiritual, to a halt.

If we consider the fish to be a kind of power animal, a guide into the unconscious, we are struck by the fact that the king has perverted a core element of shamanism—his personal and intimate relationship with a helping animal spirit. As a fisherman he hopes to snare the fish and bring it up into his world of ordinary reality, rather than allow it to lead him into its realm of spirit and mystery. In the Celtic scheme of things, the fish may be the Salmon of Wisdom; and the king is a latter-day reincarnation of the old Fisher Druid, Finegas, who initiated Finn MacCool. And the king's fate mirrors that of Finegas in yet another way. The reason he will not catch the salmon (or Grail) is that another, younger man is destined to receive the wisdom and knowledge that only the salmon (or Grail) can bestow.

The king's inability to walk suggests that he has already entered the Otherworld and returned disabled. We have seen this before. It is common for the shaman to return wounded, but it is a healed wound, making the shaman a "wounded healer." His suffering does not prevent him from continued journeys into nonordinary reality to bring back power and healing for himself or another, or in the case of the king, for the entire realm. On the contrary, his wound is the very passkey that qualifies him for entry into the Otherworld. Not so for the Fisher King. He can neither recover nor die. He is truly caught between the worlds in a severely dysfunctional way. From the vast literature on mysticism and shamanism, it is clear that once the faculties of perception have been expanded, they cannot be constricted without causing mental or even physical illness.

The malingering illness that results from denying the initial vision is well documented by reluctant shamans all over the world. Most frequently the disease clears up when they commit themselves to shamanizing. One of the clearest descriptions of this is the Yakut shaman Uno Harva, who says he became ill when he was twenty-one years old and began to see and hear things that other people could not. "For nine years I fought against the spirit, without telling anyone what had happened because I feared they might not believe me or make fun of me. In the end I became so ill that

I was close to death." So he began to shamanize and his health improved. From then on he would again feel sick if he was "inactive as a shaman over a longer period of time."[1] As Mircea Eliade puts it, "the shaman's vocation has been decided by the Gods. And, as the whole history of shamanism shows, resistance to this divine decision means death."[2] Or, in the case of the Fisher King, a malingering death.

The Fisher King is also sexually dysfunctional. In Celtic tradition this has serious implications, because the Queen is the physical representation of the Goddess of the Land, the Goddess of Sovereignty. It is only because he is her husband that the king has authority. By virtue of the royal marriage, the land is fertilized, the kingdom prospers. But the Fisher King rules over a Waste Land. We are meant to understand here that he cannot fulfill his marital duties to his true bride, the Goddess of the Land.

The Fisher King is a dysfunctional shaman. He has journeyed to the Otherworld and come back with the expected wound, and we can conclude one of two things. Either his personality was not shattered sufficiently to reorganize his understanding of reality, and thus he did not receive the shaman's intense and profound vision in which passage between ordinary and nonordinary reality is both possible and necessary or, if he did receive this vision, he was frightened by it. He refused to change his life as would be required of someone whose older paradigm of reality no longer explains the universe. Like many neophyte shamans everywhere, and like many modern Celts terrified of getting caught in Faeryland, he refused the call. As shamans in other cultures have repeatedly said, not until they accepted the call to be a shaman, not until they began to shamanize, did they recover and feel healthy again. The Fisher King will not and cannot journey into the unconscious. Nor will he, or can he, as a man, "marry" the divine feminine within himself, his anima, or soul. His marriage is fruitless. His land is wasted. He has lost his soul.

The Grail is the ultimate source of power and wholeness, and as the guardian of the Grail, the king is never far from his cure. Indeed, in some versions, the king's life is sustained by drinking from the Grail, and yet he never fully recovers. The reason for this anomaly is that although the king guards the Grail, he does not really possess it. Usually a procession of maidens carries it into the banquet hall, administers the drink to the king, and then retreats with it. These Grail priestesses, or faery women, or anima figures, are the real Keepers of the Grail, and because of that, the Grail actually resides in the Otherworld protected by the power of the feminine. Thus, like an elusive faery, the Grail, mysterious and unpredictable, appears and disappears, always just beyond one's grasp.

In their study, *The Grail Legend*, Emma Jung and Marie-Louise von Franz call attention to an important point. "When consciousness is incapable either of grasping or knowingly integrating a spontaneously emerging impulse (the lance) or content (the enemy who throws it), the individual will instead be unconsciously possessed by it. This explains the demonic nature of the Wounded King."[3] The authors state earlier that the "eternally self-renewing psychic life" requires us to utilize archetypal energy from the unconscious when it floats up. When we cannot "hold the opposites together," we must expect "the complete devastation of the land, the stagnation of psychic life."[4] When the shaman's psychic life becomes stagnant, the rich reservoir of visionary experience dries up, and with it the shaman's power to unite and reconcile opposites, to be a channel between ordinary and nonordinary realities, and to be a master of the twilight world of sacred mystery. The Wounded King remains a dysfunctional shaman.

THE GRAIL SEEKER AS SHAMAN

If the search for the Grail is about anything, it is about the search for one's identity. The core story is about the hero's continuing self-discoveries and his understanding of the meaning of life. Joseph Campbell, Mircea Eliade, and other students of myth and folklore have repeatedly noted that every quest story is an initiation in which the hero learns, in varying degrees of success, the answer to the age-old question, "Who am I?" Every quest for a life-giving talisman is a search for identity, and the search is never complete unless the searcher enters the Otherworld of spirit and eternity, for ultimately no one knows himself or herself without experiencing the primordial realm of unity and wholeness from which we emerged but which, from our ego-centered consciousness, appears filled with chaos and danger.

The Grail knights are a motley crew. They inhabit a physical world far removed from our own, but not very distant from the dreams and unconscious aspirations that motivate all spiritual seekers. Some of their stories are frustratingly unfinished. Some survive in older, pre-Christian forms with allusions and references that are difficult to appreciate from a twentieth-century viewpoint; others have been embellished by Church scribes with their own medieval Christian concerns that may prove equally obscure to modern sensibilities. For simplicity's sake, let us consider three major Grail seekers who together exemplify core themes in Celtic shamanism: Perceval (Peredur), Lancelot, and Galahad.

The character of Perceval (in some versions called Peredur) is a pagan hero who fails initially in the Grail quest, but later succeeds. Lancelot, although he seems destined to retrieve the Grail, ultimately fails because serious personality flaws make him morally unfit. Galahad fulfills the quest more fully than any other knight, but as a Christian hero he cannot accept the shaman's vision and remain true to Christian beliefs and practices. The fact that Galahad, a prime candidate for Catholic sainthood, was never elevated to this highest honor in the Church, nor did the Grail inspire a sacramental or liturgical rite, gives an interesting insight into the Grail story. In spite of the Christianizing glosses, Galahad and the Grail remained too pagan, too shamanic at heart, to become significant features in orthodox Christianity. Let us look at each of these Grail seekers individually.

Perceval is born of noble blood; the Fisher King is his grandfather. But the boy is raised in obscurity in the forest by his widowed mother and grows up as ignorant of his bloodline as he is naive about civilization beyond the edge of the forest. He bungles courtly etiquette and is an alien in the world of chivalry. Perceval has been called the "perfect fool," an epithet that renders him a prime candidate for shamanhood, since he begins his journey with eagerness, openness, and curiosity, willing to accept whatever befalls him. He sets off on his quest dressed in fool's clothing, perhaps appearing like the Fool in the Tarot deck, his worldly possessions in a small bundle carried on a stick over his shoulder, his eyes fixed on the sky, his foot about to step off a cliff. Indeed, he does not anticipate the future or seem to mind where fate might lead him, whether to the brink of an earthly precipice or to the edge of what he believes is reality.

Perceval finds the Fisher King, sees the Grail and Lance, fails to ask the questions, and so must endure a lengthy series of adventures before he once again returns to the Grail castle. This time he asks the questions, the king is healed, and the land is restored. Shortly thereafter the king dies, a further indication that the king's wound was a psychic block to transformation, as it was a physical obstacle to earthly duties. Perceval succeeds him as the next Grail King. In one version of the story, Perceval inflicts a wound in his own thigh as penance for almost having succumbed to the seductions of a fairy woman who would have lured him away from his quest. Even in his wounding he becomes the Fisher King, and assumes his rightful inheritance from his grandfather. As a story of shamanic initiation, Perceval becomes the shaman, now with his own wound, and the power to heal and restore his kingdom. Had Perceval "fallen" into the arms of the fairy temptress, he would have mirrored Lancelot's fate as Grail seeker.

Lancelot was also raised in the forest, but by faery women or witches. He was idealistic and well-intentioned, but his tragic flaws were a consuming ego enamored of worldly fame and a weakness for earthly love. By all accounts he was considered a "fallen man," a sinner, and therefore unfit to succeed in the noblest of enterprises, retrieving the holy Grail. On one adventure, Lancelot discovers the Grail chapel, looks in, and falls into a dreamlike state in which he sees a wounded knight ask to be healed by the Grail. The sacred cup appears, and the knight kisses it and recovers. Confused and disoriented, Lancelot is not sure whether he is dreaming or awake. In shamanic terms he doubts or rejects the otherworldly reality of the vision by trying to explain it in ordinary reality terms, so he wonders if it is a dream or if it is real. Of course, the vision cannot be contained in terms of ordinary reality, and proof of this is that Lancelot is stricken immobile. He cannot walk and is caught, like the Fisher King, between two views of reality, without receiving the shaman's gift of ecstasy, the ability to function in both realities as a "walker between the worlds." This is not the only time Lancelot has a vision that he does not understand. He forever lacks the ability to interpret his own visionary experience. He remains a would-be shaman, unfit for true visionary work, blinded by a love of worldly fame and his physical love for Guinevere.

Ironically, it is Lancelot's love for Arthur's queen that begets the perfect knight for the Grail quest. At the Grail King's castle Lancelot makes love to the princess Elaine, who, unbeknownst to him, is under an enchantment to make her look like Guinevere. Thinking he is with his own true love, Lancelot sires the truest and purest knight who will succeed beyond all others: Galahad.

Thus Galahad is born of the Grail Family, and like Perceval, is ignorant of his true heritage. Before arriving at Camelot, Galahad draws a sword from a stone floating in a river, similar to Arthur's feat, thus bestowing upon him a certain legitimacy. In Arthur's case, it is to be rightful king of England; for Galahad, it is to sit at the Round Table in the Seat Perilous, reserved for the noblest knight of the realm. After many adventures, Galahad finds the Grail and heals the Wounded King with blood from the Lance, and then takes the sacred objects to the Holy City of Sarras where he looks inside the Grail and beholds the sacred mysteries of the Otherworld. He immediately dies, and angels whisk his soul off to heaven. The Grail is then withdrawn from earthly view by a heavenly hand, and it is no longer present in ordinary reality.

The story makes an explicit statement about visionary experience in the Christian era. The natural world is an inhospitable environment for sacred mysteries. In Galahad's fate, the dualistic worldview that separates the sacred and the profane triumphs over the shamanic—and Celtic—notion that the two coexist. The moral is clear. Once a mortal sees the structure of nonordinary reality and its sacred mysteries, he cannot continue to live an earthly life; he must depart the physical realm and go to heaven. Neither the Grail nor the shaman can remain here.

The Grail Quest represents a private, personal journey for enlightenment and power. It is fundamentally a shaman's quest, not the path for Catholic saints. Relying on visionary experience and miraculous/magical adventures with otherworldly beings of ambiguous morality, the seeker enters a world too loosely structured for the rigid dichotomies that were fast characterizing Christian thinking. The Grail world contains shapeshifting powers, where friendly foes become foelike friends. It is the true world of the unconscious, where the conscious mind's binary categories fail to explain reality. Black and white, good and bad, ally and enemy, sacred and profane, are not easily distinguished. The Grail is a cup, not a box. There are no separate corners for saints and sinners. On the contrary, the Grail, like its pagan antecedent, the Cauldron of Mystery, contains a heady, hallucinatory brew of seekers, fools, risk-takers, failures, and fighters. Its healing power satisfies each person in terms of what he or she needs most for self-discovery. If we dare to look into the round, spherical vessel of the Grail, we become, like its contents, stirred, mixed, and intermingled, losing our sense of separateness. For ultimately, that is the lesson of self-discovery; we are not separate, but part of the whole.

Arthur: A Shaman-King

The origins of King Arthur remain mysterious. Since the life of Arthur was recorded in the twelfth century, it has attracted, like a magnet, folktales, myths, and legends from several cultural and literary sources. It continues to do so. In fact, Arthur, like the Grail, is a haunting figure in Western consciousness, a malleable hero who can serve many causes, inspire many hopes and dreams. It is not surprising, therefore, that this quasi-historical Welsh hero and the stories told about him should reflect so dramatically the major concerns of essential shamanism and the Celtic strains of shamanic lore. The "once and future" king, whose earliest beginnings may have been in the mind of a shaman, is a pivotal figure in the history and fate of Western European shamanism.

The "original Arthur" (if there was one) was probably a Welsh warlord of the fifth century A.D. or a composite hero made up of the adventures and exploits of several Welsh chieftains. When the stories about Arthur assume their literary shape, it is clear that the core epic has absorbed much of pre-Christian mythology—stories that reveal many aspects of shamanic thinking that we have already recognized as indigenous to older Celtic spirituality.

In the oldest Welsh tales, for example, Arthur possesses amazing supernatural qualities similar to those of solar deities and the same magical/
shamanic powers that we find in various shamanic traditions. Even Arthur's
name derives from *Art* or *bear,* suggesting at one point he may have been
the semidivine son of the Welsh bear god Artaius, or a theriomorphic god
himself. The bear may have become a power animal when, in the course
of many tellings and retellings of Arthur's adventures, the god-hero "lost" his
divinity and was "reduced" to a mere mortal shaman-hero. Later, as the tales
about him lost their shamanic flavor, he became an almost completely ordinary and human hero, and the only remaining trace of the bear power was
in his name.

In one of the earliest Welsh accounts, Arthur conducts an otherworldly raid into the Lower World to steal the Cauldron of Immortality,
which brings the dead back to life. On one level this journey is a shamanic
initiation in which Arthur acquires knowledge and experience by storming
seven fortresses or realms in the Otherworld. This type of journey through
multiple levels—often seven—is a common initiation trek for shamans. We
can interpret the multilevel structure of the Otherworld to reflect the need
for the initiate to encounter nonordinary reality from many different perspectives. Also, various levels or regions would impress upon the neo-
shaman that the Otherworld is multidimensional and that the cosmos
greatly exceeds our very limited perceptions of it. Arthur succeeds in his
quest (although losing many companions along the way) and brings back
the Cauldron and with it the power to restore life. The Cauldron suggests
the shaman's power to retrieve souls from the Land of the Dead.

In the Welsh tale of *Kulhwch and Olwen,* Arthur is portrayed as a type
of faery king with companions who share the same semidivine powers we
found in other mythological heroes, powers often attributed to shamans.
For example, one companion who is clairaudient can hear an ant fifty miles
away. Another can see a fly in Scotland from as far away as Cornwall. Both
these skills indicate the shaman's intimate knowledge of the natural world
and the ability to transcend ordinary geography. One warrior can walk over
the tops of trees and run through the woods and not break a stick or blade
of grass. Another can leap 300 acres at a single bound. One knight can move

so fast no human or animal can catch him (another indication of the power to fly, or to become invisible). One of Arthur's closest companions, Kai (whose character survives into later versions), possesses the shaman's heat. When he walks through the rain, whatever he carries stays dry. On cold days, the fire from his body keeps other men warm. Two other faery companions represent the extremes of beauty and ugliness, one being incredibly hideous, the other so wondrously beautiful he is thought to be an angel.

One of Arthur's original companions possesses a short dagger that becomes a bridge when laid across a river or torrent. The bridge between this world and the Otherworld is frequently described as being sharp, narrow, dangerous, or slippery, implying that anyone not worthy of entry will fall off and be killed. Spirits and angelic beings, of course, have no problem crossing such a bridge, nor would a shaman. Today among modern practitioners of witchcraft, the short dagger, or athame, is still used as a ritual tool to bridge the worlds. Witches use it to cast a circle or create sacred space by drawing or cutting the designated space in the air. The area within the circle is considered to be neither in this world nor the Otherworld, but a place between the worlds, a bridge between nonordinary and ordinary reality.

There are also indications that Arthur's knights attracted certain animal powers to them, much like Finn's men. Sir Owain had a lion, Sir Gawain a mule or horse that conducted him into otherworldly adventures. Even Arthur himself is depicted seated on a goat, surrounded by a collage of animals, humans, and zodiacal signs, in a mosaic in the Otranto Cathedral in Italy. Is the artist trying to link Arthur with the Animal Master? Does the melange of human and animal figures, along with the beasts and deities of the zodiac, suggest that Arthur has power over the realms of spirit, animal, and human, both on earth and in the heavens? What is the nature of Arthur's realm?

THE WONDERS OF CAMELOT

Many characteristics of Camelot have a faery or otherworldly quality. A brief description of the more prominent aspects and personalities of Arthur's realm will give us some insight into his magical kingdom as a place where the perilous journeys begin and end for the "knights errant."

Arthur's sister Morgan la Fay is a faery queen (la Fay means "the faery"). With eight other faery women, sometimes referred to as nine witches, she guards the Cauldron of Rebirth. She is described in a medieval text as having "learned the use of all plants in curing the ills of the body. She knows, too, the art of changing her shape, of flying through the air."[5] We can recognize in Morgan the skills and talents of a shaman, the same qualities that would later be attributed to witches. The figure of Morgan can be traced back to specific Celtic goddesses: Matrona, a mother/river deity, and the Morrigan, three Irish war goddesses. In the earlier versions of the Arthurian epic, she is portrayed as a faery godmother or benign enchantress who gives Arthur gifts and powers. Later Christian romancers transformed her into an evil witch and troublemaker, a seductress who ultimately contributes to the fall of Camelot.

The wizard-druid Merlin, Arthur's intimate advisor, has faery blood on his father's side and possesses many shamanic powers, including the ability to pass back and forth between the worlds, to see into the past and future, and to shapeshift. Since no one ever knows his real age, he is sometimes portrayed as a young man, sometimes a white-haired sage.

The name Merlin in Welsh is *Myrddin*, which is more of a title than a name for an individual person. It has been interpreted to mean a "spirit of inspiration," perhaps a form for an even older god of inspiration. In this sense, then, we begin to see how legends of Myrddin (or *a* Mryddin) building Stonehenge make mythological sense. The stone circle is from the gods; indeed it is an entry or portal to their Otherworld, a place of inspiration. Merlin is as much Arthur's spirit guide as he is the king's spiritual adviser. He functions as a spirit or shaman rather than a priestly confessor.

Before Merlin is reduced to a merely sly court magician in medieval romances, he is a shamanic spirit guide and manipulator of ordinary and nonordinary realities. He arranges Arthur's birth through magic, and steals the young baby away to be fostered and educated in metaphysical mysteries as well as the traditional warrior skills. He builds the Round Table for Arthur's father, Uther, on whose death it passes to Guinevere's father, Leodegranz. Guinevere, whose name can be translated "white shadow" or "white faery," brings the Round Table to Camelot as her dowry. Thus the

Table is faery-built, faery-guarded, and a faery-gift. Merlin himself says it is meant to represent "the roundness of the world." It is an object of power whose roundness or completeness demonstrates the totality of creation. The Round Table is an *axis mundi*, a Center of the World. It replicates the Wheel of Life and the Web of Universal Power and Energy.

According to one legend, Merlin modeled Stonehenge after the "Starry Table" of the night sky. Thus we find at Camelot three tables: the Table of the Stars (the sky and cosmic design), the Table of the Land (the earth, the natural world), and the Table of Knights (the world of human endeavors). These three "round tables" parallel the shaman's three realms of Upper World, Lower World, and Middle World. The presence of the Round Table makes Camelot, in Geoffrey Ashe's words, "a place of the imagination,"[6] rather than a historical or geographical place. It is a twilight realm bridging the Otherworld of spirit and this world of human aspirations. Camelot unites the best of the natural world and human creation beneath the celestial powers of the sky and the zodiac. At Camelot the beauty and order of the universe can flower.

We have a choice of episodes that account for Merlin's withdrawal from the earth. The newer, Christian versions attribute his downfall and death to sensuality and sorcery. A seductive protégé uses her magic to trap Merlin in a cave or tree. A more pagan and older Celtic version casts no slur on magic or sensuality, like the later retellings, but explains the disappearance of Merlin to his voluntary retirement to an *esplumoir*, a somewhat obscure word that can be interpreted as a "moulting cage" where hawks shed their feathers. Perhaps Merlin, like an elder shaman, quietly withdrew to change his feathered shaman's robe for some other spiritual uniform. Still other interpretations of the legend have him sleeping on the Isle of Bardsey off the northwest coast of Wales, or alive in his house of glass along with nine companions, the thirteen treasures of Britain, and the true British throne. It is said that Merlin, like Arthur, will return whenever the world needs him.

Arthur's sword Excalibur was a gift from the Lady of the Lake, a female guardian of the Otherworld. Forging Excalibur was undoubtedly the work of shamanic metallurgists in Avalon, perhaps the goddesses themselves. The

famous sword is both a power object and a helping spirit. From the shaman's point of view, it is the energy (or spirit) in an object that gives it its
power, and since the energy in all created things is the same substance
(mana, manitou, magic, etc.), every object can be perceived as a conscious
entity containing a spirit. Thus Excalibur is as much a spirit helper (in a shamanic sense), as it is an object with magical power (in the faery tale sense).
On his death, Arthur orders the sword to be thrown back into the lake,
since its power was a gift from the Otherworld and should rightfully be
returned there once Arthur's earthly life is completed.

The medieval accounts of Camelot, Arthur, and the Fellowship of the
Round Table strongly suggest that, near the end of his earthly life, Arthur
is himself the Wounded King, an ineffectual ruler, and a dysfunctional shaman. The marital rift between Arthur and Guinevere over Lancelot pre-
vents the king from fulfilling his sacred duties as husband. Guinevere, the
human representative of the Celtic Goddess of the Land, is childless. A malaise, or soul sickness, hangs over the court. Arthur lacks the courage or will-
power to search for the Grail, so he sends his knights in his place, a decision
that leads to the downfall of his kingdom. Most of the knights never return,
and those who do are broken, disillusioned men. Like the Fisher King waiting for the young innocent knight to come and heal him by asking the Grail
questions, Arthur mopes around Camelot, waiting for salvation. But the
knight who brings it is the dark son, Mordred, and salvation is not health,
but death.

THE DAMSELS IN DISTRESS

Most of the knights of the Round Table do not find the Grail, but they
do encounter perilous adventures on their journeys, frequently involving
young maidens held prisoner by evil knights. Who are the "damsels in dis-
tress," and what insights into Celtic shamanism do they provide?

In one version of the Grail story, the Fisher King's realm is a Waste
Land because the wells are dry and the maidens who guard them have
been abducted by wicked knights. The priestesses of the land, the goddesses of fertility, have been raped and violated. Before their abduction,

the maidens refreshed travelers with food and drink served in golden cups filled with sacred water from the well. When you drank from the cup, you received health, blessings, and power from the Otherworld, the gift of strength or courage you most needed. One day the evil King Amangons stole the cup from a well, carried off the maiden and raped her, and thus set an example that was followed by other knights at other wells. As the legend describes it, the land "lost the voices of the wells and the damsels that lived in them."[7]

What does it mean to say that the women lived "in" the wells? Obviously spirits and faery folk can live wherever they want, but what is the point of living in a well? The image often appearing in the texts as *well* has broader shamanic significance than what we commonly mean today by the word. In some versions, the word used is *puis*, meaning, in addition to well, a burial mound, a grotto, and a spring. The word is the root of the French term *puissance*, the feminine term for power. Our limited image of a well as a simple shaft sunk into the ground and containing water is, in the Arthurian world, a faery complex consisting of an entry into the Otherworld, healing waters, the Celtic nemeton or sacred grove, a darkened chamber in which shamanic initiation rites may have taken place, even a burial site, possibly a reliquary with severed heads. It is a veritable Celtic theme park vibrating with the same feminine energy and goddess spirituality found in earth-centered ceremonial sites in other lands.

The full tragedy behind the rape is the violation of an entire spiritual system. When the legend tells us that the "voices" were silent, we get a glimmer revealing the broader function of these important women. They were oracles, soothsayers, channelers, who may have used visionary states to answer the questions of seekers who came to them, in the fashion of the Oracle at Delphi.

From a metaphysical point of view, the knights' mission was more than the rescue of abducted women. It was an otherwordly journey to bring back the old religious practices and reinstate the female shamans at their sacred entries into the Otherworld. The reason the earth is dried up and dying is that something has been wrongfully stolen from nature. The land has lost its soul.

Metaphorically, the abducted women also represent the human soul. In psychological terms, their imprisonment in a high tower or a deep dungeon reflects the ennui and weariness of the person whose own soul is dried up or lost, whose life is going nowhere. Emma Jung and Marie Louise von Franz say, "The fairies and maidens in the hills . . . are, as it were, the soul of the spring or tree or place and, equally, *what man feels psychically in such places.*" (Italics mine)[8] As shamans understand it, the earth contains places of exceptional power where the human soul is infused with cosmic energy, places where the soul of the person and the soul of the universe meet. Instinctively we sense the power of these places when we enter them, even though we cannot always articulate the reasons for the shift in our sense of well being, the tingling sensation we might feel in our bodies, or the altered quality of consciousness that overtakes us there. We simply feel, as some describe it, more whole, more complete, more ensouled.

This brings us back to one of the shaman's primary healing services: soul retrieval. In *Soul Retrieval: Mending the Fragmented Self,* Sandra Ingerman relates that soul loss and/or soul retrieval ceremonies can be found in Siberia, Central Asia, Indonesia, China, India, North and South America, the Philippines, Northwest Africa, New Guinea, Melanesia, and Australia.[9] The concept is almost universal. In her own work as a shamanic counselor, Ingerman has discovered that people intuitively sense a fragmentation of soul and a corresponding loss of soul parts after a traumatic event such as divorce, rape, war, child abuse, death of a loved one, or serious illness. Ingerman's pioneering work as a teacher of soul retrieval methods is making the shamanic model a viable healing option for contemporary spiritual counseling. Traditional shamans would understand the value of her work because, as Mircea Eliade notes, the shaman is a "great specialist in the human soul; he alone 'sees' it, for he knows its 'form' and its destiny."[10]

In the vast literature on shamanism, there are widespread stories of soul loss as a cause of sickness or madness, and the necessary journey on the part of the shaman to retrieve the lost soul and restore life to the sick or dying patient. The madness of the neophyte shaman is also a kind of soul loss and retrieval, with the young initiate receiving his new or transformed soul (vision) from his or her helping spirits or from older shamans in the community. In shamanic societies, it is the business of the shaman to locate and bring back lost souls from nonordinary reality where they may have strayed or been stolen for, as Mircea Eliade puts it, "only [the shaman] can see and capture souls."[11] Perhaps the absence of shamans in modern Celtic cultures and elsewhere in the Western world helps to explain why people who have spontaneous shamanic experiences in the form of faery sickness or who have "fallen into Faerie" become so frightened and filled with insecurity. There is no one trained in visionary journey-work who can help the sufferers find meaning and purpose in their otherwise bizarre experiences.

To return to the Middle Ages, Arthur's knights, indeed every knight who journeys to find the Grail or a kidnapped woman, is symbolically on a soul journey, a quest to discover some lost part of his own being that he desperately needs to be whole. Like the Wounded King, he is fragmented. But unlike the king who wastes away on a couch, or sits and fishes, hoping that a modicum of salvation will surface now and then from the unconscious, the knights retain the fierce confidence and power of the shaman to undertake the journey and recapture the soul. Depending on how we interpret the tales, the knights are either searching for their own souls, the souls of others, or the soul of the land itself.

Soul loss can mean several things. Typically it means the loss of our vital essence that leads to the death of the body. But it can also mean dispiritedness, loss of spirit or *elan*, depression in psychiatric terms, which can lead to physical illness. Loss of soul always suggests that something has been torn or stolen from the unconscious, from nature. Eliade describes it as a "rape of the soul."[12] The Grail quests and the perilous adventures of Arthur's knights are about soul retrieval, for the woman of the well or her cup will restore the fecundity of the land, the king's health, and the adventurer's sense of self.

The Once and Future Shaman

The disspiritedness of the Fisher King gradually swept across the medieval world as Christianity dissociated spirit from nature, thus causing the greatest case of soul loss in human history. The shamanic archetype was suppressed by the triumph of "Western Civilization," and we forgot, or lost hope in, one of the most persistent and life-affirming beliefs—the belief in shamanism. We forgot that it is a human talent to be able to pass between the worlds. We grew to mistrust all techniques of ecstasy and the knowledge acquired in trance states.

So disparaged did shamanism become in the Western mind, that when it was discovered again in the preindustrial cultures of Native Americans, Siberians, Africans, Polynesians, and others, it was not recognized as something akin to what our ancestors in Europe could possibly once have practiced themselves. The modern European superiority complex made it almost impossible to recognize European shamanic practices that survived into historical times; so assured were we that our ancestors were always superior to such "primitive" religious activities and beliefs, and so certain were we, as Christians, that all native, pre-Christian spirituality was devil worship. Witness the continuing belief held almost universally in the West that witchcraft (and modern Wicca) is satanism.

Gradually, today, our arrogance is being tempered, and we are beginning to find meaning and value in so-called "primitive" spiritual practices. In a sense, we are currently retrieving the "soul of shamanism" and are even now grafting it back onto the Western psyche. Perhaps the journeys into our shamanic heritage will lead us to a new wholeness, with ourselves, with each other, and with the earth.

8

DEATH: THE CENTER
OF A LONG LIFE

We just may have to accept the notion that absolute death does not exist. Modern scientific research supports psychologist Sandor Ferenczi's suggestion that the germs of life may be present, although concealed, in human consciousness, or what he refers to as "the inorganic self." He writes, "In that case, we would have to abandon the question of the beginning and end of life once and for all, and see the whole universe, organic and inorganic, as an endless see-saw between tendencies of life and death where neither ever becomes sole ruler."[1] First-person accounts of near-death experiences (NDEs) also suggest that, at the moment of physical death, human consciousness begins a journey into a new and more radiant form of existence. In an extensive study of shamanism and near-death experiences, Holgar Kalweit concludes that what the dying (those who reach the brink of death and return) experience is not the same kind of place that theologians, philosophers, and poets have for centuries called the "realm of death," implying a radical break in consciousness with earthly existence. Kalweit believes, "There is no realm of death as such.

Instead, the Beyond consists of all those properties particular to our consciousness once it is independent of the body."[2]

The dying person, like the shaman, experiences a world composed of the same stuff of human consciousness as he or she knew "in life"; however, it is now experienced without the constraints of ego-consciousness, the "ego-blinders" the physical body requires to rivet attention on the body and its ability to manipulate physical reality for its own health and safety. Mircea Eliade has documented the rich literature on the shaman's contribution to the knowledge of death, the "funerary geography" the shaman explores on ecstatic journeys into the Otherworld.[3] In Eliade's words, "The unknown and terrifying world of death assumes form, is organized in accordance with particular patterns; finally it displays a structure and, in the course of time, becomes familiar and acceptable." This may be, in the final analysis, the greatest gift of shamanism to the history of human spirituality: the ability to find pattern and structure in death and to render it familiar and acceptable.

In this chapter we will look closely at the characteristics of the NDE and trace these components through the classic descriptions of the Celtic Otherworld, specifically in the mystical voyages to fabulous islands, in the haunting accounts of Avalon, and in the mysterious triple death that fascinated the Celtic imagination.

DEATH: THE DOORWAY TO ANOTHER LIFE

Those who survive NDEs acquire a radically transformed attitude toward life and death. With remarkable consistency, survivors lose their fear of death. They know from personal experience that there is another, friendlier universe waiting for them and that the issues of fear and control, which so mesmerize the ego, rapidly disappear when the soul dissociates from the body. Like the core elements of shamanism that recur with predictable regularity the world over, the descriptions of the NDE also contain core features, which not surprisingly correspond to many of the features of the shaman's journey.

The following are core features of the NDE (as enumerated by Kalweit) with their counterparts found in the visionary work of shamanic practitioners.

At the moment when consciousness separates from the body, the dying hear enticing sounds, often described as clicking, clacking, or rushing noises, sometimes followed by harmonious ringing or wondrous music. These acoustical conditions, which are functionally similar to the sonic driving produced by the shaman's drums, rattles, and click sticks, signal to the soul that separation from the body is now possible. The sound mesmerizes and freezes the ego-consciousness, and in some way or other releases the soul, or that part of consciousness that survives the physical death. There may be some need on the part of consciousness to have this particular type of acoustical experience in order to depart the body and the ego-constraints that characterize its ordinary state.

In spite of shamanism's reputation for being a mysterious and esoteric activity requiring years of intense training, average men and women find it rather easy, even the first time, to journey while listening to shamanic drumming, and this includes people who previously complain that they "do not visualize well" or are unable to keep their attention focused for meditative work. They "ride" the drum, as Siberian shamans put it. As for the wondrous music of the NDE, music and song are regularly part of the shaman's journey, and in many cultures a particular song or chant becomes an individual shaman's special practice that triggers the altered state of consciousness and facilitates the journey. Faery music is almost a *sine qua non* for the Celts to journey into the sidhe, the Hollow Hills, and other regions of the Celtic Otherworld.

People in NDE situations report that they are singularly unimpressed with the activities they see going on around them while they are dissociated from their bodies. In hospitals, they seem unconcerned about the doctors and nurses operating on them or what people in the room are saying; even the pronouncement of death seems unimportant. Almost as if responding to the trivial pursuits of the living, the dying quickly experience weightlessness, and then float or fly off into a timeless-placeless realm. There are significant parallels here with the physical and social behavior of people undergoing the shaman's initiatory crisis and with the behavior and experiences of people "taken" into Faerie. The lack of concern with, even the inability to pay attention to, normal human activity characterizes those taken by the faeries, and as we have noted, this condition can last for a period of several years. They lose interest in life, their families, their jobs, the things that made up their normal daily lives. They seem to exist in a world of their own. Practically speaking, many take to their beds and remain there. To family and friends, they seem to act silly and strange.

Space and time as we are familiar with them in ordinary reality do not exist on the shamanic journey. Celtic traditions are filled with "time travelers" like Taliesin, Tuan Mac Carell, and druids who claim to have been present at the events of world history, even though far removed in time and place. Many dying persons experience this, but more commonly, it is the events of their own personal lives that rush before them. Everything seems to exist in a poignant present.

Another common characteristic of the dying is that as they look at their body from above or outside its physical shape, it grows diaphanous, foggy, gaseous, or misty. It becomes what the living often describe as ghost-like. The dying may even see it as an "energy field," according to Kalweit.[4] The body seems to fade and almost disappear. All this is congruent with shamans' descriptions of matter and energy, especially their perception of physical matter as filled with, or composed of, the same energy that pervades the universe. We have a hint of this same phenomenon in the many Celtic tales of faery beings, both humans and animals, that disappear in a mist or fog, or simply fade and vanish. The literary description (actually a cliche in faery tales) is that the animal or person "vanishes in the mist." But looked at from another perspective, the vanishing creature may be *turning into* mist because the gaseous state is a type of in-between state in which the energy, formerly solidified as physical matter, is returning to a purer state. Such occurrences in Celtic folk and faery lore are invariably the beginning of a journey into the Otherworld.

One of the most striking features of NDEs, one that is an important aspect of the shamanic journey, is the cave, hole, or tunnel that leads downward into the Lower World. Many commentators point out the similarities of this tunnel to the birth canal and the traumatic similarities between birth and death. The "light at the end of the tunnel" is, in fact, something that most human beings may have experienced at the moment of birth, and it is comforting to expect a similar passage when we are "birthed" into the next life. Most cultures have tales about the worlds that exist beneath or below the earth, and tunnels are obvious entries into those worlds. The faery mounds, the sidhe, the Hollow Hills, and the cracks in the side of mountains and hills that lure mortals are recurring motifs in the Celtic tales that most likely had their origins in the ecstatic experiences of their earliest shamans, reporting the NDE-like experiences of their otherworldly journeys.

Many NDE survivors encounter a river, bridge, causeway, or some type of barrier or obstacle that must be crossed to get into the Otherworld. Some report that they saw souls, apparently in great misery, struggling unsuccessfully to get across this frontier. Shamans' descriptions of their journeys frequently include barriers and obstacles, often a threatening body of water. The same seemingly insurmountable barriers occur in Celtic accounts of quests and journeys, often including the fight against an adversary who may be a mythical beast or an evil warrior or knight. Some people who practice the shamanic journey have "difficult" or "frightening" experiences too. NDE survivors find the journey peaceful and smooth; perhaps they are exempted from the struggle since it is not their "time" yet, or maybe there are some people for whom the obstacles will not be required. If we are correct in assuming that the Otherworld is composed of the same structures and patterns of consciousness as this world, it is reasonable to expect that a person will encounter his or her own fears and doubts in the Otherworld.

A brilliant and radiant light seems to be the most characteristic feature of the next world. The dying, like the shaman journeying through the tunnel, see it ahead as a beacon that draws them onward. The spirits that are met in the Otherworld often have a radiant, diaphanous quality. Some NDE survivors refer to them simply as "light beings." Invariably they are friendly, encouraging, loving creatures who make the traveler feel at home. Shamans, too, tend to have at least a few helping spirits composed of light or brilliant colors. An Irish mystic, interviewed in the early twentieth century, claimed to have distinguished various orders of light beings: "those which are shining, and those which are opalescent and seem lit up by a light within themselves." The mystic thought the shining beings were in a lower class, and the rarely seen opalescent beings were similar to the old Irish gods and goddesses.[5]

Finally, there is unanimity on the beauty and joyousness of the next world, in spite of the pockets of struggle and misery. The overall quality of the Otherworld is extremely positive. Visitors want to remain there, and often need to be told, usually by a light being perceived as superior to the others, that it is not their "time" yet, and they must return to the land of the living. Shamans concur with this description. Black Elk, for example, reported, "I could see a beautiful land where many, many people were camping in a great circle. I could see that they were happy and had plenty."[6] Essie Parrish, a Native American shaman, described the land she journeyed to as filled with the "beautiful things of the Earth, hills and fields and flowers and everything beautiful . . . on both sides of the road, flowers and flowers and flowers out of this world. And there is a white light at the center, while you're walking."[7]

From all accounts, NDE survivors and traditional shamans concur that the process of death opens a doorway into a radiant and infinitely appealing world. Their experiences strengthen the notion that we do not need to fear the universe.

Books of the Dead

Some cultures have produced written instructions on dying to prepare their peoples for the final passage into the next world. The Egyptian and Tibetan Books of the Dead, and the medieval European *ars moriendi*, are classic documents in the literature of death. In brief, Books of the Dead encourage the dying to accept the inevitable and to leave the earthly realms with composure as they enter a new mode of existence. The descriptions of the Land of the Dead, complete with landscapes, "physical" features, personalities who will meet and guide the soul, and the tests and obstacles awaiting the new arrival may be logical forms and structures based on human consciousness, but evolved to their natural extensions once freed from the limiting perspectives of the body and the ego. Such images, independent of three-dimensional realities, can grow to exaggerated proportions. For example, two widespread features that appear in many cultures' visionary descriptions of the next world are some forms of heaven and hell, which can be viewed as the two extremes of delight and misery extended to their ultimate conclusions. Or, NDE survivors may perceive some form of severe judgment and retribution, consequences that develop (again in an exaggerated form) from the natural regrets that occur on reviewing one's past life and realizing that there is no more time to rectify the harm one caused, make amends, seek forgiveness, or recapture missed opportunities.

Books of the Dead are most likely based on the journeys of shamans. In fact, Kalweit maintains that the reports of shamans and other cultural and mythic heroes concerning their journeys into the Otherworld "provide members of a culture from early childhood onward with psychological guidance and behavioral models which also help the dying to pass safely to a new realm of consciousness."[8] Whereas older cultures, like in Egypt and Tibet, put these models down in writing, contemporary American culture is reluctant to even speak about them. Our own culture attempts to deny death and dying and to shield real death experiences from our children. As a society we are unique in this aversion to discussing and dealing with death openly and consciously. We refuse to produce and offer concrete descriptions and instructions related to one of the most important moments, if not *the* most important moment, in each human life. Even our mainstream religions supply only vague information about the Otherworld, and often this is used as a threat or bribe to control the religious beliefs and worldly behavior of their congregations. To fill this gap in our knowledge and understanding of death, the first-person accounts from NDE survivors are rapidly becoming a valuable source of information about entry into the next life. Fast on their heels, however, are the visionary experiences of modern practitioners of core shamanism.

◆

THE CELTIC "BOOK OF THE DEAD"

It was well-known in classical times that the Celtic tribes did not fear death.[9] Diordorus quotes Posidonius as saying that the Celts believed "the souls of men are immortal, and that after a definite number of years they live a second life when the soul passes to another body." From Strabo's writing at the end of the first century B.C., we learn that the druids believed that "men's souls and the universe are indestructible, although at times fire and water may prevail." Caesar, ever squinting through the eyes of a militarist, suspected that the Celtic leaders devalued death as a cynical incentive to egg their warriors on to ever greater forms of reckless bravery. As he put it, the Celts are taught that "souls do not suffer death, but after death pass from the one to the other." Lucan, trying to understand the druidic doctrine of immortality, put it simply: Death for the Celts was "the center of a long life." In his classic study of druids, Stuart Piggot calls attention to how this doctrine was at such variance with the standard popular beliefs about the next life prevalent around the Mediterranean, especially with the Celtic tribes' closest neighbors, the Greeks, Romans, and Etruscans. The classical descriptions of the soul's destination from these cultures are dreary, glum, and dank, marked by gloomy caverns, desolate marshes, or a nerve-racking carousel of transmigrations through other animate life-forms. As we will see, these negative descriptions held no sway with the Celts.

In spite of all the discussion among non-Celtic observers concerning the druids' doctrine of immortality and rebirth, native Celtic sources say almost nothing about it. As Alwyn and Brinley Rees point out, Celtic literature is "strangely silent on the subject"; and yet the "earliest and most vivid 'visions' of a Christian Other World recorded in medieval Europe appeared in the Celtic West."[10] The fact that these descriptions did not contain imagery from *other* Christian sources indicates that individual Celts were having visions of heaven *on their own*, an important clue that shamanic experiences survived and were derived from more ancient Celtic practices that had not died out. All this reinforces the notion that shamanic visionary practices survived in medieval Europe and that they became the foundation for what the Catholic church later persecuted as witchcraft.

———

◆

But how do we explain the strange silence concerning life after death in the early literature of the Celtic peoples? One way to tease forth an answer from a question such as this is to turn the tables on the dilemma by assuming there *is* native literary material dealing with immortality, but like archeological treasures, it may be hidden beneath a later literary landscape. It may also be in shards and fragments. The Reeses did precisely that, and concluded that there are "tattered remnants of an oral Celtic 'book' of the dead."[11] They can be found in the tales about fantastic voyages to otherworldly islands. Taken as a whole, the fabulous voyages to enchanted isles are stories about the soul's journey through this life and into the next, and like the classic Books of the Dead, these voyage tales (*immrama* in Irish) offered the Celtic peoples a preview of the stages and experiences that make up the transition from earthly consciousness to whatever forms of consciousness await us in the Otherworld. Psychologically the *immrama* reassure the living that the pathway into the next world has been charted and at least partially explored. In effect, the territory of death has been mapped, and as in other archaic societies, the primary explorer and mapmaker is the shaman. Even though the heroes of voyage tales are not explicitly shamans, these accounts, like other myths and legends, were most likely composed of information originally reported in the ecstatic journey experiences of tribal shamans.

How many tales, voyages, and voyagers were originally in the oral literature we will never know. In the story of Bran, a faery woman tells him there are 150 islands, but he visits only two: the Isle of Joy and the Isle of Women. The voyage of Maelduin brings back information about thirty-three islands, which he or his men have visited. Teigue, son of Cian, sailed to only one island, but it was indeed wondrous with all the standard features of the Celtic Otherworld: apple trees; leafy oaks; hazel trees with lots of nuts; flowering fields; three faery mounds; the burial sites of Irish kings; ramparts made of silver, gold, and white marble; magical cups; and so on.

Collectively, the voyage tales (specifically the three Irish tales of Bran, Teigue, and Maelduin) present certain types of information relevant to the dying, and equally important, they alert the living as to what types of earthly experiences will impact on their fate in the Otherworld after death. In short, they tell the listener how to live now and what to expect later.

One type of information concerns abstract principles, similar to Plato's concept of Ideal Forms, such as Truth, Beauty, Justice, and so on. If the afterlife is composed of the elements of human consciousness released from materiality, then Plato's Ideal Forms are, in some sense, waiting for us after we die. Just as archetypal images structure the energy sources of the unconscious, the imagery of Irish wonder voyages (like the imagery of the shaman's journey) helps to structure the "stuff" of the next life. It is not surprising, therefore, that the next life is very similar to this one. So for example, on some isles the travelers are confronted by colors, elements, feelings, and the stages of human life. These are presented in the pairs of opposites that seem endemic to human thinking, such as black-white, male-female, youth-age, sorrow-joy.

On some islands the voyagers discover specific components of life isolated into environments or categories. For example, there are islands populated primarily by ants, birds, horses, trees, swine, sheep, men, women, fire, laughter, metals, and one island with only a cat. On some islands there are strange, monstrous mutants such as a horse with clawed feet; a beast that revolves inside its skin; a river that burns like fire; shouting birds; a fountain that pours water and whey on Fridays and Wednesdays, milk on Sundays, ale and wine on other feastdays; a watery rainbow with salmon swimming along it; and trees with huge intoxicating berries that produce deep slumber. On one island Maelduin and his men see a revolving rampart of fire leading to a doorway through which they can see beautiful people, clothed in luxurious attire, drinking from golden vessels, and listening to the most beautiful music.

What do these fantastic voyages to enchanted islands tell us about death and dying?

The *immrama* confront us squarely with the major dilemma of spiritual consciousness and of Celtic spirituality in particular: the incompleteness of human life. Spiritual consciousness is characterized by longing and questing, by an eternal dreaming about what lies beyond the horizon of ordinary reality. The origins of the world's religions and spiritual practices lie in the haunting sense that life is incomplete or illusory, and that the human personality is unfulfilled, and just possibly, incapable of fulfillment in this life. A larger, grander life exists somewhere else, in the Otherworld, in a timeless-spaceless realm that transcends the laws and structures of physical reality. Similarly, one's individual personality feels capable of other forms of identity and experience, forms that expand and enrich the human spirit, but are not possible under what we think of as ordinary conditions. At the heart of the spiritual quest lies the perennial question concerning the relationship of spirit and matter, or soul and body. Our longing and questing for completeness and wholeness restructures consciousness as we follow and explore the urge to be *somewhere* else and to be *something* else. I believe this is what Holgar Kalweit means when he says that "our spiritual consciousness unconsciously plumbs its own depths by exposing itself to situations that alter its inner structure."[12]

The shaman, more than others, risks this exposure. Why? Because in the shamanic journey, the shaman assuages these two longings, at least temporarily. In ecstatic trance the shaman *goes* somewhere else, and *becomes* something else. He or she visits the worlds that lie beyond the horizon of the imagination and becomes animals, plants, and other physical objects. The paradox is that in order to explore and shapeshift into any (or every) aspect of creation, shamans must partially "uncreate" themselves, or dissociate the soul from the body, or become spirit. In short, they must "die."

The island voyages of the Celts, in effect, alter consciousness so the heroes can experience the spiritual advantages of living under conditions that do not conform to the rules of ordinary reality. The fantasy islands confront the voyagers with the emptiness of life lived solely within the categories of ordinary consciousness, while they demonstrate the possibility—and the ultimate *im*possibility—of living outside those categories. This paradox may be the heart of human existence. For example, Maelduin and his men live for three months on the Island of Women enjoying tremendous pleasures and the vision of eternal youth, but it seems like three years to them and they grow tired of it. What they are learning here is that, yes, we can imagine life with unending pleasure and fun, and yes, this seems to be what we would logically hope for in our wildest dreams, but no, this will never satisfy us. As the Irish seafarers meet the constituent elements and forms of human life, they realize that as disembodied forms (pure misery, pure joy, pure laughter, pure pleasure, pure grief, pure sex), something is missing. *What* they are lacking may remain a mystery that can only be resolved in the next life.

Disentangling the many strands of human life, however, is the first leg of the voyage to a fuller understanding of the mysteries, not just of being human, but of the universe itself. Even body and soul must be disentangled from the illusions inherent in mortal existence. We need death, just as the shaman needs the soul flight into the Otherworld. Again there appears to be a curious irony: By disentangling the soul from the body, and by isolating the components of life into separate species, we are not faced solely with a chaotic swirl of unrelated parts, but with the opportunity to experience what psychologists call the "oceanic feeling" of being one with All That Is. This is what the shaman experiences on many shamanic journeys: the energy of the universe freed from material forms in which it typically resides so that the shaman's own energy can merge with it in its totality. At other times, on other journeys, the experience may be less inclusive, less ambitious in that the shaman merges with only one particular form of energy, such as an animal, a plant, a river, or the wind.

Collectively, the voyages drive home an important spiritual message: separate and recombine, or as the alchemists put it, *solve et coagule*. In shamanic terms, dismember and reassemble. On some islands the travelers find isolated human qualities and conditions, or animal species cut off from the rest of the animal kingdom; on other islands they find combinations appearing, at first, as monstrous hybrids of the natural order of things. To our question about the nature of reality, the voyages answer resoundingly: reality is multidimensional, the view from the shores of ordinary consciousness is extremely myopic and shortsighted, and there may be infinitely more ways to construct a universe and to begin the greater voyage of the soul to the Islands of Eternity than we realize.

The Reconciliation of Opposites

The separation of ordinary reality into its fundamental parts reveals the polarities inherent in human thinking. When a voyager, or the storyteller's listener, lands upon an island that appears to be dedicated to one particular aspect of human life, such as joy, sorrow, laughter, women, or whatever, he or she is confronted with one-half of a polarity. In one sense, the voyage is telling the traveler to learn as much as he or she can about this or that quality or condition. In another sense, it is saying that such a quality or condition is not the whole of human life, and in no respect is it the totality of the human soul. Put another way, an archipelago of experience, not a single island, is needed to decondition our ordinary view of reality, to experience both the richness of this life, and to glean an insight into the richness and variety of the next life. By experiencing distinct pieces of life, we become more acutely aware of the greater picture. Each island, and its experience, is like a piece of the puzzle.

The truth learned on each island is acquired not by philosophical speculation but by psychic experience. On each island, the visitor acquires the condition of that island more fully, or realizes the opposite condition absent from the island, but which the visitor brings within himself or herself. For example, on an island of chastity, represented by a fortress with a glass bridge, Maelduin and his companions are not readily welcomed. The glass bridge repels those who try to cross it. A beautiful woman also rejects them. As it turns out, the woman is determined to protect her virginity. When the men try to woo her for Maelduin, she promises to give them her answer the next day. Her answer is unequivocal: She, the island, the great fortress and its bridge of glass have all disappeared and the men are adrift at sea. In other words, humans bring their carnal desires onto the island of chastity and are repelled.

The incompleteness of island life is painfully acute. The islands are monochromatic reflections of isolated human desires, lacking the fuller context by which we realize the value of those desires. Often the missing context is the polarity that allows us to appreciate oppositional qualities such as night and day, joy and sorrow, activity and rest, and so on. At first glance, as the boat approaches the shore, life on a particular island may look incredibly attractive, but the incompleteness of the environment stirs some longing in the human soul for a greater wholeness, or perhaps variety, or the familiar polarity by which we can appreciate the truth and value of things. Visitors instinctively feel that it is wrong to stay on any one island; for paradoxically, in order to remain there, human consciousness would be adrift without the moorings of polarity, symmetry, and variety.

In any event, experiencing the voyages is a form of death therapy designed to mitigate the shock of discovering that life after death, although it may be composed of the material of human consciousness, will be significantly altered from what we may have supposed. The *immrama* prepare us to encounter familiar categories in unfamiliar settings and to accept the breakthroughs in human understanding that such encounters will produce. After we cross the ocean of death, we will be able to understand, perhaps even appreciate, a whole world organized around just half of a concept that seemed incomplete to us while in the body. Or maybe we will learn in a more dramatic way than we have ever learned in this reality that everything really does contain its opposite.

Even the dichotomy of spirit and matter may finally prove to be an illusion. The Cartesian revolution in Western thinking has made this dichotomy the backbone of the Scientific-Industrial Revolution for the last 400 years. We who are born into this era are programmed to assume this to be true, but the antagonism between spirit and matter is a relatively new idea in the history of human understanding. Ultimately, the solution to the problem of spirit and matter may be the ultimate prize, the longed-for wisdom of the Grail. For upon our answer to this question hangs philosophy, theology, science, technology, and art. If spirit and matter compose the primary dichotomy of human existence, what is their true relationship? How does consciousness relate to nature? Is mind separate from the rest of creation, or as the shaman discovers, does mind/consciousness participate *in* and *with* nature?

It is also possible that the point of the *immrama* is to encourage us to make the most of all aspects of human life while we are still alive, so that we do not come to the end of our lives and discover that we have not lived as fully as we could have. Salvation, enlightenment, or fulfillment after death may hinge on our having made the most of the opportunities (both negative and positive) presented to us in this life.

What the soul learns as it sails through the archipelago of isolated qualities, values, and human conditions is to "separate and recombine." In alchemical terms, dissolve and coagulate. In shamanic terms, dismember and re-member. Eventually, after enough journeys, enough islands, enough dismemberments, the journeyer will know all the possible combinations, and perhaps that is what we look forward to most in the next life. But in the final analysis, Books of the Dead are not studied in order to reach a particular destination or to achieve a specific body of knowledge, but to learn a process, a process wondrously realized by the analogy of the voyage, a mode of thinking based on openness and a desire for adventure. For if the dying soul is to make the final transition into the next life with grace and composure, it must be ready for anything.

JOURNEY AND SHAPESHIFT: PARADISE REGAINED

Ultimately what we do not know about death is where we will go and what we will become. Interestingly, these are the two questions that confront the new shamanic practitioner and even experienced shamans, although for the latter, the terrain and the transformations begin to take on a predictable routine. Repeated journeys into the Otherworld and shapeshifting experiences reinforce the shaman's worldview that everything is ultimately related and that personal power is available, through the assistance of helping spirits, to make the journeys and transformations successfully.

Earlier we looked at the Celtic "boasts" as expressions of the shamanic experience. "I am the wind that blows across the sea; I am a wave in the ocean." The wind, of course, creates the wave out of air, water, and motion. The elements and the dynamic interplay among the forces of nature are not alien to the Celtic shapeshifter and journeyer. The wonder voyages, as a rough and incomplete map of the Otherworld, hold out the possibility of continuing, after death, this emersion into the qualities and states of existence that will fulfill the human longing for wholeness. Whether there are universes beyond even the Otherworld with their own forms of fulfillment remains to be seen. But from the shaman's limited human perspective, to journey into the multiple dimensions of reality available even in *this* universe is a kind of paradise, especially as he or she becomes a "master" of the ecstatic state in which we can reach the outer dimensions of the cosmos.

Joseph Campbell calls the most ancient spiritualities "religions of identity" because, stemming from shamanic experiences of unity and identity, they sought to awaken in their devotees a realization that the Divinity is within each human being.[13] Clearly, in a state of ordinary consciousness, we do not fully appreciate the implications of this, but ancient spiritual practices, especially initiatory rites and various forms of trance-inducing meditation methods, even ritual drugs, attempted to foster this realization. When it occurred, it was like an awakening or an enlightenment, similar to the mystic's awakening to his or her union with the Divine.

Our ancestors experienced reality very differently from us. Whereas we have desacralized nature, they saw in the material universe divine powers. Whereas we think of Divinity as being self-contained, transcendent from matter, remote from physical creation, our ancestors saw Divine Power permeating the physical realm and manifesting in distinct forms or attributes. And responding to the old adage that we cannot know what we cannot name, our ancestors gave those divine forms and attributes manifested in nature specific names, of gods and goddesses. Thus they created the ancient pantheons that ruled over nature and human activity. In one respect the cynic's claim that we create the gods, rather than vice versa, is correct; but we create the lesser deities in order to appreciate more fully how Divinity (the Great God/Goddess or Spirit) is immanent in daily life. If it is true that we cannot *know* what we cannot name, it is equally true that we cannot *talk* to what has no voice. In some sense shamanism is a method for taking this process of creating and naming the gods and goddesses one step further and giving voice to creation. It is a means of releasing the human spirit from ordinary consciousness so that it can merge and communicate with the Divine Power in nature and realize how that Power permeates all created things, including the human spirit itself. Thus it becomes even more clear, from the shamanic journey into visionary states of consciousness, that these divine powers are really within each of us.

What the ancient mystery religions seem to have taught their initiates was that at death we take back these powers of the gods and goddesses. They become once again internalized aspects of our own divinity. At the moment of death or shortly thereafter, we reclaim our divine identity. In the Egyptian Book of the Dead, for example, the deceased soul boasts: "My hair is the hair of Nut. My face is the face of the Disk. My eyes are the eyes of Hathor . . . There is no member of my body that is not the member of some god . . . I am Yesterday, Today, and Tomorrow, and I have the power to be born a second time. I am the divine hidden Soul who creates the gods."[14] This last line is a haunting echo of the sentiment in Amergin's boast, "I am the god who fashions thought in the mind." Nor is the claim to encompass all time—the past, present, and future—far removed from Tuan Mac Carell's boast to have been present at the entire history of Ireland, nor is it alien to Taliesin's claim that "There is nothing in which I have not been."

In all cultures the myth of the Golden Age asserts the possibility that before time began human beings realized many, if not all, of these divine powers within themselves. They could talk with animals, fly, shapeshift, understand the secret life of nature; they were strong, healthy, happy, and immortal. Descriptions of this "original paradise" contain many details found in descriptions of the next world after death. Like the Wheel of the Seasons, the human imagination expects to come full circle, and we imagine life after death to be similar to what life was like before birth. We will be young, beautiful, wise, happy, and fulfilled, containing all the wisdom and power of which we are capable. When the shaman journeys, he or she re-enters that mythical time, and these primordial conditions are re-established.

There is a belief among the Irish that Ireland escaped the Fall from grace as depicted in the Judeo-Christian tale of Adam and Eve in the garden. The popular folk belief states that Ireland is the closest one will ever get to heaven while still on earth. Hidden within this notion lies an older belief, not foreign to pagan Celtic thought, namely, that "heaven" or the Otherworld is here on earth at the present moment, perhaps everywhere, perhaps only in certain sacred groves or spectacular regions of great beauty and power. But whether it is seen as universal or localized, the Otherworld is *here*. As the Celtic tribes were Romanized and Christianized, they lost much of their ancestral territory, such as sacred groves, graves, wells, springs, and mountains. It is not hard to imagine that as the Celts watched their lands being invaded by foreigners and foreign ideologies, the ancient Celtic faith that the world of creation contains the world of spirit would become localized in the one geographic region, the one *island*, where Celtic thought and culture survived most intact.

W. B. Yeats discovered the typical Irish peasant at the turn of the century still believing "that the utmost he can dream was once or still is a reality by his own door. He will point to some mountain and tell you that some famous hero or beauty lived and sorrowed there, or he will tell you that Tir-na-nog, the Country of the Young, the old Celtic paradise—the Land of the Living Heart, as it used to be called—is all about him."[15] What strikes us here in terms of shamanic sensibilities is not just the idea that "heaven is on earth," but that what is seen in dreams, or in imaginative revery, is vital information in visionary form, and that the vision is, in fact, a *fact*—a spiritual fact, not apparent to those who have lost this older, Celtic faith.

The Celts were never at a loss for descriptive terms for the Otherworld. Tir-na-nog means the Land of Youth. Other favorite terms were the Land of the Living, the Land of Promise, the Other Land, the Great Plain, the Plain Agreeable or Happy. In the Christian era, the Tir-na-nog became the Land of the Saints, but the old pagan paradise underwent only the slightest alterations. In *Adamnan's Vision*, it is still described as an island, still attainable only by a long sea voyage. Once there the visitor finds no pride, disease, falsehood, envy, or death; instead there is the "delight of every goodness."[16] There is also the wondrous music of magical birds and heavenly fragrances, redolent of apple blossoms.

As time went on, the Christianized versions of the Otherworld acquired the Catholic subdivisions of purgatory and hell. The birds are transformed into shrieking harpies with ferocious beaks and talons to torture sinners. There is no longer music or sweet perfumes, but wailing and shrieking as the wicked are punished for the transgressions of their past lives. But with or without the Christian glosses, the pagan belief that the Otherworld is here on earth, on some remote island across the sea, continued to fascinate even Christianized Celts. At some point, of course, orthodox Christianity triumphed over pagan beliefs. The doctrines that God was transcendant and heaven was nonphysical replaced the pagan faith in the immanence of God in all creation, and the belief that heaven, or the next life, contained human pleasures writ larger than the imagination could ever conceive. This gradual transition from pagan to Christian occurred in many places over many years. Perhaps it happened now and then as in the curious tale about St. Malo and Brandan, his mentor, who, even though they were Christians, set sail to find the actual pagan Otherworld. After several days, the waves drove them back to shore, and an angel appeared to tell them that if they sought a land of youth and happiness, they had best wait until death. In other words, you can't get there from here anymore.

AVALON

Of all the islands in the literature concerning the Celtic Otherworld, Avalon holds a paramount position in the Western imagination. The name is believed to be derived from the Welsh *Avallach*, meaning apple. The Irish called the Isle of Women, *Emain Ablach*, (another term for apple) because it was famous for the wonderful apples that grew there. Geoffrey of Monmouth describes Avalon: "The Isle of Apples was also called Fortunate Isle, because all the vegetation there grew naturally with no need of cultivation . . . the harvests were rich and the forests thick with apples and grapes."[17] It may seem strange to contemporary readers that the Celts placed so much emphasis on vegetation, particularly apples. Why apples?

We must remember that until trade routes were established with warmer lands to the south, northern Europeans had a very limited selection of fruit, sugar, and spices. For centuries after trade routes were opened, there were still no reliable methods of refrigeration to transport perishable commodities cheaply and in significant quantities. Only the wealthy could afford exotic fruits from the Mediterranean. The sweetness and fragrance of fruit, not to mention its delicate nature, made it a rare commodity. But the hardy apple grew naturally in the northern climate and seemed to be a gift from the Goddess herself. The apple tree was sturdy and predictable, the wood burned sweet, and the blossoms in the springtime turned an orchard into a veritable faeryland of color and fragrance.

Descriptions of Avalon call attention to the absence of pain, suffering, and the usual problems of human society. In the *Gest Regum Britanniae*, we read, "This island in the midst of the ocean was not affected by any sickness. There were no thieves or criminals, no snow, fog, or extreme heat. Eternal peace reigned. There were always flowers and fruits under their foliage. The inhabitants were without fault and always young. A royal virgin, fairer than the fairest, governed that island."[18] It is obvious from such descriptions that the Celtic Otherworld is not an actual Land of the Dead in the sense that other cultures imagine a place inhabited by souls of the departed and characterized by misery and an unbearable longing for the life that has ended. How radically different is the Celtic Otherworld, populated not by the dead, but by the living, by handsome, radiant beings whom the Celts have called by different names over the centuries: Gods, Goddesses, the Good People, the Gentry, the Faery Folk.

By calling the Otherworld "The Land of the Living," the Celts express their strong belief in the immortality of the human soul, that death is not the end, but a doorway into another kind of life. Avalon is the Living Land, the Summer Land, where people are young, happy, and free of worry. But is Avalon (or heaven, for that matter) meant to last forever? Celtic traditions seem to say that the world beyond death may not be permanent, that it, too, might only be the center of even further lives. We find this idea in the many tales admonishing visitors to the Otherworld not to get caught or stay there. Often the traveler is warned, for example, not to eat the food of the faeries, or be lured, as was Thomas the Rhymer, into the sexual entrapments of the Faery Queen. Sir Owain, who journeyed into St. Patrick's Purgatory, was told not to eat angel food because the result would be similar to eating the food of Faerie. If you eat the food, you stay.

Another insight into the perennial warnings against getting caught in the Otherworld, an insight quintessentially Celtic, is that there is always something wrong or unnatural about *staying* in the Otherworld. Even

Arthur is not expected to stay in Avalon forever. He will return when the world once again needs him. The Grail, too, does not remain in the invisible realms. It appears, brings its blessings, restores human strength and environmental health, then departs. Could this be an offshoot of a shamanic tradition of journeying to the Otherworld, but always for the purpose of returning to share one's power and knowledge with the living? The call to "come away" is not an escape, but a mission, almost shamanic in its implications, to bring back healing and wisdom. It is part of the Celtic spirit to bridge the "spaceless space" between this world and the Otherworld, to keep the lines of communication open, and not to burn even the Perilous Bridges behind you.

In the first century A.D., Pomponious Mela described an island off the Celtic coast that seems to have been a destination for spiritual seekers, but not a place where one remained. The island was ruled by nine women. We hear in his description traces of the Celtic description of Avalon, ruled by Morgan and her nine sisters. Pomponius Mela describes the women in very shamanic terms. He writes that the women "have the power to unleash the winds and storms by their spells, to metamorphose any animal according to their whim, to cure all diseases said to be incurable, and finally, to know and predict the future."[19] What is so intriguing about his account of these women's shamanic practice is that they "reserved their remedies and predictions *exclusively for those who had traveled over the sea expressly to consult them.*" (Italics mine.) We have seen that "traveling over the sea" or "going under the sea" is a common expression meaning to journey into nonordinary reality.

If the women bestowed their powers only on those who had traveled over the sea "expressly to consult them," then there must have been people who traveled over the sea expressly to consult with them. There must have been shamans. Exclusivity and intentionality are hallmarks of shamanism, setting it off from other forms of mysticism and visionary experience, for the shaman can journey where others cannot, and can do it at will, with intention, purpose, and success, all of which are implied in Pomponious Mela's description. He seems to say what shamans everywhere believe: that healing knowledge and predictions are *available*, that they are gifts from

helping spirits, and all it takes is the journey or voyage into the spirit world
to acquire them. From Pomponious's account, it would appear that there
was a tradition of this along the Celtic coast.

Avalon continues to shine in the Western imagination as a deep and
richly faceted jewel, illuminating the great mysteries of human existence. It
may have begun its own journey in Western spirituality as an island of
apples, or the alchemical workshops where priestesses forged Excalibur, or
the temporary resting place of Arthur, but Avalon is to Western imagination what Bali Hai is to the Polynesian—an image of perfection, a place of
perfect happiness, a state of being. It is the Western equivalent of nirvana.
It is the dream within our dreaming.

Can Avalon be located geographically? Many have tried, and failed, to
provide convincing evidence. Glastonbury in Somerset, however, remains
a strong contender, and even if the evidence is more whimsical than historical, there is good reason to treasure this age-old power spot in southwestern
England. Originally, the area was referred to as Summerland, a common
name for the Otherworld, suggesting the pleasantness and fecundity of
summer. At one time the area around Glastonbury was a marshy swamp,
and what today is a large hill with a ruined tower, or Tor, was once an
island, requiring a boat to reach it. It seems to have always been apple-
growing country, as far back as anyone can remember, and it still is.

An older Welsh name for the island at Glastonbury was *Ynys-Witrin*,
the Isle of Glass. Like metallurgy, glass making was originally considered a
magical skill, and for many centuries glass was an expensive and impressive
commodity. It is also possible that terms for glass and crystal were used
interchangeably, both having the wonderful properties of translucence and
sometimes the ability to splay light into the colors of the rainbow. Indeed,
many people, even today, consider crystal to be solidified sunlight with magical, healing powers.

Tradition claims that the first Christian church in Britain was built at
Glastonbury by Joseph of Arimethea, and so the site is intimately associated
with the Grail legends. The actual Tor is the remains of a medieval church
built to St. Michael, but even more ancient beliefs hold that the tower
stands above the entrance to the Celtic Lower World where Arthur and his

men quested for the Cauldron of Immortality. Thus Glastonbury seems to have always exerted a spiritual pull on the Western mind, from pre-Celtic and pagan Celtic times through the early Christian era down to the present.

Glastonbury continues to attract spiritual seekers, New Age enthusiasts, and modern followers of the occult and older pagan religions. The belief that it is, or was, Avalon, or the entrance to Avalon, keeps this ancient site in the forefront of mythic consciousness. Whether Arthur is buried beneath the Tor, whether at certain times of the year the mists return and the hill once again becomes an island, whether, as some have suggested, the remains of the prehistoric track winding around the hill to the top was at one time a labyrinth used for initiations into a pre-Celtic mystery religion, we may never know. But from a shamanic point of view, and from the perspective of Celtic shamanism, Glastonbury will remain a place wrapped in mystery where the world of time and matter meets the world of eternity and spirit. It is a place to begin the shamanic journey.

THE SHAMAN'S DEATH

Once, Merlin's sister, Ganieda, the wife of king Rhydderch, hoped to prove that her brother, who was going through his "madman of the forest" period, was a fool. This was her plot: She hired a young boy to appear in court on three different occasions. The first time he came dressed in his normal clothing. The second time he cut his hair and wore a disguise. The third time he appeared dressed as a young girl. On each appearance, Ganieda asked Merlin to predict how the boy would die. On the boy's first visit, Merlin predicted he would fall from a high rock. When the boy returned in disguise, Merlin said he would go out of his mind and meet a violent death in a tree. For the "young girl," Merlin foresaw a death by drowning in a river. Ganieda, delighted at her brother's apparent confusion, tried to persuade her husband, the king, not to trust Merlin's predictions, nor his disclosure that Ganieda was having an affair with another man.

Little did Ganieda suspect that years later, when the boy had grown up, he would indeed die a triple death just as Merlin had predicted. It happened this way. The boy, now a man, was hunting one day when his dogs startled a deer who led them on a furious chase up and down the side of a mountain. Caught up in the frenzied madness of the hunt, the boy spurred his horse faster than was safe for the rocky terrain. The horse stumbled, and the boy fell from the cliff and caught his foot in a tree limb that grew out over a fast-running stream. Suspended from the tree, and with his head underwater, he drowned. So Merlin had the last laugh with his sister.

When the Celtic warriors swore their oaths on the elements, they were risking a triple death of their own: by fire (from the falling sun and stars), by water (in the raging sea), and by earth (from earthquakes or landslides). In swearing thus, they may have been hoping to identify themselves with their chieftains, for the death of a chief, and later Irish kings, was always described as a triple death. Let us look at one kingly death, that of Diarmait, son of Fergus. Earlier in his life St. Ciaran prophesied that Diarmait would die from being wounded, drowned, and burned. The king, displaying that Celtic mix of pagan and Christian sensibilities, or simply hoping to hedge his bets, asked his druids what they thought of the matter. The first druid predicted "slaughter"; the second foretold "drowning"; the third said "burning." In spite of these concurring opinions, Diarmait scoffed at the prediction. But it too came true. Lured to a feast by a treacherous foe, Diarmait was killed after the foe hurled a lance through his chest while he was about to leave the hall. The king, stunned but not dead, re-entered the building, which had by this time been set on fire, so he dived into a vat of ale to escape the flames. But in vain. The roof beam fell on him and killed him. So how did Diarmait die? He was speared to death, drowned in ale, burned up in a conflagration, and crushed by a roof beam.

There is something peculiarly shamanic about the notion that the elements will be on hand to cause the death of a famous person. The animistic view that the wind, rain, stars, or sun takes an active interest in human life presupposes an intelligent, indwelling spirit in nature, and, in the individual elements of nature, a spirit responsive to human concerns. The shaman, of course, understands this well, for this mystical insight is at the heart of shamanic activity, and it explains the shaman's personal relationship with his or her power animal, the spirits of nature, and by extension, all of nature.

It is quite possible that the triple death was originally the shaman's death, and only later attributed to kings and heroes. For in causing the shaman's death, the elements of nature symbolically announce that they have closed the three worlds in which the shaman journeys. The worlds are now hostile; the journeying is over. The Upper World of stars and sky falls upon the shaman's head. The Lower World beneath the sea rises up to drown the shaman. The Middle World cracks open and swallows the shaman. There is to be no more "walking between the worlds." The shaman becomes a person without a spiritual country.

And yet how fitting that the regions of the shaman's otherworldly journeys into nonordinary reality serve as the midwives of the shaman's birth into the next life, providing the final passage for this last journey. The triple death closes off the elements of nature once and for all, so the shaman is forced to go farther than on any previous journey of the imagination. Now the shaman must truly go beyond the upper and lower regions of nature, even beyond nature herself, beyond creation, seeking the journey for which all the others were preparation—the Journey into the Great Beyond.

The triple death has haunted the Celtic imagination for good reason, for the Celtic imagination is intensely shamanic. On some level of consciousness, the Celtic spirit knows what the shaman knows: that beyond the beauties and terrors of the three worlds of nature lies another world that is our real home; that as hospitable, stimulating, satisfying, and adventurous as nature has been for our earthly sojourn, it is not our final destination. The migration will and must continue, as we search for our place of resurrection. The destination called Avalon is always just beyond the reach of myth and memory. For in the final analysis, Avalon is not a geographical spot, nor a spiritual retreat from the hardships of life. It is the song of hope in the human heart calling, "Come away, come away."

EPILOGUE

THE LURE BEYOND
THE ENDS OF THE EARTH

Patty Flynn, an Irish storyteller at
the turn of the last century, lived in a leaky little one-room cabin in the village Ballisodare, which he described as one of "the most gentle" faery places
in the whole of County Sligo. W. B. Yeats, who knew Flynn, described him
as "a great teller of tales [who] knew how to empty heaven, hell, purgatory,
faeryland, and earth to people his stories." [1] He could "mix heaven, hell,
purgatory, and faeryland together, or even to set the heads of beasts to the
bodies of men, or thrust the souls of men into the heart of rocks." Yeats
found him on occasion cooking mushrooms for himself, or "asleep under
a hedge, smiling in his sleep," a description that could indicate a trancelike
state for this "little bright-eyed old man" who had, according to W. B. Yeats,
"the visionary melancholy of purely instinctive natures and of all animals."

Was Paddy Flynn a shaman? He might very well have been, using his
mushroom meals and ecstatic sleeps beneath a hedge to journey into the
Otherworld where he found his Catholic realms of heaven, hell, and purgatory, and the older pagan realms of the Irish faeryland, and where he
learned to put animal heads onto human bodies and to discover how the

human soul could enter the consciousness of rocks. Paddy Flynn journeyed shamanically into nonordinary reality and shapeshifted into the spiritual forms of other natural phenomena. Then he returned to tell entrancing stories of his journeys.

The Celtic spirit has always been alive to the possibility of sharing and becoming conscious with the spirit of other places and creatures. Amergin's boast is inherent in the Celtic scheme of things: "I am the wind that blows across the sea, I am a wave of the deep, I am the stag of seven battles, I am the hawk overhead." It is a boast of travel to enchanted isles, magical lands, the secret places deep in the Hollow Hills, and the private clearings in our souls. It is a boast of participating in the thoughts and feelings of all creation, as if human beings were kith and kin of rocks, streams, plants, stars, trees, animals, and gods and goddesses.

The Celtic spirit has persisted through time and space over many centuries, bridging the worlds of ordinary and nonordinary realities. In fact, the Celtic spirit thrives in that moment between the worlds when reality is as thin as gossamer and truth is as delicate as twilight, when day and night seem to fold gently into each other, and the world of Faerie and the world of mortals share a common terrain. Each time some faery voice calls, "Come away, come away," it lures the Celtic imagination into the borderlands of life and death, where we are haunted by the two most important questions in the history of the human spirit and, indeed, in the personal history of each man and woman: Where, at death, do we go, and what do we become?

In every culture men and women have wrestled with those two questions; and for the shaman, the answers are in the form of experience, rather than verbal statements. For ultimately, no one can tell us with certainty where we will go and what we will become after death. But the first-person accounts of shamans the world over attest to the experiences that await the person crossing the threshhold from this life into the next. We will journey into another reality; we will recognize our common heritage and share our common spirit with all of creation. The journey is into a state of consciousness that expands beyond the narrow confines of ordinary reality, beyond those walls of space, time, and ego that hedge our lives and over which we

◆

have such difficulty seeing and leaping. But the shaman knows how to escape those walls, how to spring free and find the worlds that lie just beyond the world of ordinary daily life.

W. B. Yeats said the Celtic people know how to "keep a little fire on our hearths and in our souls, and welcome with open hand whatever [may] come to warm itself, whether it be man or phantom." [2] Perhaps the Celts have kept their doors open to the spirits from the Otherworld because they have always harbored the strong belief that those spirits or phantoms were never far beyond the realms of everyday existence to begin with; and since they share so much with us already, it is foolhardy to try to keep them at bay.

The Irish mystic A. E. named the larger, expansive identity that we have in common with all created things, the "majestical Self," the infinite and eternal "It." [3] He wrote that in visionary work "we imagine ourselves into Its vastness. We conceive ourselves . . . as moving in all things, as living in all beings, in earth, water, air, fire, aether. We try to know as It knows, to live as It lives, to be compassionate as It is compassionate." A. E. called his own form of meditation a "fiery brooding" that expanded his imagination into the realms of spirit and energy familiar to shamans everywhere.

With remarkable consistency the shaman and the mystic of every century recognize the special flame of vision that illuminates the worlds beyond our ordinary realm of time and space. Each of us, if we are determined to mine the riches of visionary experience, can learn personal ways to journey into those Other Worlds and share in the spiritual knowledge of all created things. Accompanied by helping spirits, we pass through invisible doorways and partake of the Divine Power that transcends the mysterious bodies of animals, the fire in our heads, the soul of nature itself. Then in our journeying, we discover Amergin's ancient truth: We *are* the lure beyond the ends of the earth.

NOTES

Introduction

1. Caitlin Matthews, *The Celtic Tradition* (Longmead, Shaftesbury, Dorset: Element Books, 1989), 13.

2. Robert Van de Weyer, ed., *Celtic Fire: The Passionate Religious Vision of Ancient Britain and Ireland* (New York: Doubleday, 1991), 167.

3. Mircea Eliade, *Shamanism: Archaic Techniques of Ecstasy* (Princeton: Princeton University Press, 1964), 3.

4. Anne Ross, *The Pagan Celts* (Totowa: Barnes and Noble Books, 1986), 103–104.

5. Barry Cunliffe, *The Celtic World: An Illustrated History of the Celtic Race: Their Culture, Customs and Legends* (New York: Greenwich House, 1986), 156.

6. M. L. Rosenthal, ed., *Selected Poems and Two Plays of William Butler Yeats* (New York: Collier Books, 1962), 22.

Chapter One: Varieties of Shamanic Experience

1. Carlo Ginzburg, *Ecstasies: Deciphering the Witches' Sabbath* (New York: Pantheon Books, 1991), 103.

2. Joseph Campbell, *The Way of the Animal Powers* (London: Summerfield Press, 1983), 157.

3. Michael Harner, *The Way of the Shaman* (New York: Bantam, 1980), xiii.

4. Campbell, *The Way of the Animal Powers*, 156.

5. Eliade, *Shamanism*, 1.

6. Holgar Kalweit, *Dreamtime and Inner Space: The World of the Shaman* (Boston and London: Shambhala, 1988), 76.

7. Margaret Murray, *The God of the Witches* (London: Oxford University Press, 1952), 48.

8. Diarmaid Mac Manus, *Irish Earth Folk* (New York: Devin-Adair, 1959), 14.

9. W. B. Yeats, *Irish Fairy and Folk Tales* (New York: Dorset Press, 1986), 11.

10. Mac Manus, *Irish Earth Folk*, 180.

11. Lady Gregory, *Visions and Beliefs in the West of Ireland* (New York and London: G. P. Putnam and Sons, 1920), 63.

12. *Visions and Beliefs*, 37.

13. *Visions and Beliefs*, 66.

14. Joan Halifax, *Shamanic Voices: A Survey of Visionary Narratives* (New York: E. P. Dutton, 1979), 5.

15. Christopher Bamford and William Parker Marsh, *Celtic Christianity: Ecology and Holiness* (West Stockbridge: Lindisfarne Press, 1987), 126–29.

16. Eliade, *Shamanism*, 113.

17. *Shamanism*, 59–60.

18. W. Y. Evans-Wentz, *The Fairy Faith in Celtic Countries* (New York: Citadel Press, 1990), 236.

19. *Fairy Faith*, 345–46.

20. Halifax, *Shamanic Voices*, 49.

21. Kalweit, *Dreamtime and Inner Space*, 191.

22. John Matthews, *Taliesin: Shamanism and the Bardic Mysteries in Britain and Ireland* (London: Aquarian Press, 1991), 161.

23. Eliade, *Shamanism*, 510.

24. Joseph Campbell, *The Flight of the Wild Gander* (Chicago: Regnery Gateway, 1969), 157.

25. Eliade, *Shamanism*, 486.

Chapter Two: Shapeshifting, Severed Heads, and the Web of Life

1. This quote from Amergin and the following from Taliesin can be found in many sources. Translators take considerable latitude when rendering these texts into English. Both are quoted in Charles Squire, *Celtic Myth and Legend* (Newcastle: Newcastle, 1975), 123–24. The versions presented here are my own adaptations.

2. Ward Rutherford, *The Druids: Magicians of the West* (Wellingborough, Northamptonshire: Aquarian Press, 1978), 71.

3. Matthews, *The Celtic Tradition*, 108.

4. *Celtic Tradition*, 7.

5. Matthews, *Taliesin*, 283–85.

6. Evans-Wentz, *The Fairy Faith in Celtic Countries*, 377.

7. Alwyn Rees and Brinley Rees, *Celtic Heritage: Ancient Tradition in Ireland and Wales* (London: Thames and Hudson, 1961), 98.

8. Robert Graves, *The White Goddess* (New York: Farrar, Straus and Giroux, 1966), 13.

9. T. W. Rolleston, *Celtic* (New York: Avenel Books, 1986), 134.

10. Morgan Llywelyn, *Bard: The Odyssey of the Irish* (New York: Tor, 1987), 65.

11. Cunliffe, *The Celtic World*, 83.

12. Ross, *The Pagan Celts*, 121.

13. Halifax, *Shamanic Voices*, 73.

14. Marie-Louse Sjoestedt, *Gods and Heroes of the Celts* (Berkeley: Turtle Island Foundation, 1982), 74–75.

15. Proinsias Mac Cana, *Celtic Mythology* (New York: Peter Bedrick Books, 1987), 63.

16. Kalweit, *Dreamtime and Inner Space*, 203.

17. Harner, *Way of the Shaman*, 29.

18. Ross, *The Pagan Celts*, 121.

19. Cunliffe, *The Celtic World*, 82.

20. Ginzburg, *Ecstasies*, 208.

21. Stuart Piggot, *The Druids* (London: Thames and Hudson, 1961), 79.

22. Eliade, *Shamanism*, 245.

23. Van de Weyer, *Celtic Fire*, 170–71.

24. Rees, *Celtic Heritage*, 76.

25. Bamford and Marsh, *Celtic Christianity*, 12–13.

26. Joan Halifax, *Shaman: The Wounded Healer* (New York: Crossroad, 1982), 11, and Campbell, *The Way of the Animal Powers*, 169.

Chapter Three: The Edges of Twilight

1. Yeats, *The Celtic Twilight*, 47–48.

2. Alexi Kondratiev, "The Coming of Lugh," in *An Gael* (New York: Irish Arts Center, 1990), 11.

3. Harner, *The Way of the Shaman*, 9.

4. Rolleston, *Celtic*, 36–37.

5. Arthur Evans, *Witchcraft and the Gay Counterculture* (Boston: Fag Rag Books, 1978), 19.

6. Fred Fuller, "The Fool, The Clown, The Jester," in *Gnosis* (Spring 1991), 17.

7. Enid Welsford, *The Fool: His Social and Literary History* (Gloucester: Peter Smith, 1966), 326.

8. Yeats, *The Celtic Twilight*, 41.

Chapter Four: The Music of Enchantment

1. Kalweit, *Dreamtime and Inner Space*, 145.

2. Halifax, *Shamanic Voices*, 108.

3. Evans-Wentz, *The Fairy Faith in Celtic Countries*, 57.

4. Ruth Murray Underhill, *Singing for Power: The Song Magic of the Pagago Indians of Southern Arizona* (Berkeley: University of California Press, 1938), 6.

5. Halifax, *Shamanic Voices*, 32.

6. *Shamanic Voices*, 6–7.

7. *Shamanic Voices*, 33.

8. Evans-Wentz, *The Fairy Faith in Celtic Countries*, 118.

9. Eliade, *Shamanism*, 98.

10. Ross, *The Pagan Celts*, 89.

11. John G. Neihardt, *Black Elk Speaks* (New York: Simon and Schuster, 1975), 36.

12. Halifax, *Shamanic Voices*, 118.

13. *Shamanic Voices*, 75.

14. *Shamanic Voices*, 250.

15. *Shamanic Voices*, 182.

16. Evans-Wentz, *The Fairy Faith in Celtic Countries*, 40.

17. *Fairy Faith*, 298–99.

18. Donal O'Sullivan, *Carolan: The Life, Times, and Music of an Irish Harper* (London: Routledge and Kegan Paul, 1958).

19. *Carolan*, 160.

20. *Carolan*, 155.

21. Campbell, *The Way of the Animal Powers*, 98.

22. Eliade, *Shamanism*, 156–58.

23. Ross, *The Pagan Celts*, 129.

24. *Pagan Celts*, 270.

25. Van de Weyer, *Celtic Fire*, 155.

26. Bamford and Marsh, *Celtic Christianity*, 105.

27. Halifax, *Shaman*, 24.

28. Eliade, *Shamanism*, 480.

29. Van de Weyer, *Celtic Fire*, 150–51.

30. Bamford and Marsh, *Celtic Christianity*, 49.

31. Donald Sander, *Navaho Symbols of Healing* (New York: Harcourt Brace Jovanovich, 1979), 63.

32. Matthews, *The Celtic Tradition*, 103.

33. Bamford and Marsh, *Celtic Christianity*, 48.

34. *Celtic Christianity*, 54.

35. Rolleston, *Celtic*, 108.

36. Matthews, *Taliesin*, 140.

37. Halifax, *Shamanic Voices*, 69.

38. Rees, *Celtic Heritage*, 142.

39. *Celtic Heritage*, 331.

40. Ginzburg, *Ecstasies*, 230–66.

41. *Ecstasies*, 240.

42. Yeats, *Celtic Twilight*, 66.

43. Jack Maguire, *Hopscotch, Hangman, Hot Potato, and Ha Ha Ha: A Rulebook of Children's Games* (New York: Prentice Hall, 1990), 4.

44. Ginzburg, *Ecstasies*, 255–57.

45. Halifax, *Shamanic Voices*, 20.

46. Matthews, *Taliesin*, 80–81.

47. Ross, *Pagan Celtic Britain*, 288.

48. Rees, *Celtic Heritage*, 210.

49. *Celtic Heritage*, 212.

50. *Celtic Heritage*, 235.

51. Matthews, *Taliesin*, 130–32.

52. Van de Weyer, *Celtic Fire*, 209–11.

Chapter Five: The Soul of Nature

1. Piggot, *The Druids*, 80.

2. Halifax, *Shaman*, 9.

3. *Shaman*, 14.

4. Stephen Larsen, *The Mythic Imagination: Your Quest for Meaning through Personal Mythology* (New York: Bantam Books, 1990), 71.

5. R. J. Stewart, *The Mystic Life of Merlin* (London: Arkana, 1986), 212.

6. Evans-Wentz, *The Fairy Faith in Celtic Countries*, 17.

7. Halifax, *Shamanic Voices*, 251.

8. Evans-Wentz, *The Fairy Faith in Celtic Countries*, 227.

9. Cunliffe, *The Celtic World*, 90.

10. Matthews, *Taliesin*, 234.

11. Philip Carr-Gomm, *The Druid Tradition* (Longmead, Shaftesbury, Dorset: Element Books, 1991), 112.

12. Rutherford, *The Druids*, 67.

13. Piggot, *The Druids*, 108.

14. Quoted in Rutherford, *The Druids*, 67.

15. Kaledon Naddair, *Keltic Folk and Faerie Tales: Their Hidden Meaning Explored* (London: Century, 1987), 68.

16. Eliot Cowan, "Interview with an Irish Shaman," in *Shamanism: Quarterly of the Foundation for Shamanic Studies* (Summer 1992), 17.

17. Naddair, *Keltic Folk and Faerie Tales*, 69.

18. William Anderson, *Green Man: The Archetype of Our Oneness with the Earth* (London: HarperCollins, 1990), 45.

19. Ross, *Pagan Celtic Britain*, 137.

20. Timothy Taylor, "The Gundestrup Cauldron," in *Scientific American* (March 1992), 88.

21. Bamford and Marsh, *Celtic Christianity*, 125.

22. *Celtic Christianity*, 10.

23. Stewart, *The Mystic Life of Merlin*, 85.

24. *Mystic Life*, 38.

25. Eliade, *Shamanism*, 184.

26. Anderson, *Green Man*, 3.

27. John E. Pfeiffer, *The Creative Explosion: An Inquiry into the Origins of Art and Religion*, (Ithaca: Cornell University Press, 1982), 177.

28. Evans-Wentz, *The Fairy Faith in Celtic Countries*, 443.

29. James Bonwick, *Irish Druids and Old Irish Religions* (Dorset: Dorset Press, 1986), 239.

30. Stewart, *The Mystic Life of Merlin*, 143–44.

31. Jean Markale, *Women of the Celts* (Rochester: Inner Traditions International, 1986), 46.

32. *Women of the Celts*, 60–61.

33. Quoted in Bonwick, *Irish Druids and Old Irish Religions*, 241.

Chapter Six: Forest Folk

1. Serge Kahili King, *Urban Shaman: A Handbook for Personal and Planetary Transformation Based on the Hawaiian Way of the Adventurer* (New York: Simon and Schuster, 1990), 14–16.

2. Mac Cana, *Celtic Mythology*, 107.

3. Robert Jerome Smith, "Irish Mythology," in *Irish History and Culture*, ed. Harold Orel (University of Kansas Press, 1976), 17–18.

4. Mac Cana, *Celtic Mythology*, 107.

5. Sjoestedt, *Gods and Heroes of the Celts,* 104.

6. *Gods and Heroes,* 113.

7. Matthews, *The Celtic Tradition,* 82.

8. Rolleston, *Celtic,* 267.

9. Ross, *Pagan Celtic Britain,* 337.

10. Eliade, *Shamanism,* 154.

11. *Shamanism,* 154.

12. Murray, *The God of the Witches,* 59.

13. Rolleston, *Celtic,* 264.

14. Andras Corban Arthen, "The Witch as Shaman," in *FireHeart* (Spring/Summer 1989), 29–30.

15. Ginzburg, *Ecstasies,* 104.

16. *Ecstasies,* 155.

17. *Ecstasies,* 170.

18. Arthen, "The Witch as Shaman," in *FireHeart* (Spring/Summer 1989), 29.

19. Murray, *The God of the Witches,* 52.

20. Ginzburg, *Ecstasies,* 161.

21. Eliade, *Shamanism,* 175.

22. Pfeiffer, *The Creative Explosion,* 177–80.

23. *Creative Explosion,* 162–63.

24. Murray, *The God of the Witches,* 78.

25. *God of the Witches,* 92.

26. *God of the Witches,* 108.

27. *God of the Witches,* 110.

28. There is no evidence for a Europeanwide witch cult dating back into pre-Christian times, as Margaret Murray suggested. Critics point out that she overstated her case regarding the extent to which practitioners of the Old Religion and folk magic were organized into covens and associations. Obviously some witches were solitary practitioners. Many witches, then and now, practice a

craft that has only tenuous similarities with others. Here I am using the phrase, "witch cult," to mean the image of the witch in the popular mind, that is, the assumptions, whether true or not, in a given locality, that witches banded together for ceremonial work.

29. Eliade, *Shamanism*, 314.

30. Cowan, "Interview with an Irish Shaman," in *Shamanism: Quarterly of the Foundation for Shamanic Studies* (Summer 1992), 11.

31. Campbell, *The Flight of the Wild Gander*, 159.

32. Mircea Eliade, *The Quest: History and Meaning in Religion* (Chicago: University of Chicago Press, 1969), 115.

33. Arthen, "The Witch as Shaman," in *FireHeart* (Spring/Summer 1989), 55.

Chapter Seven: Perilous Journeys

1. Kalweit, *Dreamtime and Inner Space*, 88.

2. Mircea Eliade, *The Two and the One* (New York: Harper Torchbooks, 1965), 169.

3. Emma Jung and Marie-Louise von Franz, *The Grail Legend* (Boston: Sigo Press, 1986), 210.

4. *Grail Legend*, 194.

5. Matthews, *The Celtic Tradition*, 12.

6. Geoffrey Ashe, *King Arthur: The Dream of the Golden Age* (London: Thames and Hudson, 1990), 15.

7. John Matthews, *The Grail Tradition* (Longmead, Shaftesbury, Dorset: Element Books, 1989), 94.

8. Jung and von Franz, *The Grail Legend*, 204.

9. Sandra Ingerman, *Soul Retrieval: Mending the Fragmented Self* (San Francisco: HarperSanFrancisco, 1991), 78.

10. Eliade, *Shamanism*, 8.

11. *Shamanism*, 300.

12. *Shamanism*, 215.

Chapter Eight: Death: The Center of a Long Life

1. Quoted in Markale, *Women of the Celts*, 82.

2. Kalweit, *Dreamtime and Inner Space*, 67.

3. Eliade, *Shamanism*, 509–10.

4. Kalweit, *Dreamtime and Inner Space*, 4.

5. Evans-Wentz, *The Fairy Faith in Celtic Countries*, 60.

6. Neihardt, *Black Elk Speaks*, 170.

7. Kalweit, *Dreamtime and Inner Space*, 44–45.

8. *Dreamtime*, 71.

9. Piggot, *The Druids*, 113.

10. Rees, *Celtic Heritage*, 324.

11. *Celtic Heritage*, 325.

12. Kalweit, *Dreamtime and Inner Space*, 19.

13. Campbell, *The Flight of the Wild Gander*, 198.

14. *Flight of the Wild Gander*, 199.

15. Evans-Wentz, *The Fairy Faith in Celtic Countries*, 357.

16. *Fairy Faith*, 356.

17. Markale, *Women of the Celts*, 79.

18. *Women of the Celts*, 80.

19. *Women of the Celts*, 81.

Epilogue: The Lure Beyond the Ends of the Earth

1. Yeats, *The Celtic Twilight*, 3–4.

2. *Celtic Twilight*, 6.

3. A. E., *The Candle of Vision: Inner Worlds of the Imagination* (Dorset: Prism Books, 1990), 14.

BIBLIOGRAPHY

A. E. *The Candle of Vision: Inner Worlds of the Imagination*. Dorset: Prism Books, 1990.

Anderson, William. *Green Man: The Archetype of Our Oneness with the Earth*. London: HarperCollins, 1990.

Arthen, Andras Corban. "The Witch as Shaman." *FireHeart* (Spring/Summer 1989): 27.

Ashe, Geoffrey. *King Arthur: The Dream of the Golden Age*. London: Thames and Hudson, 1990.

Bamford, Christopher. "The Heritage of Celtic Christianity: Ecology and Holiness." In *Irish History and Culture*, edited by Harold Orel. University of Kansas Press, 1976.

Bamford, Christopher and William Parker Marsh. *Celtic Christianity: Ecology and Holiness*. West Stockbridge, MA: Lindisfarne Press, 1987.

Bonwick, James. *Irish Druids and Old Irish Religions*. Dorset: Dorset Press, 1986.

Campbell, Joseph. *The Flight of the Wild Gander*. Chicago: Regnery Gateway, n.d.

_____ . *The Way of the Animal Powers*. London: Summerfield Press, 1983.

Carr-Gomm, Philip. *The Druid Tradition*. Longmead, Shaftesbury, Dorset: Element Books, 1991.

Cowan, Eliot. "Interview with an Irish Shaman." *Shamanism: Quarterly of the Foundation for Shamanic Studies*, vol.5, no. 1 (Summer 1992): 4.

Cunliffe, Barry. *The Celtic World: An Illustrated History of the Celtic Race: Their Culture, Customs and Legends*. New York: Greenwich House, 1986.

Eliade, Mircea. *The Quest: History and Meaning in Religion*. Chicago: University of Chicago Press, 1969.

_____ . *Shamanism: Archaic Techniques of Ecstasy*. Princeton University Press, 1964.

_____ . *The Two and the One*. New York: Harper Torchbooks, 1965.

Evans, Arthur. *Witchcraft and the Gay Counterculture*. Boston: Fag Rag Books, 1978.

Evans-Wentz, W. Y. *The Fairy Faith in Celtic Countries*. New York: Citadel Press, 1990.

Fuller, Fred. "The Fool, The Clown, The Jester." *Gnosis*, no. 19 (Spring 1991).

Ginzburg, Carlo. *Ecstasies: Deciphering the Witches' Sabbath*. New York: Pantheon Books, 1991.

Graves, Robert. *The White Goddess*. New York: Farrar, Straus and Giroux, 1966.

Gregory, Lady. *Visions and Beliefs in the West of Ireland*. New York and London: G. P. Putnam and Sons, 1920.

Halifax, Joan. *Shaman: The Wounded Healer*. New York: Crossroad, 1982.

──────────── . *Shamanic Voices: A Survey of Visionary Narratives*. New York: E. P. Dutton, 1979.

Harner, Michael. *The Way of the Shaman*. New York: Bantam Books, 1980.

Ingerman, Sandra. *Soul Retrieval: Mending the Fragmented Self*. San Francisco: HarperSanFrancisco, 1991.

Jung, Emma and Marie-Louise von Franz. *The Grail Legend*. Boston: Sigo Press, 1986.

Kalweit, Holgar. *Dreamtime and Inner Space: The World of the Shaman*. Boston and London: Shambhala, 1988.

King, Serge Kahili. *Urban Shaman: A Handbook for Personal and Planetary Transformation Based on the Hawaiian Way of the Adventurer*. New York: Simon and Schuster, 1990.

Kondratiev, Alexi. "The Coming of Lugh." *An Gael*. New York: Irish Arts Center, 1990.

Larsen, Stephen. *The Mythic Imagination: Your Quest for Meaning Through Personal Mythology*. New York: Bantam Books, 1990.

Llywelyn, Morgan. *Bard: The Odyssey of the Irish*. New York: Tor, 1987.

Mac Cana, Proinsias. *Celtic Mythology*. New York: Peter Bedrick Books, 1987.

Mac Manus, Diarmaid. *Irish Earth Folk*. New York: Devin-Adair, 1959.

Maguire, Jack. *Hopscotch, Hangman, Hot Potato, and Ha Ha Ha: A Rulebook of Children's Games*. New York: Prentice Hall, 1990.

Markale, Jean. *Women of the Celts*. Rochester: Inner Traditions International, 1986.

Matthews, Caitlin. *The Celtic Tradition*. Longmead, Shaftesbury, Dorset: Element Books, 1989.

Matthews, John. *The Grail Tradition*. Longmead, Shaftesbury, Dorset: Element Books, 1990.

———. *Taliesin: Shamanism and the Bardic Mysteries in Britain and Ireland*. London: Aquarian Press, 1991.

Murray, Margaret A. *The God of the Witches*. London: Oxford University Press, 1952.

Naddair, Kaledon. *Keltic Folk and Faerie Tales: Their Hidden Meaning Explored*. London: Century, 1987.

Neihardt, John G. *Black Elk Speaks*. New York: Simon and Schuster, 1975.

O'Sullivan, Donal. *Carolan: The Life, Times, and Music of an Irish Harper*. London: Routledge and Kegan Paul, 1958.

Pfeiffer, John E. *The Creative Explosion: An Inquiry into the Origins of Art and Religion*. Ithaca: Cornell University Press, 1982.

Piggot, Stuart. *The Druids*. London: Thames and Hudson, 1975.

Rees, Alwyn and Brinley. *Celtic Heritage: Ancient Tradition in Ireland and Wales*. London: Thames and Hudson, 1961.

Rolleston, T. W. *Celtic*. New York: Avenel Books, 1986.

Rosenthal, M. L., ed. *Selected Poems and Two Plays of William Butler Yeats*. New York: Collier Books, 1962.

Ross, Anne. *Pagan Celtic Britain: Studies in Iconography and Tradition*. New York: Columbia University Press, 1967.

———. *The Pagan Celts*. Totowa, NJ: Barnes and Noble Books, 1986.

Rutherford, Ward. *The Druids: Magicians of the West*. Wellingborough, Northamptonshire: Aquarian Press, 1978.

Sander, Donald. *Navaho Symbols of Healing*. New York: Harcourt Brace Jovanovich, 1979.

Sjoestedt, Marie-Louise. *Gods and Heroes of the Celts*. Berkeley: Turtle Island Foundation, 1982.

Smith, Robert Jerome. "Irish Mythology." In *Irish History and Culture*, edited by Harold Orel. University of Kansas Press, 1976.

◆

Squire, Charles. *Celtic Myth and Legend*. Newcastle: Newcastle, 1975.

Stewart, R. J. *The Mystic Life of Merlin*. London: Arkana, 1986.

Taylor, Timothy. "The Gundestrup Cauldron." *Scientific American*, vol. 266, no. 3 (March 1992): 84.

Underhill, Ruth Murray. *Singing for Power: The Song Magic of the Papago Indians of Southern Arizona*. Berkeley: University of California Press, 1938.

Van de Weyer, Robert, ed. *Celtic Fire: The Passionate Religious Vision of Ancient Britain and Ireland*. New York: Doubleday, 1991.

Welsford, Enid. *The Fool: His Social and Literary History*. Gloucester: Peter Smith, 1966.

Yeats, W. B. *The Celtic Twilight: Myth, Fantasy and Folklore*. Dorset: Prism Press, 1990.

_____ . ed. *Irish Fairy and Folk Tales*. New York: Dorset Press, 1986.